The Paradox of Countertransference

Also by Carol A. V. Holmes

There Is No Such Thing as a Therapist:
An Introduction to the Therapeutic Process

The Paradox of Countertransference: You and me, here and now

Carol A. V. Holmes Ph.D

palgrave
macmillan

First published 2005 by
PALGRAVE MACMILLAN
Houndmills, Basingstoke, Hampshire RG21 6XS and
175 Fifth Avenue, New York, N.Y. 10010
Companies and representatives throughout the world

PALGRAVE MACMILLAN is the global academic imprint of the Palgrave
Macmillan division of St. Martin's Press LLC and of Palgrave Macmillan Ltd.
Macmillan® is a registered trademark in the United States, United Kingdom
and other countries. Palgrave is a registered trademark in the European
Union and other countries.

ISBN–13: 978 0–3333–92964–3 hardback
ISBN–10: 0–333–92964–0 hardback
ISBN–13: 978 0–3333–92965–0 paperback
ISBN–10: 0–333–92965–9 paperback

This book is printed on paper suitable for recycling and made from fully
managed and sustained forest sources.

A catalogue record for this book is available from the British Library.

Library of Congress Cataloging-in-Publication Data

Holmes, Carol A. V.
  The paradox of countertransference : you and me, here and
  now / Carol A. V. Holmes.
    p. cm.
  Includes bibliographical references (p.) and index.
  ISBN 0–333–92964–0 (cloth) – ISBN 0–333–92965–9 (pbk.)
  1. Countertransference (Psychology) I. Title.

  RC489.C68H655 2004
  616.89′14–dc22   2004054822

10 9 8 7 6 5 4 3 2 1
14 13 12 11 10 09 08 07 06 05

Printed in China

To Gae

'Human kind cannot bear very much reality'
T. S. Eliot

Contents

Acknowledgements

I would like to express my gratitude to Andrew McAleer for his generous and consistent support. I would also like to extend my gratitude to Rosalind Oliver for her expert, knowledgeable and thorough editorial and proofreading recommendations.

A special thank you to all the following practitioners who gave up their valuable time and agreed to be interviewed for the book: Jonathan Bradley, Professor Emmy van Deurzen, Fakhry Davids, Lesley Murdin, Helen Davis, Dr John Byng-Hall, Dr Mary Harris, and Professor David Smith.

Many thanks to Kate Oaten for her speedy response and technical assistance whenever the gremlins(!) in my computer appeared to take possession.

Finally I would like to thank Gae Oaten for everything.

Introduction

The field of psychotherapy overall is readily distinguishable by its lack of homogeneity, although many therapists from these competing schools would probably agree that the substance of their work relies on the quality of the relationship at the centre of that work. This lack of unity and the need to formalize and authenticate their axioms have led some practitioners to turn to scientific models as a means of dealing with this absence. This trend can be traced back to Freud, who was the first person to utilise the hydraulic method of late nineteenth-century physics as a symbolic means of demonstrating the credibility of the dynamics of his metapsychological theory of the mind. Following in Freud's footsteps, Robert Langs has attempted to raise the status of his own controversial psychoanalytic model by harnessing knowledge drawn from evolutionary psychology and twentieth-century physics. In direct contrast, therapists from other schools of thought, such as the humanistic tradition, consider that psychotherapy should be viewed as a creative, rather than scientific, endeavour.

The world of science and scientific knowledge, especially at the quantum level, has undergone some extraordinary changes during the past eighty years, which has led researchers in the field to doubt and wonder at the puzzling and strange nature of their findings. Quantum mechanics are concerned with the unobservable microscopic world of the electron. An electron is an elementary particle in all atoms, and as such is the most basic unit of energy in nuclear physics. Studies devoted to the behaviour of electrons found that they could function as a wave or a particle depending on how they were observed. This contradiction was of particular interest to the remarkable scientist Niels Bohr, especially in terms of the notion of complementarity, as it was found that it was not possible to measure in any precise way the movement of an electron in isolation from its position. Bohr's emphasis on the dynamic interaction between the observer and the observed followed from the fact that change occurred simply by observation of the electron's movement. These findings suggest that the notion of objective observation is something of a misnomer, and, further, that the nature of scientific research is limited, uncertain and contingent.

This author believes that these same ideas, more than ever before, are fitting and useful metaphors which can help to explain and make sense of what happens between people both in and out of therapy. Further, the principles of complementarity and uncertainty point to an important link that exists between science and creativity, as the ability to embrace and integrate contradictions is considered to play a significant role in the creative process and in psychological well being as well as in the field of quantum mechanics.

The realization of the senselessness of studying the elements of a system in isolation from the system as a whole is also particularly pertinent to the contradictory principles that underlie chaos theory. Research has shown that all living systems are created from and characterized by both chaotic and orderly features, which has compelled scientists in this area also to accept the holistic and creative features of their findings. The inaccuracy of the notion of objectivity, which even science has now been forced to embrace, is also supported by studies into self-deception and deception in the relatively new area of evolutionary psychology.

These ideas also seem eminently well suited as explanatory vehicles that can help to unravel the problems associated with the contradictory definitions surrounding the notion of countertransference, as they reinforce the need to focus on the significance of the therapeutic system in a more holistic light. The concept of countertransference is specifically associated with psychoanalysis. It is also a term that can be considered to have paradoxical features, as it is used to denote either the experience of interpersonal insight or a lack of it. Freud's concerns regarding interpersonal entanglement and the problem of maintaining an objective neutral stance can also be inferred from his original formulation of countertransference, which he described as the analyst's 'blind spot' (Freud, 1912a, p. 116). Bearing these ideas in mind, the author decided to interview seasoned psychoanalytic practitioners as well as therapists from other traditions in order to explore their beliefs about the relational features of these approaches and their ideas about countertransference.

This book is therefore primarily concerned with the investigation of some of the more innovative and interpersonal developments in the realm of countertransference that are also coherent with the tenets of holism and the principles of complementarity and uncertainty. The interface between the competing schools of psychotherapy and their attitudes to the therapeutic relationship are also considered from this overlapping perspective.

The more obvious difficulty of this remit centered around the specific theme of countertransference, which is of course directly aligned with the psychoanalytic tradition, and around the need to examine this notion in the light of other traditions which for their different reasons do not incorporate, have eschewed or do not see fit to include such a distinctive term into their model. The question naturally arises, why bother to attempt such a task at all if the connections are so obscure? However, when Freud developed his rudimentary ideas on countertransference, he was in fact attesting to the significance of the interpersonal and to the primacy of the automatic influence that each of us has in our interactions with others. Freud's legacy, however oblique, and whether acknowledged or not, is one of the primary sources from which all other schools have developed, or fled.

From this author's point of view the central theme of counter-transference of this book is related to some of the current ideas on the subject which endorse the relational, complementary qualities of the therapeutic encounter. I would further suggest that the therapist's focus on the vicissitudes of the relational aspects of the interaction should therefore be an important feature of the therapeutic task. Nevertheless, it is precisely these vicissitudes, which arise in the immediate encounter, that tend to be the very areas that are the most problematical and disturbing for both parties of the dyad.

This book has also sought tentatively to extend the dilemmas that arise in the relational paradigm between therapist and client, to include the ongoing disagreements that support and sustain the separation and lack of engagement between opposing schools of psychotherapy.

Freud's eventual, albeit rudimentary, inclusion of countertransference in his theory of human nature reflects a belief in a commonality between analyst and patient in terms of both their transference antecedents affecting and infecting one another. All the therapeutic schools presented in this text, however far removed from the psychoanalytic tradition, would agree on the significance of the relational component, even though each is likely to define 'relational' in its different way; and it is by means of the concept of countertransference that the text examines the way in which psychoanalysis and some other models of therapy understand and explain what they mean by the importance of the relationship.

The interview for each of the participating therapists consisted of a communicative presentation, followed by six open-ended questions and the therapists' responses; these questions are presented in the body of the text. In order to get a flavour of the practice of their approaches, all the therapists were finally asked to give an example of how they would address the brief case-study vignette outlined below. The clinical material pertaining to this vignette that appears in Chapter 3 was offered anonymously.

Case-study vignette

Client information

- Age. 32.

- Gender. Female.

- Ethnic Group/Nationality. White/American.

- Relationship. Unattached.

- Living Arrangements. Shares a flat with two female friends.

- Profession and Employment Details. Client has a biology degree and has worked in this field in her country of origin. At present in London, she has been working on a temporary basis in administration.

- Referral. One of her flatmates suggested that psychotherapy might be of help. The friend accompanied the client to the centre for her first session.

- Presenting Problem. Client locks herself in her room for days on end. Gets angry for apparently no reason (trashes her room and breaks her friends' belongings). Cries a lot for no obvious reason. Refuses to discuss any of these matters and finds it difficult to talk with her friends and people in general. Client stated she feels very frightened most of the time and said that she 'wants to feel alright'.

- Setting. A clinical organization run on a charitable basis.

- Fees. Offered on a sliding scale.

- Clinical arrangements. The clinic provides a waiting room for clients. Therapists are required to collect clients from the waiting room at their allotted time. If a client arrives late for their session they are told to inform the receptionist, who then informs the therapist of the clients arrival. The therapist then collects the client from the waiting area.

- The therapist was informed by the agency prior to meeting the client that she would be difficult and challenging to work with.

Progress of sessions

The first two sessions were reported to be slow and painful, the client hardly spoke and the sessions were relatively silent. On the occasion of the third session, the therapist went to the waiting room at the appointed time to find that the client had not arrived and then returned to the consulting room. After twenty minutes had elapsed the therapist returned to the waiting room to check if the client had arrived, having had no indication from the previous session that the client would not attend. The therapist then saw the client going to the reception desk and duly returned to the consulting room to receive the receptionist's call. When the receptionist called she apologized and told the therapist that the client had in fact arrived only two minutes late for her session and had registered at the desk, but owing to other pressures she had forgotten to inform the therapist. Thus, when the therapist went to check on the second occasion, the client had actually been waiting for eighteen minutes. The therapist returned to collect the client and nothing was said on the way up. When both were seated, the therapist apologized to the client, who shrugged and mumbled 'it's all right' and then fell silent. The therapist then asked: 'I wonder what is coming to mind for you?'

Client

'I have had a very bad week, I walked out of my job, I didn't even turn off my computer, I just got up and walked out. I am worried that I will lose a day's pay. [Pause.]
'It's the people I work with, they refuse to call me by my name, they can't pronounce it and say it should be Milly. They say 'her'. I don't know why they can't take time to think about my name, Michaela; they talk about it saying how funny it is.' [Pause.]
   The client's body language indicated that she was angry, she clenched her fists, the expression on her face appeared sulky and set hard. 'It's, like, I am invisible.' [Pause.]
'Not a person, just not there. I hate them. I hate being treated like that. I can't afford to lose the money.' [Pause.]

In the author's view, there is a paucity of literature devoted to the underlying factors and motivations that may predispose the individual to choose psychotherapy as a career. It was therefore decided to interview three highly experienced trainers from three different training institutes. The interview consisted of seven questions which attempted to tap into the way in which the notion of countertransference might be applied in the selection procedure for potential trainees, as well as in the actual training programmes themselves. The interview questions are included in Chapter 8, Psychotherapy Training.

There have been a number of notable scholarly texts devoted to the examination of countertransference, as well as a myriad of journal papers and conference presentations on this same topic. Chapter 1 opens with a basic outline of transference, followed by a précis of the developments and major changes that have occurred in the history of the notion of countertransference.

Chapter 2 discusses some of the more recent countertransference issues raised by contemporary authors. Developments in the field of evolutionary psychology have grown considerably during the past decade. This relatively new and controversial area of research has brought the nature/nurture debate to the forefront yet again, addressing questions about, and finding genetic explanations for, human nature, based on the Darwinian perspective of natural selection. David Smith is one of the leading psychologists of this movement; his work has been dedicated to examining countertransference in relation to deception and self-deception from an evolutionary and survival perspective. This chapter outlines some of his most recent and radical ideas on this subject.

Although there has been enormous interest in the topic of countertransference in general, David Mann is one of the few people to have written extensively and in depth on the theme of erotic transference and countertransference. The dearth of literature and lack of clinical material on this theme, as well as my own experience, indicate strongly that erotic countertransference is still a taboo subject which many psychotherapists would prefer to ignore. This lack is even more paradoxical given the fact that one of the fundamental principles of psychoanalytic thought is the momentous significance of the erotic. This is one of the reasons that I chose to include Mann's work here; however, his thesis has also, and importantly, broken new ground by illuminating both the positive as well as negative aspects of erotic countertransference in the therapeutic relationship.

The term 'counterresistance' refers to the resistances in the therapist that often impede and interfere with the therapeutic process. The expression 'countertransference enactment' has been used to explain how staff in institutional settings often repeat and replicate the disturbances of the patients under their care. Both of these ideas are also outlined in Chapter 2.

Chapter 3 is a presentation of the communicative approach to psychoanalytic psychotherapy, which I have described as a radical reformulation of psychoanalysis. This is the tradition in which I have myself been trained, and in which I have for many years been closely involved, including lecturing, developing professional training programmes and writing in the area. More precisely, my particular area of interest is in the interface between systems theory, Existential philosophy and communicative principles.

Chapter 4 is an investigation of the life and work of three psycho-analytic mavericks, Sándor Ferenczi, Harold Searles and Robert Langs, who saw fit to reformulate and extend the concept of counter-transference and its usage within the clinical situation.

Chapters 5, 6, 7 and 8 set out an elucidation of four therapeutic models: the existential, humanistic, integrative and systemic. The significance of the notion of countertransference is also addressed from each of these perspectives.

Chapter 9 focuses on the topic of countertransference in relation to training. It features interviews with three experts in the field of psychotherapy training: child psychotherapist Jonathan Bradley, who teaches on the child psychotherapy programme at the Tavistock Centre, London, and who explains the ethos of the Tavistock's psycho-analytic approach; Lesley Murdin, Director of psychotherapy training at the Westminister Pastoral Foundation; and David Smith, former psychotherapist and head of psychotherapy training, now Lecturer in philosophy at the University of New England, who submits his case for a radical reappraisal of current psychotherapy teaching methods.

Chapter 10 is a summation of my own ideas and research into the subject of the therapeutic interaction. Here I have attempted to integrate ideas taken from competing therapeutic ideologies and amalgamate some of their specific interpersonal premises with current scientific precepts.

The process of writing a book from a number of different perspectives on a topic that is principally associated with one school of thought has been a challenging but ultimately invaluable experience.

There were moments when I felt particularly fortunate after emerging from a chaotic period to have the opportunity to re-evaluate and reconsider my own professional beliefs, personal philosophy and prejudices. In the main this has been due to the generous, thoughtful and open attitude on the part of all the practitioners and trainers who willingly and voluntarily agreed to give up a substantial proportion of time to be interviewed for this book. Once again I would like to extend my thanks to you all; your collaboration has added immensely to this book.

Chapter 1

Countertransference

During the past fifty years the concept of countertransference has become a topic of considerable interest, debate and controversy in the field of psychoanalysis, as witnessed by the increasing number of publications on the subject. At the same time, it is interesting to note that even though countertransference is now considered to be a salient and ongoing element of the psychoanalytic interaction, the major dictionaries devoted to psychoanalytic terminology do not reflect this significance. This inconsistency is particularly noticeable given the fact that over this period of time many of the refinements that have occurred within the psychoanalytic tradition have focused on elaborating the more reciprocal and interpersonal aspects of the analytic relationship. It is further unexpected because many of the scientific breakthroughs that occurred at this time have also revealed and explained the ubiquity of interdependence.

It is therefore somewhat surprising to note that in Rycroft's *A Critical Dictionary of Psychoanalysis* (1968) only nine lines are given to countertransference compared to almost two pages to the notion of transference. Similarly, in Laplanche and Pontalis' *The Language of Psychoanalysis* (1973) transference warrants eight pages compared to only a one-and-a-quarter pages afforded to countertransference. In Sandler, Dare and Holder's classic reference text, *The Patient and the Analyst* (1973), two whole chapters are given over to transference and a mere sixteen pages to its counterpart. Finally, Joseph Schwartz's recent scholarly book, *Cassandra's Daughter* (1999), which explores the history of psychoanalysis in Europe and America, has a thirteen-page discussion of the notion of transference and only a single, perfunctory page on countertransference.

Given the noted growth of the focus on countertransference this resilient weighting in favour of transference calls for some explanation. In part this may be related to the tacit agreement that exists between psychoanalysis and certain other therapeutic approaches which tend to view the patient's ability to perceive reality as less trustworthy than the therapist's. After all, it is the client who requires the services of the therapist, and not the other way round, so not surprisingly it is the client's problems that take pride of place. This idea is also contained within the developmental history of psychoanalysis. Once Freud had clearly formulated the transference foundations which supported his overall model, his subsequent theoretical development of countertransference was likely to be seen as the second string. Freud was relatively clear about his definition of countertransference as a flawed aspect of the analyst, and of its occasional but inevitable interference in the analysis. The subsequent hundred years of clinical research and psychoanalytic literature, however, reveal at least two, somewhat opposing, positions on countertransference.

Despite the preponderance of literature available on this theme, the dispute between these positions remains just as prevalent today. It appears to be related to an ongoing disagreement about both the definition and the importance of the *counter* aspect that Freud (1910) appended to his original transference nomenclature. The term *counter* is defined in the following ways: (1) 'In a contrary direction or manner'; (2) 'In a wrong or reverse direction'; (3) 'Run counter to'; 'To have a contrary effect or action to'; (4) 'opposing; opposite; contrary'; (5) 'Something that is contrary or opposite to some other thing' (*Collins English Dictionary*, 1986, p. 195). Other synonyms include 'reverse; contrast; conflicting; and antithesis' (*Roget's Thesaurus*, 1972, p. 14). The original psychoanalytic definition of the term countertransference refers to a process in the analyst that is the counterpart of the patient's transference. However, etymologically the term itself could be construed in a variety of different ways. In order to understand these different readings, and before outlining the developments that have occurred in the history of the use of the term, it is helpful to consider first the evolution and disagreements that have occurred in the development of the concept of transference.

Transference

The term transference underpins and encapsulates both the theory and the practice of psychoanalysis and was first defined by Freud in a limited and specific way. Early in the development of his ideas, Freud (1895) noticed that his patients unconsciously transferred ideas and affects onto the practitioner. He described this activity as a 'false connection'. Laplanche and Pontalis provide the following succinct definition: 'In the transference, infantile prototypes re-emerge and are experienced with a strong sensation of immediacy' (1973, p. 455). At first Freud considered transference to be a transitory phenomenon, related more to the personality of the physician than to the patient's psychopathology. In this early phase in the development of his ideas he therefore felt that transference interfered with the therapeutic process. However, by 1912 Freud's clinical observations had convinced him that these transferred psychic contents were by far the most significant issue in the psychoanalytic process and the most important and useful clinical tool. He realised, too, that the intense transference phenomena could be discerned in other relationships outside the clinical setting, such as between tutor and pupil or in any relationship where one person is in a position of authority over the other.

From a classical perspective everything is played out around the patient's unconscious infantile longings, love, hate and disappointments, usually related to parental figures yet re-experienced and transferred spontaneously by the patient onto the here-and-now relationship with the analyst.

Transference and reality

The problem of differentiating between transference, as a distortion or illusion, and the patient's real perceptions towards the analyst continues to be the subject of debate. Laplanche and Pontalis (1973) raise the question of the difficulty caused by such a loosely defined notion that leaves the analyst in the decisive position to make the judgment as to whether the patient's material is either transferential or based on a real perception of the analyst. Sandler, Dare and Holder (1973) emphasize the inevitably idiosyncratic influence of the analyst's personality on the expression of the patient's transference and further point out that the analyst is, of course, a real person and an active participant in the interaction. The French analyst Daniel Lagache (1993) also refers to the same dilemma of some authors who reject the idea that everything that occurs in the patient's communications is a consequence of transference. Other practitioners maintain that the unconscious is not only able to perceive reality but also possessed of a natural curative capacity (see Chapter 4).

Displacement

Transference refers to the unconscious, automatic intrapsychic capacity to carry across ideas and images connected with an early significant figure into the relationship with the person of the analyst.

Essentially, transference is a description of and type of displacement, which functions as a defensive mechanism for the patient as a means to conceal and deny the true origin and source of a forbidden wish. Displacement is the process in which an image of one person is replaced by another, who then becomes synonymous with the first. In 1900 Freud published his major work, *The Interpretation of Dreams*, in which he explains the two fundamental mechanisms of defence, displacement and disguise. These mechanisms conceal from the dreamer the true source of his or her concern and the identity of the person associated with it.

Transference resistance
The defence of displacement manifests itself as resistance and refers to the resistances within the patient when he or she is antagonistic towards or refutes the analyst's interpretations. Such opposition is viewed as an indication of transference and denotes the patient's anxiety, which has been prompted by the analyst's interpretation, as the latter attempts to uncover the unconscious material that the patient struggles to keep repressed. It has also been noted that transference resistance encompasses undisclosed conscious ideas that the patient has about the analyst (Sandler, Dare and Holder, 1973).

Positive transference
By 1912 Freud had divided transference into two affective categories (Freud, 1912b). Positive transference denotes the warm, loving, affectionate emotions the patient feels toward the analyst. Freud considered that these positive affects played a significant role in the treatment process and counted as a major contributing factor in the successful outcome of the work. He believed that the continuation of patients' tender, benign feelings predisposed them to accept the analyst's interpretations. In this sense Freud acknowledged that analytic success was based upon the influence of the analyst and the suggestibility of the patient. Freud made a further distinction between affectionate and erotic transference. While the patient could consciously admit to having warm, benevolent feelings towards the analyst, erotic feelings tended to be subject to repression. At the same time he asserted, somewhat paradoxically, that any and all positive affects towards another person had at their base an erotic component, and yet a qualitative difference could be observed between the two. He further noted that although the erotic transference appeared at some point during the treatment, the positive aspect was apparent from the onset.

Negative transference

The patient's experience of hostile and aggressive feelings towards the analyst are manifestations of negative transference. The mobilization of the patient's antagonistic feelings transferred onto the analyst are seen as a defensive strategy, as a means of avoiding the more disturbing erotic transference emotions. The ability to hold in mind conflicting impulses and emotions in relation to one person is known as ambivalence. Freud believed that the inability to acknowledge contradictory impulses of love and hate towards the same object lay at the heart of the problems that psychoanalysis attempts to address.

Transference and repetition

The concept of repetition offers an explanation for the phenomenon of resistance. Freud coined the term 'repetition compulsion' to illustrate the dynamic nature of the unconscious. Under the sway of the unconscious the individual is at one and the same time compelled to repress disturbing material from the past and also driven to re-enact the conflict in the present. Repetitions from the past may take on the guise of current symptoms, as a form of what is termed 'acting out', or may be symbolized in dreams. By definition repetitions are unconscious and will therefore continue to be enacted in the present. The Freudian notion of the compulsion to repeat offers supporting evidence for the theory of transference and the way in which the patient's past is reproduced in the analytic relationship.

Transference neurosis

The compulsion to repeat is linked to the patient's neurosis in relation to the analyst. This reproduction of the patient's neurosis within the psychoanalytic setting is one of the fundamental aims of psychoanalytic treatment, as the patient is then considered to be amenable to interpretations and explanations that reveal their underlying infantile neurosis. Transference neurosis refers to patients' tendency to develop an intense transference relationship with their analyst, which is constituted out of their childhood conflicts and their current neurosis, replicated and re-enacted in the analysis.

Transference revisions

The classical Freudian position views the appearance of transference as a phenomenon that occurs from time to time in the analytic setting and is noted from the patient's remarks about or alluding to the analyst or when there is an indication of the patient's resistance.

Melanie Klein (1952) put forward a broader view than Freud's original definition of transference. It has been suggested (Hinshelwood, 1989) that Klein's transference revisions were based on her clinical observations from working with very young children. Klein considered that the appearance of transference phenomena in this patient group indicated the presence of matching anxieties in the children's day-to-day lives. Furthermore, her observations led her to elaborate her conception of unconscious phantasy, as her attention was drawn to the conspicuous strength of these transference enactments. This thinking subsequently became part of her work with her adult patients. For Klein, transference was a ubiquitous phenomenon that inevitably occurred in all relationships. As a consequence, Kleinian analysts will tend to concentrate their interpretations around the here-and-now transference interaction and the patient's immediate phantasy experiences as these occur for the patient with the analyst in the consulting room.

Klein's theoretical revisions, which included a re-conceptualization of infantile development, demarcated into the paranoid/schizoid and depressive positions, paved the way for her alternative technical procedures. Her approach contrasts with the Freudian tradition, which aims to curtail the patient's anxiety by gradually timing and addressing the transference as it appears in the form of resistance.

The notion of splitting is central to Klein's thesis and to her notion of the infantile paranoid/schizoid position, dominated by the need to perceive others in terms of either good or bad. Paranoid or persecutory anxiety is understood to arise in response to the person's need to deflect their fear of disintegration (death anxiety) onto an external object. Splitting is placed firmly in the category of defences employed to ward off this persecutory anxiety. From a Kleinian perspective, an intense positive transference may therefore be viewed as an idealization of the analyst and in this sense used as a defensive procedure against more negative, aggressive feelings. To continue this line of thought, interpreting patients' immediate manifest or underlying, anxieties is considered, paradoxically, to provide them with some relief, as it is a closer representation of reality.

Contemporary transference revisions

The interpersonal approach to psychoanalysis was founded by the American psychiatrist Harry Stack Sullivan (1953, 1964) and has been described as a 'two-person' psychology. Sullivan's extensive clinical work with schizophrenic patients led him to the view that human beings are constituted through their interactions with others. Interpersonal psychoanalysis is therefore essentially interested in the phenomenological aspects of the therapeutic encounter. The approach is characterized by its focus on the reciprocal examination of the patient–therapist interaction.

The exploration of transference is also considered from this same interpersonal, two-person perspective. According to Eric Singer,

Interpersonalists believe that it is particularly crucial to the understanding of transference to understand that the analyst is an active participant in the engagement with the patient, not simply a neutral figure on to whom distortions are projected. In this view, the analyst brings to the therapeutic engagement his or her personality, replete with all its human foibles. This dictum is the sine qua non of inter-personal psychoanalysis. (1998, pp. 95–96)

The interpersonal position takes into consideration both the accurate perceptions and the distorted features of the patient's interpersonal reflections. In order to distinguish between these alternatives the analyst is expected consistently to check how his or her own involvement is influencing the interaction. Nevertheless, as the reader will appreciate, it is an uphill struggle to achieve such a balance given that a great deal of immediate interpersonal activity takes place outside of conscious awareness.

The Freudian method of working with transference was also challenged by Heinz Kohut, the founder of 'self-psychology', which he developed from his clinical work with patients who were defined as narcissistically disturbed – although his model came to be much more widely applied across the field of psychopathology as a whole. Kohut described three kinds of 'selfobject transferences', which the infant needs to experience in order to develop a stable sense of self. 'Mirroring' refers to the experience of being validated and confirmed by the caretaker. 'Idealizing' entails the perception of being able to depend on a significant person, who is felt to be powerful and perfect. 'Twinship' pertains to the soothing experience of feeling similar to and approved of by another person. Kohut (1977, 1984) tendered very much of an alternative view of transference compared to Freud's original definition. He felt that transference was the patient's attempts to reawaken an early-disrupted developmental stage, which the patient must be allowed to experience with the analyst. The analyst, at this stage is expected to empathize with, rather than interpret, the patient's experience. This is in direct contrast to the classical position and the dictum that the analyst must not respond to, or gratify, the patient's transference wishes. Realistically, the analyst is unable always to fulfil the patient's needs, which reactivates and recapitulates the patient's early disappointments. The analyst is expected to maintain an empathic stance, which also involves the realistic provision of 'optimal frustration' in order to enable the patient to internalize the analyst's selfobject capacities independent of the analyst.

Kohut placed enormous emphasis on the individual's early environment. He also believed that human beings have an innate tendency to develop and grow; in this sense his ideas are evocative of fundamental humanistic and Rogerian principles. What is known as the relational school of psychoanalysis has developed from a variety of converging theoretical models, and incorporates ideas from British object relations, Sullivan and Kohut. As its name suggests, the relational school emphasizes the reciprocal and mutual participatory nature of the analytic relationship.

Countertransference

Freud first introduced the concept of countertransference fifteen years after the first reference to transference appeared in his writing. He stated: 'We have become aware of the "counter-transference", which arises in [the analyst] as a result of the patient's influence on his unconscious feelings, and we are almost inclined to insist that he shall recognize this countertransference in himself and overcome it' (1910, pp. 144–5). Further on, Freud strongly recommends that practitioners be required to subject themselves to regular periods of self-analysis in order to 'overcome' their countertransference reactions.

It has been proposed, by Charles Rycroft, that countertransference is most accurately defined as the analyst's transference onto his patient. 'In this, the correct sense', Rycroft writes, countertransference is a disturbing, distorting element in the treatment' (1968, p. 25). Freud viewed the concept of countertransference in a similar light to his early ideas on transference: that it was an affect that needed to be excluded as quickly as possible from the analysis. However, unlike his subsequent re-evaluation of transference, in which it became an essential therapeutic tool, Freud did not redefine his ideas on the usefulness of countertransference in the treatment procedure.

Yet over time the notion of countertransference has undergone various adulterations and expansions since its original, distinct Freudian formulation. These revisions to the meaning of countertransference have led to some confusion and resulted in at least two alternative definitions which can be said to have contradictory features. On the one hand, the analyst's feelings are used as a form of evidence, and countertransference reactions are assumed to be based on the analyst's valid perception of the patient's true feelings and intentions. On the other hand, countertransference responses are viewed as an impediment, a distorting factor and a resistant element in the analyst's ability to maintain a neutral position in relation to the patient, which, as we have seen, Freud referred to as the analyst's 'blind spot'.

It is interesting to note that there are only five references to countertransference in the entire twenty-three volumes of Freud's complete works. There is also no mention of countertransference in Volume 14, *On The History of the Psycho-Analytic Movement* (Freud, 1914). Furthermore, although Freud introduced the term, he did not give a clear definition of the concept, except to say that it was an unconscious process that was triggered in the analyst by the patient. He did, however, lay stress on the psychoanalytic rule of abstinence as a means of curtailing the countertransference: 'In my opinion, therefore, we ought not give up the neutrality towards the patient, which we have acquired through keeping the counter-transference in check' (1915, p. 164).

As I mentioned earlier in this chapter, countertransference appears almost as an afterthought in the main reference books and dictionaries of psychoanalysis, and this may, in part, be due to the small role that the concept has played in the classical ego model developed by Freud. This trend is, however, reversed in the *Dictionary of Kleinian Thought* (Hinshelwood, 1989), which dedicates seven pages to countertransference and only five pages to transference. This tendency continues in the reference text *The Independent Mind in British Psychoanalysis* (Rayner, 1991), which extends ten pages to countertransference, compared to only six on transference. The striking difference can be attributed to the emphasis that was placed on countertransference both conceptually and clinically by the Object Relations school and by the Independent school, which drew many of its adherents from the Kleinian tradition.

It has been suggested that the history of countertransference and its developments can be categorized into three phases (Young, 1994), beginning with the classical Freudian position, which assumed that the presence of countertransference constituted an impediment to the treatment process, owing to the analyst's inability to maintain a professionally necessary neutral position. A significant change occurred between the late nineteen forties and early nineteen fifties, which may be attributed to the burgeoning developments in object relations theory. D. W. Winnicott (1949) and Paula Heimann (1950) in the Kleinian tradition and Margaret Little (1951) were all responsible for bringing the issue of countertransference into the foreground of the psychoanalytic arena. Their groundbreaking and controversial work postulated how the analyst's often unwieldy feelings, instead of being seen as an obstacle, could be used as a measure or a barometer for understanding the patient. Subsequent research, in what has been called the third phase, prioritized the alternating, reciprocal transference–countertransference connection between patient and analyst. In the transference the patient projects into the analyst, which brings to light the countertransference vulnerabilities, disturbances and proclivities of the analyst.

The developments that have occurred in the history of the term countertransference have been lucidly documented and debated, both chronologically and critically, by a number of eminent authors in the field (Sandler, Dare and Holder, 1973; Wolstein, 1988; Alexandris and Vaslamatzis, 1993; Maroda, 1994; Mitchell and Black, 1995). As mentioned earlier, I will select and discuss the main protagonists, their contributions, similarities and differences. I will also show how the debate addresses the matter of how these countertransference innovations appear to have led to deterioration in the clarity and refinement of the notion, and the inherent risks that this poses for practitioners in their clinical work.

Winnicott's formative paper, 'Hate in the Countertransference' (1949), which he presented to the British Psychoanalytic Society in 1947, stressed the therapeutic value of the analyst's realistic feelings of hatred towards his patients. He based this supposition on the duality of love and hate – on the ambivalent mixture of feelings that inevitably exists in all relationships. The analyst's ability to acknowledge hatred toward the patient was seen as therapeutic from two perspectives: on the one hand because the patient's behaviour was 'objectively' hateful; on the other hand because if the analyst denied, or repressed, their hostile feelings, they would be compelled (by the force of their unconscious) to act them out in relation to the patient. In this paper Winnicott cites as an example his clinical work with a very disturbed young orphan boy: 'Did I hit him? The answer is no, I never hit. But I should have had to have done so if I had not known all about my hate and if I had not let him know about it too' (p. 200). Winnicott's assertion and the rationale he gives for expressing his feelings to the patient in this brief vignette are clearly a radical departure from Freud's original intentions.

Winnicott's early contribution to the debate is important and for our purposes significant in as much as he fearlessly admits to and acknowledges the impossibility of the analyst as an impassively and impartially benign observer in the therapeutic interaction. He further suggests that it is appropriate and helpful for the patient if the analyst discloses his or her hostile feelings because the former is thereby enabled to become aware of their influence on or projections onto the analyst. More recently, other clinicians have endorsed the therapeutic value of the occasional use of this type of self-disclosure with intensely hostile patients (Coltart, 1992; Bollas, 1987; Maroda, 1994). However, in this particular example, Winnicott is using countertransference as the analyst's awareness of negative affects towards his or her patient and does not take into consideration any other possible underlying or unconscious motivations on his part. Furthermore, we may note for the sake of democracy that had the patient expressed similar views towards the analyst, it would be the analyst alone who had the power to judge whether the communication was a transference distortion, a rationalization or a valid observation.

Some analysts have criticized this imbalance and what they see as a potential bias in the application of these two major psychoanalytic concepts – which remain open to definition and can therefore be used by the analyst in idiosyncratic or defensive ways with patients (see Ferenczi, 1933; Little, 1951; Szasz, 1965; Langs, 1992; Smith, 1999a). As Karen Maroda notes: 'What is distinctive about psychoanalysis is that the defenses used by the therapist to protect himself are highly intellectualized and that this protection was built into the system at its conception' (1994, p. 17).

The innovative ideas presented by Paula Heimann in her brief paper on countertransference in 1950 had an enormous impact on this debate, so much so that the perspective she outlined has now become firmly established and assimilated into psychoanalytic thought and practice. She attributed the analyst's countertransference feelings to the patient's unconscious unexpressed emotions. Heimann's position is in stark opposition to Freud, who claimed that countertransference was an analyst-centered disturbance that could detrimentally influence the patient and interfere with the treatment. Instead, Heimann believed that it was the patient who created these disturbances in the analyst. In this sense countertransference could now be seen as a source of important information, which could be employed significantly to enhance the analyst's understanding of the patient's unconscious.

On 7 June 1950 Margaret Little delivered a scholarly, impartial and candidly self-reflective essay on the problematical nature of counter-transference to the British Psycho-analytical Society. In this presenta-tion she expressed her concerns about both Winnicott and Heimann's theoretical and technical assertions on this topic. Her paper seems to be primarily concerned with two issues. First she accents the uncon-scious quality of countertransference and links this to the arbitrary nature of its meaning and to the analyst's reluctance to plumb the murky depths of his or her own psyche:

> The attitude of most analysts towards countertransference is precisely the same, that it is a known and recognized phenomenon but that it is unnecessary and even dangerous ever to interpret it. In any case, what is unconscious one cannot easily be aware of (if at all), and to try to observe and interpret something unconscious in oneself is rather like trying to see the back of one's own head – it is a lot easier to see the back of someone else's. The fact of the patient's transference lends itself readily to avoidance by projection and rationalization. (Little, 1951, p. 33)

She then proceeds to address the issue in a most refreshing manner and attempts to redress the balance of power between patient and analyst by showing the essential interconnectedness in the transference–countertransference relationship:

> Any analysis (even self-analysis) postulates both an analysand and an analyst: in a sense they are inseparable. And similarly trans-ference and countertransference are inseparable; something which is suggested in the fact that what is written about one can so largely be applied to the other. (p. 33)

Little continues her thesis in a spirit of equality by giving credence to the neglected topic of the patient's real, rather than purely distorted, perceptions of the analyst. For Little, the analyst is a real person, not an impartial observer. This mitigates their being the only person in the interaction to have the right to define what counts as reality. Further-more, her discourse also implies that the analyst, as well as the patient, will experience periods of resistance. Her ideas are reminiscent of systemic principles and of the research that was evolving in the physical sciences around this time.

Ten years later both Heimann and Little wrote again on this same topic from their differing perspectives (Heimann, 1959–60; Little, 1960). However, in the interim Roger Money-Kyrle (1956) took up the subject and broadened the definition to include 'normal countertransference'. For Money-Kyrle, normal countertranference is seen as an ideal which is likely to fail when there is too close a correspondence between the patient's and the analyst's psychopathology, resulting in the analyst's inability to offer an appropriate interpretation.

Normal countertransference also refers to those moments of understanding by the analyst which lead to an interpretation that enhances the patient's understanding and can therefore be regarded as a form of empathy. As well as contributing to the patient's self-knowledge, normal countertransference is viewed as advancing the analyst's understanding of his own difficulties. Money-Kyrle's account of normal countertransference is to some extent equivalent to the definition of transference, in so far as it relates to the analyst's early childhood relationships that are now impinging on the encounter with the patient. However, the difference between normal countertransference and transference is that it can be used as a form of empathy if the analyst has some conscious awareness of it and can contain it in the interest of the patient. Money-Kyrle appears to imply that normal countertransference interferes with the analytic process when it remains outside of the analyst's awareness and is too akin to the patient's transference. This type of normal countertransference may be described as the analyst's transference, triggered off by the patient's transference and psychopathology (unlike the patient's transference, which occurs more unilaterally in the sense of being generally activated in the patient relatively independently of the analyst's person and behaviour).

Little (1951) and also Mabel Cohen (1952) have opted for consistency, clarity and uniformity in their formulations of countertransference as the counterpart of transference. In straightforward fashion Cohen notes:

On the whole, countertransference responses are reflections of permanent neurotic difficulties of the analyst, in which the patient is often not a real object but rather is used as a tool by means of which some need of the analyst is gratified. (1952, p. 67)

Both authors, however, accept and acknowledge the relevance of including the insightful and therapeutic functions of the analyst under the descriptive umbrella of countertransference.

In general, one of the most apparent and consistent features of the explanatory writing on countertransference has been the explicitly paradoxical highlighting of the concept's components. This, however, begs the question. Cohen attempts to deal with this by suggesting an operational definition: 'When, in the patient–analyst relationship, anxiety is aroused in the analyst with the effect that communication between the two is interfered with by some alteration in the analyst's behaviour (verbal or otherwise), then countertransference is present' (p. 70). Although Cohen concedes that the presence of the analyst's anxiety may be denied and defended against when it is outside awareness, she also makes the (to my mind) somewhat unsubstantiated and merely hopeful claim that this is less likely to occur because of analysts' lengthy training analyses.

Money-Kyrle's examination of the implicit and often unconscious motivational factors that predispose individuals to devote themselves to the relief of others, as well as of the stresses and strains that are part and parcel of the work, suggests that the negotiation between normal countertransference and its disturbances will remain an on-going difficulty. He cites some of the basic human drives that attract, stimulate, gratify but also enable the analyst to empathize with their patients, such as the reparative and parental needs. However, as reparation and aggression are shown to go hand in hand (reparation described as a means of assuaging individuals' innate aggressive drives), it is claimed that when the work becomes difficult, as undoubtedly it always will do, there is the risk of the analyst's aggression coming to the fore. This same principle applies to the dynamics that underlie the parental drive, and to the intimate link that exists between it and our own (often unconscious) childhood difficulties that are played out and repeated in the parental role.

The theoretical assumptions that underpin psychoanalysis challenge the claim that the analyst is in the advantaged position owing to his or her extensive training analysis, as human vulnerability, anxiety and the sway of the unconscious are the stock-in-trade of all therapeutic work, to which both analyst and patient are subject. These funda-mental premises endorse the idea that human beings never relinquish, or totally resolve, their childhood issues and, therefore, as adults, will continue to be neurotic to some degree or other.

Harold Searles has written extensively on the topic of counter-transference (see Chapter 4). His view is that there is an intimate tie between the patient's transference neurosis and the analyst's counter-transference neurosis, so much so that in the course of the treatment both parties' emotions and attitudes towards one other become significantly altered (Searles, 1959). The Argentinian analyst Heinrich Racker expressed a similar idea of the close relationship between the patient's transference responses and the analyst's countertransference reactions as early as 1948. Racker declared: 'Although the neurotic reactions of countertransference may be sporadic, the predisposition to them is continuous' (1968, p. 111). What we might call this egalitarian stance has been elaborated in a recent paper by David Smith, 'Understanding Patients' Countertransference' (Smith, 1999a), in which the author logically and creatively argues that if the analyst's countertransference responses are viewed as emanating from the patient then the reverse must also be true: that is, the patient must also unconsciously perceive and react to the emotional affects that emanate from the analyst.

Extended periods of normal countertransference are described by Money-Kyrle as countertransference disturbances, which he regards as unavoidable exaggerations of normal countertransference issues. As far as Winnicott is concerned, whenever practitioners deviate from their professional analytic stance, by, as he says, behaving as rescuers, teachers, allies, or moralists, countertransference is present: 'In so far as all this is true the meaning of the word countertransference can only be the neurotic features which *spoil the professional attitude* and disturb the course of the analytic process as determined by the patient' (1960, p. 162). This clear-cut approach to countertransference as a description of the analyst's inappropriate behaviour towards the patient is supported by Ralph Greenson in his classic text on psycho-analytic technique:

> Errors due to countertransference arise when the analyst reacts to his patient as though the patient were a significant person in the analyst's early history. Countertransference is a transference reac-tion of an analyst to a patient, a parallel to transference, a counter-part of transference. The counter in countertransference means analogue, duplicate of, like the counter in counterpart. It is not like counter in counteract or counterattack, where it means opposed to or contrary, etc. Countertransference reactions can lead to persistent

inappropriate behavior toward the patient in the form of constant misunderstanding or some unconscious rewarding, seductive or permissive behavior by the analyst. (1967, p. 348)

Maxwell Gitelson (1952) made the distinction between the analyst's transference and countertransference by describing the former as the analyst's total reaction to the patient and the latter as his or her limited reactions to specific facets of the patient. Nevertheless, Gitelson's explanation of the difference between patient and analyst assumes a general willingness to give credence to the analyst's state of mind in contrast to that of the patient.

Whether analysts should disclose their countertransference difficulties to their patients has and continues to be the subject of debate and disagreement. For Little (1951) and Gitelson (1952), the analyst's use of self-disclosure is seen as an important therapeutic procedure. Whereas for Money-Kyrle (1956) and Heimann (1959–60), the analyst's self-disclosure places an unnecessary burden on the patient, tantamount to a confession of impotence, which the patient may then identify with rather than appreciate. To further complicate the debate, Robert Langs's development of the Communicative approach (see Chapter 3) is founded on the premise that patients consistently reveal their concerns about the analyst's behaviour towards them in the stories they tell – concerns which the analyst is then obliged to acknowledge in the interpretations he or she gives. From this perspective all the analyst's interventions may be deemed countertransference responses. In fact, it is these relatively undefended interpersonal acknowledgements which are seen as the most useful and appropriate therapeutic intervention for the patient to internalize.

The need to be loved has been mentioned as just one of the personal incentives that tacitly motivate individuals to opt for the arduous profession of psychotherapy (Racker, 1968). On this view there is no attempt to deny countertransference issues interfering with the treatment process. The analyst's frustration in the presence of a patient who has developed a strong negative transference will be assumed to elicit feelings of anger and resentment or an attempt to placate the patient. As such, the analyst's idiosyncratic response is likely to be thought dependent on his or her own early interactions, and all behaviour from the patient that comes under the heading of resistance almost guaranteed to influence the attitude and behaviour of the analyst towards the patient by impeding his or her ability to remain neutral.

Projective identification

It was Melanie Klein who first introduced the concept of projective identification (Klein, 1946); however, the term itself did not emerge in the literature until 1952. It has been described by Robert Young as the most significant contribution to psychoanalysis since the development of the role of the unconscious. Etymologically the word projection means literally *to throw in front of*. Psychoanalytically, projection refers to an unconscious defensive mechanism which enables individuals to reject an unacceptable aspect of themselves and instead perceive it as part of or emanating from an external object. Because the primary features that distinguish the concept of projection from projective identification are rather blurred, each term has been used to represent the other.

Some authors have suggested either that it is too difficult to attempt to clarify the difference between the two notions or that the concept of projective identification has become too vaguely defined (Meissner, 1980; Spillius, 1983; Hinshelwood, 1989). Projection is clearly a significant element of projective identification; however, the concept tends to be used to capture a more powerful kind of process that also relies on the entanglement of the recipient of the projection.

The notion of identification is arranged under four different headings in the *Critical Dictionary of Psychoanalysis* (Rycroft, 1968), and includes projective identification, defined as 'the process by which a person imagines himself to be inside some object external to himself'. This, the author emphasizes, is a defence 'since it creates the ILLUSION of control over the object and enables the subject to deny his powerlessness over it and to gain vicarious satisfaction from its activities' (pp. 67–68). Rycroft's description of projective identification is focused primarily in terms of the subject's intrapsychic, primitive defensive strategies, and is very much in keeping with Klein's original conceptualization of the term, as a process that takes place within the subject's phantasy world.

Part of the continuing controversy and debate surrounding the meaning of the concept of projective identification is related to the broadening of its original definition, which has come to concentrate more on the interpersonal properties of the concept. As Julia Segal explains: 'projective identification involves a more active *getting rid of* something belonging to the self into someone else. Projective identification involves evoking in someone else aspects of the self which one cannot bear' (1992, p. 36). In this sense the subject of the projective identification relies on finding a suitable object into or onto which to project the disturbing aspects of the self.

The loosening of the concept of projective identification to include both phantasy and reality is also reminiscent of the fate that befell the concepts of transference and countertransference and the ensuing confusion. The American interpersonal analyst James Grotstein makes his position very clear: 'Projective identification never occurs in a vacuum. There must always be an external realization which justifies the projection so that the projection can take place' (1987, p. 70). Thomas Ogden (1982) also lays stress on the interpersonal quality of these ubiquitous, complex and subtle communications, while also emphasizing the manipulative proclivity of the subject over the external object.

The Kleinian term projective identification has now become an established concept, employed by practitioners from a variety of other psychoanalytical traditions. This widening of usage may in part have also contributed to the skewing and deviations that have occurred away from the meaning Klein originally gave the term.

Klein anchors the concept of projective identification firmly to the earliest, paranoid/schizoid, developmental position. The tiny infant's intense vulnerability and lack of a cohesive sense of self gives rise to the first and most primitive defence of splitting. The need to split bad, aggressive, disturbing internal affects is a function of the death instinct, or death anxiety. Splitting enables the baby to deflect anxieties concerning its survival into the mother through the mechanism of projective identification. The strategy of projective identification activates omnipotent phantasies and buffers the infant's awareness of its dangerous and separate position in the world. This is the price that the infant and adult must pay when they need to deny the reality of their mortal and precarious place in the world.

The Kleinian analyst Wilfrid Bion made a considerable contribution to understanding the link between the underlying dynamics that influence the mother–baby interaction and the analyst–patient encounter. In 1959 Bion expanded and augmented Klein's original concept by describing two distinct and contradictory modes of projective identification. It has been suggested that Bion's differentiation between normal and pathological types of projective identification helped to sharpen and clarify the confusion surrounding its definition (Hinshelwood, 1989). Pathological projective identification refers to Klein's seminal description – to the expelling of violent, aggressive, unbearable, primitive impulses and images into an external object. Normal projective identification, by contrast, refers to the therapeutic capacity to empathize – to project into an external object in order to communicate with, understand and 'be with' the object in a more benevolent mode. If pathological projective identification is the leading response in the paranoid/schizoid position, then normal projective identification can be identified with the depressive position and the ability to experience the object in a more holistic, realistic and compassionate way.

The concept of containment developed by Bion is now firmly established as a crucial aspect of the therapeutic process throughout the schools of psychoanalytic psychotherapy. The mother's ability to contain the infant's early intense aggressive projections as they are described in Klein's initial developmental position is vital to the baby's continuing emotional and mental development and provides the template for the capacity the infant will eventually develop to contain its own unwieldy anxieties. Bion (1962) characterized the role that the mother's state of mind plays in the carrying out of this maternal task as one of *reverie*. A newly born infant, having been propelled into a totally unknown, disturbing and noisy world, is likely to experience many occasions of overwhelming chaos and anxiety. The mother's primary role is to moderate the baby's distress, which requires her to be in a sufficiently calm and receptive state of mind to be able to take in the baby's highly toxic projections and to project them back in a less noxious, more manageable form. It is the mother's state of mind that acts as a container for the baby's aggressive impulses and fragmented experience of being.

Bion extrapolated these ideas about the mother–infant interaction to explain also the significant dynamics of the patient–analyst encounter. This is what Bion means by normal projective identification – the mother/analyst's capacity to empathize with the baby's/patient's turbulence and disarray by allowing this to wash over, or indeed through, them without reacting and then returning it in a more meaningful and bearable form. Bion advised analysts to develop a state of mind towards their patients that is free from memory or desire (1970) – an injunction that may be considered to be the equivalent of the mother's state of *reverie*. By relinquishing memory and desire, the analysts can free themselves to be with the patient in the immediate situation, and give themselves also the mental space to be aware of their own reciprocal experience.

Abnormal or pathological projective identification, by contrast, has as its aim to obliterate meaning, to impede creativity and instead to replace thought with confusion. The reader may be able to identify with the utter confusion, dismay and general lack of thought that accompany moments of intense emotion when one is interacting with a person who superficially appears calm and rational but who also conveys a sense of something dangerous and out of control. It is those moments when nothing makes sense, when it is neither possible to think or reflect, almost paralysed by confusion. After the event there may be a vague awareness that something inappropriate or contra-dictory occurred but that was difficult to put one's finger on when, as it felt, there was nothing else to do but just respond automatically. It may take days or weeks after the event to untangle what lay beneath the disturbing encounter and may indeed be a process that is never fully realized, as the feelings experienced were (to some extent) forced upon one from an external source, yet had also been evoked by some internal recognition. The patient who is unable to bear or acknowledge their anger may be able to 'get under the skin' of the analyst who then finds himself or herself experiencing strong feelings of anger. Although the patient's unconscious motivation to disown their aggression has impacted on the analyst, nevertheless the hostile affects subsequently brought to the fore are still a reflection of the analyst's own feelings. A focus on the interpersonal, rather than purely intrapsychic, per-spective will, it is to be hoped, militate against the projective process being used by the analyst to deny the essential interdependence of the relationship.

Projective identification is one of the primary modes of human communication. Normal projective identification enhances rapport and meaning and is essential to the establishment and maintenance of a sound therapeutic relationship. Abnormal projective identification can destroy meaning and create a pathological form of merging and dependence between the subject and the recipient of his or her pro-jections. Both kinds of projective identification are implicated in all relationships. The analyst, like the mother, has the formidable task of containing the patient's/baby's abnormal projective identifications and through the mobilizing of a capacity to empathize, enables them both to experience a more normal, less defensive mode of interaction.

Projective Counteridentification

Projective counteridentification is a term coined by Leon Grinberg (1993) to describe 'disturbances caused in analytical technique by the excessive intervention of projective identification on the part of the analysand, which gives rise in the analyst to a specific reaction' (p. 47). To explain what he means, Grinberg makes a distinction between two different modes of being with a patient – an active mode and a passive mode. In the former, the analyst's activity is likened to normal projective identification, the analyst taking in the patient's projections and then returning them to the patient in a modified form. By contrast, projective counteridentification refers to situations where the patient projects into the analyst and compels the analyst to feel and respond in exactly the same way as he or she is unconsciously feeling and wanting to behave. Grinberg notes: 'It is as though he ceases to be himself and turns unavoidably into what the patient unconsciously wants him to be' (p. 48). Under these conditions, Grinberg suggests, analysts will tend either to replicate the patient's projections, and almost certainly rationalize this behaviour, or resort to other defensive strategies, depending on their own, individual level of tolerance to the specific projection they have received. It is these essentially defensive reactions on the part of the analyst that are the counteridentifying' component of Grinberg's concept, and they lead to a hiatus in normal communication between patient and analyst.

Owing to the distinctive features of the analytic process and the need for the practitioner to understand and contain the analysand's often unbearable emotions, the risk of empathy being corrupted remains an occupational hazard. Although Grinberg appears to make room for the analyst's ability to tolerate the patient's intense projections, his concept of projective counteridentification offers a somewhat one-dimensional view of the analyst as someone who is at times swamped by, and unable to resist, the patient's projections.

Grinberg has recognized some clinically important features of the way in which the patient projects into the analyst and how this can influence the analyst and the analytic work. Normal projective identification, for Grinberg, appears to be the order of the day. It seems that analysts are generally able to tolerate their patients' intense projections and therefore actively to carry out the necessary detoxifying process for their patients to reintroject. However, on occasion patients *are* able to immobilize their analyst by unconsciously forcing their projections into them. The analyst is therefore viewed by Grinberg as either actively helpful and containing or as the passive, manipulated recipient in the encounter – two very distinct responses to the patient's projections. In the active mode the analyst responds appropriately to the patient; in the passive mode countertransference responses and pathological projective identification take over, here defined as counteridentification.

Freud's original definition of countertransference seems at first glance to place the ball firmly in the analyst's court. By providing a 'counter', or equivalent, to the patient's transference, Freud appears to have counterbalanced the bias that has favoured the analyst as the more reality-based member of the analytic dyad. However, on closer inspection of his first mention on the topic (see above p. 2), it is clear that Freud is saying that it is the patient who has elicited the analyst's unconscious countertransference. This reading may be seen as somewhat at odds with Rycroft's definition, which asserts that countertransference is 'the analyst's transference on his patient' (1968, p. 25) The expectation is that the patient will transfer material from his or her past onto a relatively neutral analyst. The analyst's countertransference is more readily expected to arise in response to the patient's transference.

Paula Heimann's contributions on the subject endorse this idealized image of the analyst as the enlightened one, who is capable not only of internally experiencing the patient's genuine feelings but also of differentiating them from his or her own affects. This view took root and flourished with the introduction and establishing of the Kleinian notion of projective identification. There have, however, been some erudite and more balanced dissenting voices in the dark, among them Little, Racker, Ferenczi, Searles and Langs. Nevertheless, the subsequent 'counter' appendage to the Kleinian term by Grinberg is also in keeping with this somewhat unilateral position in tending to imply that it is only the patient who has the capacity actively to evoke emotions in the analyst, who is as a result at times forced to accept them in a passive way.

The classification of projective identification to include both normal and pathological phenomena has paradoxically increased the theoretical and technical force of the term while also adding to its ambiguity – a method of communication (empathy) or of the eradication of meaning. Yet it is the patient who is generally expected to produce material which is conducive to abnormal projective identification (to which the analyst is expected to respond empathically, as in 'normal projective identification'). This simplification not only loses the interpersonal complexity of the notion but also adds to the risk of it being used technically by the analyst in a more shallow and defensive way. This risk is also applicable to, and in many ways overlaps with, the separation of countertransference into normal and abnormal categories.

This brief review of the major turning points in the history of the concept of countertransference implies that the concept has developed into a convoluted and highly sophisticated theoretical idea which may be difficult to recognize in action and is in danger of being employed disingenuously and even deviously in the consulting room by the therapist. Nevertheless, the likelihood of jettisoning the two defining concepts that underpin the psychoanalytic paradigm remains remote. It may be possible instead to employ the notions of transference and countertransference in a more judicious and equitable manner, if we are prepared to concede that transference (defined as a distorting influence in the present that relates to the individual's past) can apply to both members of the therapeutic dyad. By the same token, counter-transference (defined here as the unconscious capacity to perceive and understand the other) could also be considered to be something inherently attributable to the patient as much as to the therapist.

Chapter 2

Contemporary Views of Countertransference

The previous chapter reviewed some of the major turning points in the history and development of the concept of countertransference. This chapter will focus on some of the more recent developments and innovative ideas that are currently emerging from research carried out into specialized areas of countertransference.

Evolutionary theory and neo-Darwinian ideas have become a particular area of interest in the field of psychology. Darwinism has also inspired some psychoanalytic writers, among whom is Christopher Badcock, who has examined and integrated Darwin's discoveries with psychoanalytic principles, notably in his book *PsychoDarwinism* (1995). Meanwhile, David Smith (2002) has investigated the unconscious from an evolutionary perspective and developed an alternative psychoanalytic hypothesis which takes into consideration an understanding of the patient's as well as the therapist's countertransference.

There is general agreement in psychoanalytic circles that the subject of erotic transference is a significant element of the analytic encounter. Nevertheless, there is a paucity of case-study material and literature on this theme. Until recently, writing on the topic was even more difficult to locate, which implied that erotic countertransference was either an unlikely occurrence or perhaps taboo. The psychotherapist David Mann is one of the few people to have addressed this discrepancy in some depth, and has done so in two recent books on this theme (1997, 1999). In the early nineteen fifties Elliott Jacques headed a research project which examined the dynamics of the organizational setting from a Kleinian perspective (Jacques, 1953). This groundbreaking work was then extended in the late fifties by Isabel Menzies-Lyth and culminated in her seminal text, *Containing Anxiety in Institutions* (1988). Both these authors were primarily interested in considering in a systematic way how an organization or institution was structured in order to protect the individuals within it from primitive existential concerns and anxieties (see further Jacques, 1955). The theme of Richard Shur's contemporary work, *Counter-transference Enactment* (Schur, 1994), also addresses the institutional environment. He further elaborates these early ideas by explaining how the organization and management of psychiatric settings, as well as associated staff procedures, reinforce abusive treatment regimes. The difficulty of working under such distressing conditions almost ensures the need for defensive measures as a protection against the anxiety and depression that abound in such environments.

Finally, the relatively innovative concept of 'counterresistance', developed by Gerald Schoenewolf, will also be reviewed. This term seems to offer an alternative and less ambiguous definition of countertransference, referring as it does to obstructions by the therapist that impede the therapeutic process.

Countertransference and evolutionary theory

The theory of evolution states that all living organisms have developed from common primitive origins and have survived or perished through a process of natural selection due to pressures from an ever changing environment. The naturalist Charles Darwin published his far reaching claims in his book *On the Origins of Species* in 1859. This work, which was first unveiled at a time that was deeply ingrained with religious principles, offered the world an entirely new paradigm of the process of creation – one which did not require a God to explain the origins of the universe and all its components. The theory of evolution is now accepted as a unified biological, scientific explanation. This interest in survival strategies has been employed by researchers across a variety of diverse disciplines, including psychology and psychotherapy, which have used Darwinian principles to make sense of certain dilemmas in the field of human relations. However, as far as human behaviour and motivation are concerned, unlike in the biological and physical domain, these applications remain far more hypothetical.

The Darwinian thesis asserts that successful organisms, defined as those that survive, have developed characteristics by chance that are best fitted to their environment. Natural selection refers to those organisms that are able to adapt to the changing conditions in the environment. The particular attributes that enable an organism to survive would gradually be passed on over a long period of time and eventually become genetically assimilated as a capacity of that particular species. A selection pressure refers to a changing aspect of the environment that brings about natural selection. The term 'survival of the fittest' applies to those organisms and species that are best suited to adapting to the vicissitudes of a given environment.

Altruism

The general definition of altruism is an unselfish concern for others; whereas the biological definition describes altruism as 'self destructive behaviour performed for the benefit of others' (Wilson, 1975, p. 306). In evolutionary terms survival is dependent upon reproductive success, which means that any living organism, human or otherwise is ruthlessly compelled to pass on its basic units of heredity (genes) in order to ensure its survival. This process was famously documented by Richard Dawkins in his post-Darwinian book, *The Selfish Gene* (1976). It is therefore understandable why parents will in many instances act to protect their offspring at their own expense: their genes can be passed on to future generations even if they perish in the process – behaviour that has been described as both kin-altruism and kin selection. Nevertheless, an explanation has also been needed to understand why many kinds of living organisms, animals and human individuals who are not related also exhibit altruistic behaviour towards one another.

Reciprocal altruism

The expression 'reciprocal altruism' was first propounded by Robert Trivers (1971) to solve the evolutionary dilemma of why unselfish behaviour can regularly be recognized between individuals who are unrelated. The term 'reciprocal' relates to actions between people that are equivalent, mutual or shared. In this respect so-called altruistic acts are more likely to occur between individuals who expect that their generosity will be returned. Clearly the individual who is able to discern whether or not another will co-operate in this sense of returning their generosity is afforded an evolutionary advantage. If individuals band together and support one another there is more chance that each will survive. However, it is also common knowledge that people will often renege and instead exploit others to their advantage. This has led to the suggestion that the propagation of reciprocal altruism would of necessity stimulate the need for an evolutionary mechanism that could detect the probability of self-misrepresentation in others.

Deception and self-deception

The strategy of 'you scratch my back and I'll scratch yours' is a fitting description of reciprocal altruism, as it is a co-operative transaction that relies on honesty. It therefore came as no surprise that developments in the study of altruism also inspired researchers to take a keen interest in the field of deception. The evolutionary imperative for the development of subtle devices that would help select out fraudulent behaviour is graphically encapsulated in this statement from an unpublished paper by David Smith:

> Altruism thus exerts a selection pressure for the evolution of cheating repertoires, and cheating is facilitated by deception, which explains why 'dishonest signaling', the biological synonym for lying, is so widespread in nature (Alexander, 1975; Dawkins, 1976; Dawkins and Krebs, 1978; Otte, 1975; Wickler, 1968). (2002, p. 9)

In this paper, 'The Evolution of the Unconscious', Smith carefully examines the psychoanalytic paradigm in the light of current findings arising from evolutionary theory. The thesis Smith pursues is specifically concerned with the evolutionary predisposition for self-deception as an expedient means for denying our proclivity to deceive others. The notion of deception as a necessary survival capacity is then linked to the concept of countertransference, which Smith illuminates in a very different way from the more traditional psychoanalytic research that has been carried out on the topic.

The theory and practice of psychoanalysis is predicated upon the assumption that we are by our natures predisposed to relegate emotionally significant and disturbing issues about ourselves and our interactions with others to an area of the mind that is outside conscious awareness. From a post-Darwinian perspective, recent evidence suggests that the inclination to deceive is an innate characteristic that can routinely be recognized in many living organisms, including insects and animals as well as human beings. As a consequence of the struggle to survive, each person, species and grouping is on this view biologically compelled to deceive others in order to secure an advantage, which means that each must also in principle be capable of anticipating the deception of others. The ubiquity of human deception is potently reflected in the following quotation by Eduardo Giannetti: 'The principle defensive weapon in this struggle consists in anticipating the manipulations planned by the deceiver so as to catch him in the act, detect and decode all the suspect signals that might indicate dishonesty and hypocrisy in those we interact with' (1997, p. 40). Deception, says Giannetti, is a pervasive phenomenon: 'All human animals are, at some time or other, active deceivers and victims of deceit; we are all intermittently confronted with both situations' (ibid.).

The relationship between deception and self-deception becomes more apparent when we recognize that our deceptive manoeuvres are more likely to succeed if as deceivers we are able to remain unaware of our true intentions and our need to deceive others. Research into non-verbal communication seems to have confirmed our worst fears – that when we set out to deceive we nevertheless tend automatically to 'give the game away' through our behaviour (Ekman and Friesen, 1974; Ekman, 1992). These give-away signs arise involuntarily owing to the anxiety and pressure that generally ensue when we are trying to pull the wool over another person's eyes, and they leave us even more vulnerable and anxious about being 'found out', as our awareness adds to the risk we sense of being discovered and thus exposed to the likelihood of punishment and retaliation.

From an evolutionary perspective, it seems the best liars would be those who are able to lie unselfconsciously. Christopher Badcock (1995) refers to this ability as 'cryptic consciousness', and claims that natural selection has been shown to reward animals who are able to deceive and to detect their predators. The work of Trivers (1988) has helped to explain the evolutionary development of the capacity for interpersonal deception in the human realm. Badcock neatly sums up the survival benefit of self-deception when an attempt is made to mislead others: 'The most effective liars would be those who had convinced themselves that their lies were in fact the truth. Having achieved the feat of self-deception, duping others would be all the more easy. Now they could lie in total sincerity!' (1995, p. 72). This evolutionary strategy is further supported by Smith (2002): 'Biologists propose that the overriding function of self-deception is the more fluid deception of others. That is, hiding aspects of reality from the conscious mind also hides these aspects more deeply from others' (p. 11).

These ideas of the need to exclude anxiety-provoking stimuli from conscious awareness, and the intimate relationship between the deception of others and self-deception are also in accord with the fundamental principles of psychoanalysis. Unlike Darwin, Freud developed his theory from clinical observation, from conflicts perceived to arise in the nurturing process and from Greek mythology. Moreover, Darwin's theory of natural selection and the development of more and more sophisticated strategies of deception have been clearly discerned in plants and animals as well as in humans. Researchers in this area therefore suggest that the capacity to deceive is unavoidable for the survival of the individual as well as the species. This argument is underscored in the following statement from Smith: 'The ruthless logic of Darwinian evolution sees to it that those organisms best able to identify deceit and take appropriate action to prevent being exploited are more likely to survive and reproduce than those who are not' (Smith, ibid., p. 9)

Countertransference

The unpublished paper from Smith mentioned above and also an earlier published paper (1999a) were groundbreaking. In these papers Smith sets out to examine systematically the notion of countertransference in the light of current findings from evolutionary theory on deception and self-deception. The need to deceive is not only considered to be ubiquitous but seen as a necessary survival characteristic. Furthermore, it is suggested that we have become more and more able to carry out these deceptive tasks effectively owing to the adaptive function of the mind, which reduces the guilt and tension that emerge when we set out to deceive, by banishing them to the unconscious. The premise that deception is a comprehensive human trait has been considered by Smith in relation to the matter of a predisposition towards countertransference:

> As we have seen, evolutionary theory implies that psychoanalysts' tendency to self-deceive is not a residue of infantile conflicts and anxieties, and therefore cannot be eliminated by self-analysis, psychoanalytic treatment or redefinition. It implies that countertransference is *inevitably* present and *inevitably* obscured by self-deception. (2002, p. 21)

Moreover, as it is the patient who is by definition the more vulnerable person in the interaction, it is the patient rather than the therapist who would need to be more alert unconsciously to any deceptive or potentially harmful behaviour from the therapist. This claim is borne out by observations made in both group interactions and one-to-one psychotherapy sessions by Robert Haskell (1999) and Robert Langs (1980). These ideas were initially pioneered and documented by the analyst Sándor Ferenczi (1933), who discovered that his patients' covert communications revealed valid criticisms about his erroneous therapeutic activities. Patients unilaterally supply very personal and sensitive information about themselves, which they entrust with the therapist. One of the primary ongoing responsibilities of the therapist is to ensure that the ground rules of the relationship are sufficiently well structured and maintained that the patient can feel safe enough to trust the therapist and therapeutic process. In this sense it is the patient, in contrast to the therapist, who is the one who empowers the practitioner and as a consequence places themselves in a theoretically high-risk situation. By and large, narrative, 'subliteral' (a term coined by Haskell) communication deals with issues that are usually prohibited by social convention. These messages appear to be unconscious, as they are for the most part denied consciously by the communicator. The oblique themes expressed in patients' stories usually coalesce around issues related to the patient's experience of boundary discrepancies, deception, disloyalty and the like.

The evolutionary discourse on the pervasiveness of deception and self-deception in human interaction has been used by Smith to empha-size the innately exploitative rather than caring aspect of human nature and human interaction. As far as the therapeutic relationship is concerned, Smith then makes a case for considering the patient's narrative communications as an incisive adaptive tool – a tool that has developed over time and which lets the patient's true concerns about the therapist's trustworthiness (to honour their part of the bargain) be known. As a consequence, the definition of countertransference developed by Heimann in 1950, which presented the analyst's counter-transference reactions as a reflection of the patient's difficulties, can now be seen as a process that also applies to the patient. This body of work also implies that a great deal of human communication, includ-ing the therapeutic encounter, will be taken up with the consistent checking and monitoring on the part of one person of the behaviour and honesty of the more advantaged other.

In conclusion, these ideas support the argument that the patient's countertransference reactions about the therapist that are disclosed through their oblique messages should become one the most significant elements of the therapeutic process. Whether or not one accepts the evidence from the Darwinian theory of deception, the substance of its message offers a valuable warning to those in the caring professions, as it suggests that human interaction is characterized by suspicion, misrepresentation and the struggle for power.

The evolutionary theory of countertransference asserts that human nature is innately deceptive and self-deceptive and that this is the way it has to be for the individual and the species to survive. However, the critics of evolutionary psychology (Rose and Rose, 2001) consider this intense focus on driven biological principles to be a reactionary, backward and rather one-sided view of the human condition. These commentators claim that the evolutionary thesis engenders and fosters the dangerous idea that human nature is determined and does not therefore allow for other kinds of human possibilities, notably free-will and responsibility.

Erotic transference and countertransference

The conflicts that arise between loving, or erotic, and aggressive impulses are firmly entrenched in Freud's developmental model. In his account Freud traces the origins of the first sexual impulses, which are directed towards the mother and which subsequently induce in the infant hateful and murderous feelings towards the father. The tension and negotiation between loving and hateful affects continue to exert an influence (often unconscious) throughout the individual's life and are for that reason the primary cause of many of our personal and interpersonal difficulties. This may reveal itself in psychosomatic symptoms, in depression and in more radical disorders such as schizophrenia. Psychoanalysis is dedicated to addressing and bringing to light the underlying dilemmas associated with these concerns, with the aim of ameliorating the symptoms in question.

The Freudian model of human nature is obviously applicable to both patient and therapist; both are subject to conscious, and especially unconscious, erotic and aggressive desires. The exploration of the patient's aggressive transference is one of the fundamental components of the therapeutic process; the significance of this hostility is borne out by the extreme abundance of case-study material and publications on this topic. The same can be said of the literature (albeit there is less of that literature) dealing with the patient's incestuous erotic impulses. However, the extent of written material, seminars or conferences on the theme of the therapist's countertransference difficulties in both these areas is conspicuously limited. This neglect was further borne out by my own experience a few years ago when it was suggested to me by a group of psychotherapists that a conference on the subject of erotic countertransference was long overdue. My attempt to organize such a project initially met with great enthusiasm, as well as with some interesting smutty Freudian humour. Nevertheless, the conference never got off the ground owing to the reluctance of presenters to speak publicly and personally on this clearly sensitive and taboo subject.

The psychotherapist David Mann (1997, 1999) is one of the very few people to have dealt with this glaring omission. In his two major publications Mann firstly explores the Oedipus myth in great depth in order to highlight its overriding theme and then parallels this theme to the profession's silence in this area. For Mann, the fundamental communication expressed in the incestuous tragedy is: 'Either it should be eschewed, disavowed and repressed as quickly as possible (as in Oedipus' flight from his adopted parents), or, alternatively, it will be acted upon.' This, he continues, is a duality 'also characteristic of the classical and traditional psychoanalytic attitude regarding the erotic transference and even more so the erotic countertransference: it is a problem that should be repressed or it will be acted out' (1999, pp. 74–75).

It is Mann's view that the subjectivity of the therapist is just as significant to the therapeutic process as is the patient's internal world. Adult erotic wishes on the part of both members of the dyad – which wishes have originated out of primitive incestuous desires – must be recognized to play an important role (however unconsciously) in the therapeutic interaction, as they do in all intimate relationships. Mann's assertions reinforce the need to examine these salient issues within the encounter, and yet these issues appear to be viewed in a similar light – that is, with the same trepidation and resistance – as they are viewed within the Oedipal drama. As Mann states: 'We could say that the psychoanalytic encounter at this deeply unconscious level is where the unconscious incestuous and murderous desires of one individual meet the unconscious incestuous and murderous desires of another' (ibid., p. 77).

Good enough erotic subjectivity

'Good enough erotic subjectivity' refers to the therapist's integrated awareness of their own erotic and murderous impulses, since it is this awareness that enables the therapist to contain their desires. The therapist's ability to acknowledge these deeply conflicting, and often shameful, feelings is also containing for the patient, as it enables them to follow suit and reduces the likelihood of needing to project these feelings onto others, or to act them out in other ways. The therapist's recognition of these sometimes unwieldy affects also plays an important role in the therapeutic process, as it enables the development and maintenance of appropriate levels of intimacy and separateness between both parties. The patient's participation in a relationship that has appropriate boundaries may be an entirely new and enabling experience that can allow them subsequently to re-organize their relationships in the outside world, instead of repeating the matching interpersonal scenarios that have initially prompted them to seek treatment and that are remnants of unconscious infantile dilemmas. Mann bravely confronts the controversy head-on by reasoning that this is the fundamental task of therapy – to provide the opportunity for a different kind of relationship, which does not shy away from exploring two of the most disturbing elements of human nature, namely love and hate.

The psychoanalytic paradigm does, however, throw up some glaring and curious paradoxes in relation to these two cardinal emotions. If the patient reveals erotic desires (either overtly or obliquely) towards the therapist, this response is likely to be defined as an expression of transference and a form of resistance to the work. If, however, the therapist experiences erotic desires towards the patient, this may be described as projective identification, with its source in the patient's desires. The evidence suggests that therapists and trainees are generally reluctant to admit to such experiences owing to the need to appear professional and to the shame attached to these desires, which is why these issues are rarely raised in training, supervision and case-study examples. This reaction has been referred to as 'erotic horror' (Kumin, 1985). As for the countertransference responses, Mann points out: 'In my opinion, to see the erotic as essentially fabricated and as resistance is more often an indication of *resistance in the therapist* rather than in what is happening to the patient' (1999, p. 86). Furthermore, it is not surprising to note, given the intense and intimate nature of the psychoanalytic encounter, that the history of psychoanalysis reveals examples (from Jung to Margaret Mahler) of celebrated and pioneering analysts who have had sexual relationships with their patients (see Jung, 1908).

It is even more difficult to come to terms with how this most weighty of all the elements of human interaction could be excised from the therapeutic process when it comprises the very core of the mother–baby relationship. Furthermore, it is common psychoanalytic parlance that the denial of erotic and hateful emotions prohibits the development of a truly loving relationship.

The principal and radical message which Mann emphasizes in his thesis concerns the positive, rather than resistant, factors of the patient, and the therapist's aggressive and, especially, erotic transference and countertransference responses. Mann is also at pains to point out that the same priorities apply not only to the heterosexual elements of the encounter but also to the homoerotic impulses that inevitably emerge.

Transference and countertransference are for Mann a joint creation and the most powerful component of the therapeutic process; therefore thinking the unthinkable must be confronted at all costs, or these will be acted out.

Countertransference enactment

The term 'countertransference enactment', coined by Richard Schur (1994), describes certain types of defences that are mobilized and established by therapists and staff in psychiatric institutions as protection from the distressing primitive impulses that are aroused in them by their patients. Schur's text offers a lucid and graphic account of the way in which the pathology of severely disturbed patients detrimentally, and often unconsciously, influences and is mirrored in the reactions of their caretakers. This process is defined by Schur as follows:

> The term *countertransference defense* refers to an intrapsychic operation, the purpose of which is to establish or sustain the staff person's psychological equilibrium under conditions of threat. Hospital structures may facilitate this process. These structures augment defenses by providing a disguised institutionally sanctioned discharge channel and/or distancing procedure. (1994, p. 14)

Omnipotence is a common symptomatic feature in patients with severe psychopathology. What is less obvious is how this powerful defence is employed by staff members to cope with their patients' and their own uncontainable anxieties through the release of their (the staff members') omnipotence towards both patients and other staff members. This process is examined and explicitly clarified by Schur via an abundance of case-study illustrations. For example, staff may use the defence of splitting: one group internalizes the idealized aspect of omnipotence, while the remaining staff members identify with the persecutory elements of patients' omnipotence. These defensive actions are used as a means of staving off and defending against patients' vengeful emotions, which they, the staff members, feel unable to contain.

The creation of strong security measures to protect staff from threatening and potentially harmful situations is also cited as an example of how psychiatric staff attempt to harness omnipotent control from psychotic patients. These security precautions are generally put in place after patients have attempted to deal with their extreme anxiety and anger by acting out their omnipotent fantasies. In his important text Schur also highlights the fact that the psychological issues and implications that underlie staff members' practical attempts to deal with these ongoing, critically stressful conditions are rarely, if ever, explored. From his work and research experience in this area, Schur has been led to the disturbing conclusion that the habituation to countertransference enactments on the part of therapists and auxiliary staff in psychiatric inpatient settings is the rule rather than the exception.

The consistent focus on organizational methods is shown to contribute to the overall management design of these institutions. These tactics foster and maintain defensive strategies in patients and staff alike and shield them from transference and countertransference anxieties. The gravity of Schur's message is accentuated by his assertion that because of staff members' reluctance to address these issues, these common modes of hospital practice not only continue to be seen as acceptable but also remain unrecognized. It is also both worrying and paradoxical that the promotion of countertransference defences through enactment supports and sustains the caretaker's avoidance of anxiety by tacitly encouraging a regression to an earlier stage of development. In conclusion, it is disturbingly ironic that these are the very symptoms that have necessitated the patient's hospitalization in the first place and placed them in the care of professionals who are sadly unable to contain either their patients' or their own anxieties.

Counterresistance

The professional role requirements and ethical duties of therapists are formidable, as not only are they expected to address their patients' resistances but they must also do all they can to overcome their own. As Little (1951) noted, it is far less problematical to investigate the back of someone else's head compared to exploring one's own. It was mentioned earlier that the term 'counterresistance' was introduced by Gerald Schoenewolf (1993). His thesis starts from the position that the therapeutic encounter is characterized by an inter-actional conflict between the patient's and the therapist's resistances. The transference–countertransference matrix is the arena in which this struggle is played out. The challenge and process of the therapeutic task requires both members to confront and work through their hostilities (resistances) in order to strengthen the transparency of the alliance and to create an environment that is based more on trust. Just as the patient's resistances are reflected in their transference reactions to the therapist, so the therapist's resistances, or 'counter-resistances', are seen as a product of their countertransference responses. As Schoenewolf explains, there are various problems for the therapist to surmount before they can penetrate these resistances: 'Indeed, there are four battles of resistance going on simultaneously: the patient's battle with self-resistance, the therapist's battle with self-resistance, the patient's battle with the therapist's resistance, and the therapist's battle with patient's resistance' (1993, p. 16). Schoenewolf underscores the enigma that is part and parcel of the therapist's role and of the dilemma of grappling with both the patient's resistances as well as their own.

The author continues his discussion of counterresistance by drawing on ideas taken from Eastern philosophy and especially the notion of the development of harmony between patient and therapist, which he sees as a primary aim and that can only materialize as both patient and therapist begin to let go of their long-held resistances. In keeping with this Eastern tradition, Schoenewolf highlights the significance of the therapist's self-reflective responsibilities as an aid to the patient's progress, thus emphasizing the reciprocal nature of resistance:

Therapists need to focus less on analysing the patient's resistances and more on analysing their own. Indeed, whenever therapists become aware of a resistance on the patient's part, they should look for the counterresistance before attempting to interpret the patient's resistance. Often, once the therapist has overcome the counterresistance, the patient's resistance will be easy to resolve. (ibid., p. 18)

Schoenewolf then proceeds to outline and classify three specific categories of counterresistance. The first of these, 'countertransference resistance', emerges only in response to certain patients and is related to the patient's resistances. The author comments: 'Generally counter-transference resistance is provoked when some aspect of the patient's personality or behavior is reminiscent of a primary figure in the therapist's past' (ibid., pp. 58–59). The second, 'characterological counterresistance', is seen as entirely related to the personality of the therapist and to resistances that are characteristic of the therapist in all areas of their life. The third category of counterresistance is not linked to the therapist's past but is cultural – 'a displacement and projection of social pressures and values onto the patient' (ibid., p. 56). Here Schoenewolf is referring to strong beliefs or political, religious and racial biases held by some therapists, which are unlikely to be reflected on by the therapist and which may compromise their ability to maintain a relatively neutral therapeutic attitude and therefore may detrimentally influence the therapeutic process.

Each of these types of resistance in the therapist is considered to hamper the progress of the therapy as they must inevitably impede and inhibit the development of intimacy. In other words, it may be inferred that therapists who tend to cling to dogmatic beliefs are likely to need these kinds of resistances to keep their patients at arm's length. The objectification of people into rigid categories enables the individual to maintain an image of themselves as powerful; by using the defensive mechanism of projection they are able to deny their own vulnerabilities and view these as present in the other person. What we might call this type of 'privileged' omnipotence can be seen to be quite readily available to those who practise psychotherapy and may therefore be considered to constitute one of its major risks.

Psychotherapy, for Schoenewolf, is fundamentally a learning process in which to practise and improve one's capacity for love and intimacy. However, as all resistance can be seen as an expression of hate, and all types of countertransference resistance as expressions of the therapist's hate, then all countertransference resistance will by definition be seen to obstruct the primary purpose of the therapy and so deprive the patient of their right to experience a loving and intimate relationship. I would add that this would also deprive the patient of the equally important and necessary, albeit painful, experience of separation, which is obviously bypassed when the patient has not had the advantage of bonding in the first place. The human tendency to disavow hate (often owing to the terror of retaliation) and either to project it onto others or to displace it, so that it is less obvious to others and ourselves, remains a constant threat in the therapeutic arena. There are, however, many give-away clues that may indicate that countertransference resistance is present: for example, when the therapist is bored, or arrives late for a session; when the therapist speaks too much, or is too silent; or when the therapist runs over time – in other words, those occasions when the therapist feels compelled to disturb a boundary.

The subject of objective transference and objective countertransference is also explored in Schoenewolf's book; these are the aspects of the interaction that constitute the real relationship. On the difference between the subjective and objective Schoenewolf writes:

> If a patient fears being entrapped by a therapist when, in fact, the therapist has never given any indication of such desires, this is transference. If, on the other hand, a patient fears being entrapped by a therapist who stares menacingly at the patient, this is at least in part a real relationship. (ibid., p. 57)

Likewise, Schoenewolf gives similar examples of the difference between countertransference and the therapist's genuine concern, interest, and care for the patient. Objective countertransference is seen by him as entirely elicited by the patient's transference, which requires an interpretation. As far as Schoenewolf is concerned, the patient's awareness of being stared at by the therapist is viewed as either an outright distortion or only a partially insightful reaction, in contrast to the therapist's objective countertransference, which is accepted as an objective, conscious and reality-based reaction, that can be readily interpreted. This ambiguity is also implied by Kenneth Frank, who states: 'Analysts must continually assess the meaning of patients' transference against their own self-perceptions, rather than assuming that their baseline participation is appropriate, or that their readings are correct' (1999, p. 94).

Schoenewolf's work is important to the continuing countertransference debate, as he has been prepared to take a theoretical, philosophical and practical stand by placing the countertransference responsibilities more firmly in the therapist's lap. The Eastern-derived, humanistic emphasis on being-with-the-patient also reinforces the significance of the therapist's attitude and its influence on the quality of the interaction. The work on countertransference resistance is also of importance, as it expects therapists to acknowledge, recognize and reflect more deeply on their own, rather than their patients', resistances and the unpalatable motives that underlie them. There is, however, less stress placed on the essential value of working through these interpersonal resistances as a cardinal component of the therapeutic process. For example, Frank states: 'The insight provided into counterproductive transference–countertransference interactions creates a pathway to new relational experience' (1999, p. 95).

Psychoanalytic interview

M. Fakhry Davids is a psychoanalyst in full-time private practice in London. He qualified as a clinical psychologist at the University of Cape Town, where he was subsequently Lecturer in Psychology. Davids trained as an adult psychotherapist at the Tavistock Clinic, and as a psychoanalyst at the Institute of Psychoanalysis in London. Until recently, Davids was Honorary Consultant Psychologist at the London Clinic of Psychoanalysis.

The discipline of psychoanalysis encompasses a range of varying foci; I therefore began the psychoanalytic interview by asking the practitioner first to describe the particular area of psychoanalysis that informs his practice and the philosophy that underlines it.

Fakhry Davids described his approach as fundamentally psychoanalytic, tending toward the Kleinian school of thought:

> I make an assumption that the patient has a mind and that the reason that they have come to see me is that something has gone wrong there. I use the notion of pathology to try to conceptualize what has gone wrong. This is an investigative procedure that can take time, but once I get the pathology clear, then I develop ways of trying to intervene.

The term pathology is often associated with medical procedures and for this reason is sometimes rejected by practitioners in the field of psychotherapy. This prompted my next question as to the specific meaning he placed on the expression:

> I use the concept in a private way, as part of an ongoing internal dialogue, to capture the idea that the patient's symptoms – whatever troubles them and brings them to treatment – is connected meaningfully with a more general set of issues inside the mind. This general set of issues is the psychopathology, which I tend to conceptualize in terms of problematic object relations.

The following example from Davids helped to clarify what he meant by pathology from an object relations perspective:

> A patient with a history of frequenting prostitutes entered a new relationship that he really wanted to succeed, and recognized that

his perversion would threaten this. My patient was in most respects successful and well functioning. I assumed the problem with prostitutes was a symptom of something deeper, and the investigation I conducted revealed that a problematic relationship with his mother lay at the core of it. The patient lost her at a very early age and I hypothesized that unconscious hatred towards the mother who had abandoned him could not be fully experienced in his mind. Instead, it was split off from the relationship with her and played out repeatedly in the degrading relationships with prostitutes – all of this outside his conscious awareness. The hypothesis took a long time to clarify and confirm, but, once formed, my key interventions specifically addressed this issue.

I asked Davids to say something about what it meant to describe himself as a Kleinian. He said he was probably Kleinian in two respects, both related to his practice. The first concerns therapeutic technique:

Having identified the dynamics that underpin a patient's pathology, I try to find a version of it that is real and alive between the patient and me. Until one can get to that, I wouldn't think one has much of a chance of bringing about real change in the way things are organized in the mind. With respect to the patient I mentioned, the next step was to find how he used me as a prostitute – ways in which, contrary to his conscious intention, he devalued my work or me. When I could identify that, which took time, its meaning could be properly faced in the lived relationship between us. It is this immediacy and aliveness that enables one to really tackle internal problems – you can confront the forces involved, and work out what function they serve, much more directly than by just talking about them at a remove. That approach is associated with the here-and-now technique developed within the Kleinian tradition. The second Kleinian strand is that my conceptualization of the patient's pathology tends to be underpinned by an understanding of early (infantile) object relationships. Having said all that, today many people who are not Kleinians also tend to think and work in this way, and in British psychoanalysis generally it is difficult for any one school to lay exclusive claim to a particular conceptualization or technique. What we end up with is the product of a rich interchange within the discipline, so the actual labels we use to characterize ourselves sometimes turn out to be rather trivial.

In commenting on the interpersonal focus of the work, Davids remarked:

From the beginning, it is easily apparent that you influence the patient – that is more or less what we all expect – but the patient also influences you, making you think, feel and repond in particular ways. This often yields information about the patient's mental functioning that is not accessible in any other way, and can prove vital in filling out the picture of the patient's psychopathology. The relationship is therefore a very important field of observation, and the effect a patient has on one is an important element of observation.

The patient I mentioned a moment ago tended to make me feel pleased with myself, satisfied that I was doing a good job for him, and in turn he was a good patient. This was an idealized transference, and recognizing it as such allowed me to investigate its defensive function. It turned out that it protected both of us from having to face the impact on him of my absences, which cut to the heart of the unresolved mourning for his mother that underpinned his perverse acts. Of course work on this underlying issue was complex and difficult, but recognizing that I felt pleased with myself was an important first step in the process that eventually drew attention to it in the here-and-now.

Returning to the interpersonal field, I would expect every patient to influence me, and believe that one can't really work properly in the here-and-now without attending to such thoughts and feelings. That said, however, this is complicated, for we are talking about our own responses after all – what I think and feel in the room, as well as responses involving the patient that occur outside the consulting room – such as ones that might arise as I drive home at night.

Davids emphasized the significance of countertransference in relation to the clinical situation:

Working with the countertransference depends on being aware of what one feels, what one doesn't feel, and what one thinks in relation to the patient. But I make a distinction between being aware of such reactions and talking to a patient about them. I would not, on the whole, talk spontaneously to a patient about my countertransference responses. Instead, once I am aware of them I first try to create space for reflection: are they my own idiosyncratic reactions, or are they responses that can be said to 'belong' to the patient? It is only the latter that may be considered as countertransference proper. One's idiosyncratic response to the patient is one's own transference to that patient – it comes from what we ourselves bring to the analytic encounter, rather than essentially from the patient. They are inevitabilities mobilized in the analytic encounter since we cannot be neutral observers of the analytic process in which we are involved. To distinguish our own transferences from countertransference can involve much ongoing work. This is especially true of responses we are not fully aware of.

Davids stated that the expression 'transference reactions' referred to what the analyst brings, which means that if the analyst is aware of feeling or even of not feeling something in relation to the patient then that becomes a problem that has to be analysed first, before the practitioner can discuss it with the patient:

> I very rarely speak to a patient immediately about what I feel in response to them (even if I am convinced that it is indeed a counter-transference response). I would want to think about it first. Otherwise, the danger of attributing to a patient any wild response in the analyst is too great and can be damaging. I would, however, hold onto my responses, and go back to the material to see whether these can be linked in a meaningful way to other facts known about the patient – about the patient's past, about the way the patient is with me, previous material, dreams and so forth.

The practitioner here clearly expresses the view that both patient and analyst are prone to transference responses. He does, however, reserve the term countertransference for reactions that are evoked primarily by the patient. He is also at pains to point out that these reactions in the analyst must initially be thought of as highly tentative and tempered with a great deal of caution.

My interviewee then clarified how he would technically use his countertransference reactions in his clinical practice:

> In trying to work all this out, what I might do is to float an inter-pretation involving the meaning of a countertransference reaction, but I would be clear in my mind that the interpretation has the status of a hypothesis. I speak about it to find out if the patient can be en-gaged in the process of trying to ascertain two things: whether it is

indeed a countertransference response, and if so, what its meaning (with reference to the patient's psychopathology) is.

In terms of practice, Davids asserted that he believed it was fundamental for the therapist not only to be aware of their thoughts and feelings but, and very importantly, to process that material internally prior to considering any overt communication to the patient. He emphasized in particular the necessity of talking about it with the patient.

Pursuing it with the patient in some way is vital: if it is counter-transferential then it is probably a split-off aspect of the patient's mind that finds its way into you, the analyst. If you are going to help integrate split-off parts, then they must be addressed in one way or another. Of course this is not an overnight thing; it takes time and is part of the essence of the whole of analysis.

From this Kleinian perspective, it may be assumed that counter-transference, as defined here, is the pivot on which the analytic process is organized: that it consists of projections on the part of the patient, experienced by the analyst, which must be processed and in time reflected back in ways that can enable the patient to become aware of them, and to begin working through them.

I asked whether by 'floating' an interpretation Davids meant it would be couched as a suggestion:

Not necessarily. Whilst being clear in my mind that it is a hypo-thesis – that is, I wouldn't put my money on it – I might nonetheless put it firmly and unambiguously to the patient. Really, I am asking; but the form of the question has to take account of the fact that what I am enquiring after is likely to be split off, and hence unavailable to consciousness. If you frame it as a question, you are likely to get an intellectual response, so you 'ask' by way of a clear and unambig-uous interpretation.

For example, a patient seemed to ignore an interpretation I had made by changing the subject. At first I treated her response as an association and tried to figure out how it connected to my interven-tion; while doing so, I realized that I felt angry and impatient with her. Reflecting on this revealed that I felt dismissed with contempt. Was this feeling a consequence of my overvaluing my intervention, or had I indeed been dismissed? If so, was it because she felt that the interpretation did not take account of – that is, dismissed – some aspect of her own initial communication (to which it was a response), or did she not like the interpretation?

As means of starting to investigate this, I said simply: 'I think that you view what I have just said with total contempt.' If it was her contempt that her ego could not tolerate, and was therefore split off and lodged in me, I would expect massive defences against it: the patient might feel accused of doing something terrible, which would find us in paranoid terrain. If, however, it were tolerable, the response would be quite different. This patient, after some hesitation, said she thought my interpretation had been wrong, but she knew I tried hard and didn't want to hurt my feelings directly. This confirmed that her aggression was not so intense as to necessitate splitting and projection into her object, and we could then investigate more fully the meaning of her ignoring my interpretation.

If the patient were to respond in a powerful way, I asked, would that confirm the hypothesis? 'It would be one piece of data that supports it', Davids replied, 'and would have to be put side by side with other data relating to that particular issue to obtain a fuller picture. But a strong response would help to decide how to take the therapeutic process forward at that point.'

Although the question of countertransference was one I had already raised, I asked Davids to elaborate on what the notion meant to him. 'As I have already said, within the psychoanalytic setting one thinks and feels many things, but not all of it is countertransference.' I reiterated my understanding of his definition – that he designated the feelings that related to him rather than to the patient as his own transference issues, whereas the reactions that he felt emanated from the patient he defined as countertransference.

Yes, I would tend to stick with that definition. To jump to the conclusion that the feelings evoked in the analyst always emanate from the patient is dangerous, and I don't think that any analysts today do so. You know sometimes you just get out of the wrong side of the bed and anyone who crosses your path that day may elicit all kinds of feelings that you otherwise would not have. Now, the interesting thing is that even in such a situation not all patients evoke the same reaction in one, so theoretically one's response within the session must have at least something to do with the particular patient. But clearly the bulk of it comes from you, and I don't find it clinically useful to put too much weight on what may be the patient's contribution.

Davids remarked that although his preceding comments were theoretically interesting, because they said something important about ordinary human relating, this was not, for him, the focus of the clinical domain. Here, he said, the job is to focus on the patient's psychopathology. It is the analyst's responsibility to decide which observations, and conceptualizations flowing from them, are helpful in illuminating or working on aspects of that pathology:

> I think it is very important to know what is you and what is the patient. I would want to be aware of how I am feeling with the patient, but I would be very careful about about viewing a feeling of mine as coming exclusively from the patient. It is of course salient to notice one's feelings, especially when one is feeling rather vulnerable, but it is also often at those times that something from the patient is able to get through.

Thus it is not always possible to differentiate categorically between what belongs to whom, but the attempt to do so is a fundamental part of the complexity of the work.

> I do talk too patients about this, about what they might think I think. For example, I have a disturbed patient who has taken a very long time to bring just an ordinary observation about me – namely that she thinks that on Mondays I am usually in a foul mood. This is probably true – in so far as I don't particularly like Mondays and my patient appears to have observed me reasonably accurately. The real therapeutic issue is whether this observation is based on her projecting into me her own dislike of the aftermath of the weekend, which is to be faced on Monday, or whether she is in tune with my emotional reality. To my mind this is the therapeutic question that flows from her important observation.

I asked my interviewee for his position on disclosing this type of personal information to the patient and how he would deal with it in practice:

> I would probably never say, 'Yes, I'm in a foul mood', or 'No, I'm not', because to me the gold dust of the session is the patient's perception: this is a key to understanding her mind, which is the therapeutic task. That said, one has to be aware that patients can feel

terribly hurt and rejected by one's lack of response, and this may need to be acknowledged and worked with. It could feel like saying hello to someone who then simply ignores you, and one has to take responsibility for this therapeutic stance.

In commenting on how he would respond, Davids said he would talk about the fact that he had not responded, and that the patient had then become quiet, which suggested to him that she may have felt hurt and had withdrawn in anger.

In response to my request for an example of a typical intervention that he might employ, Davids said:

If I consider the example of the patient with the prostitutes, his perversion has been outside the analysis for a long time. What I mean is that he tended to idealize the treatment, he was the good patient; but eventually I began to feel impatient in the sessions. He seemed content, but I felt that the analysis had got a little stuck. He seemed to have pencilled me in for life as his advisor as to what goes on in his mind, and seemed quite happy to come here five days a week on that basis. Now I certainly didn't feel that this was in his interest, nor was it the kind of work that I wanted to be doing. I liked to think that we are working together to affect some kind of change in the way things were inside his mind that would give him more insight into himself, so that he might in time become his own advisor. I therefore began to think that I needed to move this analysis along a bit, and of course when you think that, you have to wonder whether this is countertransferential: had my patient's impatience been projected onto me? Having thought about this, on balance I considered that it was time for things to be moved on.

A week later he mentioned that during intercourse with his partner they had used drugs. Up to then I had been rather tolerant in dealing with this kind of material. Having resolved that things needed to be moved on, however, this time I thought I had to refer more directly to the aggression that it involved. So I spoke to him about how I thought that this was an attack on his partner's capacity to stimulate him and make him feel alive and potent in order to penetrate her. The patient went away and came back in his usual manner, but beneath the surface he was absolutely furious with me for disrupting the notion that I would be the advisor. From his point of view I should have said something different, such as 'Don't you think that it may be that you feel a bit resentful towards your partner, perhaps because she is not totally available to you all the time?' I should have put it that way instead of saying, 'When you do this, it is an attack on her capacity', and so on.

Davids explained that this was an example of where he felt that the analysis had got into a 'bit of an enclave', where things had become 'a bit too cosy' and there was 'not enough turbulence necessary for growth'. He continued:

This was how I brought in a bit of turbulence. The patient's usual response to any interpretation about his internal state was 'I don't know how I feel and, since we know that I'm cut off, I shall take your word for it. You are the expert.' This protected him from having to face his hatred of me for pushing him away, for breaking his idealized dependency on me. Subsequently his attempts to recruit me as the expert on his side intensified, so that the fact that he had felt my interpretation to be a cruel penetration into our cosy relationship nearly got lost. Paradoxically, whenever I tried to bring this fact back, the discussion would become both more interesting and animated and more difficult. When I left at the end of one of these sessions I found myself saying that I would see him tomorrow. Given that I don't usually say this to patients I wondered afterwards why I reassured him so. This alerted me to the fact that he had been involved in an intercourse with me, and in doing so I had literally become the partner who mattered but who had other fish to fry (that is, I was a separate person), which stirred hostile impulses in him; and I was being nudged to reassure him in order to conceal this fact.

Davids also mentioned that the patient's deep attachment to an artificial relationship that looks like a real one was a central feature of his pathology. This comment reminds us of the patient's need to visit prostitutes, and of the similarities that exist between the relationship between client and prostitute and between client and therapist. In both there is a necessity to pay to be in an 'intimate' situation. Davids agreed that this artificiality was likely to be reflected in the therapeutic process but pointed out that there are bound to be similarities and differences between any two relationships. If, as in his experience, the patient privileges only one aspect, that should be investigated. Might it be too threatening to look at the differences – that this therapeutic relationship is one which he hopes will help him overcome his problems and find the capacity to hold onto the new relationship by which he sets such store? If so, that would help to understand why he was drawn to prostitutes in the first place: being the purchaser of a service puts one nominally in control, and protects one from the awareness of needing others – it is the analyst, like the prostitute, who needs the business.

My interviewee implied that offering the particular intervention he had mentioned earlier had in fact created some sort of turning point in the analysis. 'Yes, it had all sorts of ripples, because an analysis has a course; and following that series of sessions we found ourselves at the end of the beginning. Following that, some substantive and gainful work was done, which resulted in my patient setting up home with his new partner.'

I asked if he was also suggesting that had he presented his patient with a subtler, milder intervention, the analysis would not have moved along as it did:

Yes, I wouldn't have caused enough turbulence in him. On the other hand, if I'd have talked about this earlier I would have been a bit more tentative and it would not have had the same effect. It was important at this stage to begin to shake things up a bit otherwise the 'advisory' transference could just continue in the same vein and any self-respecting analyst would not be content with this state of affairs.

Discussion of case-study vignette

Fakry Davids commented on the material of the vignette he was shown.

This is a very interesting piece, but I want to say two things. The first is that it is short-term therapy, which influences the reality of the therapeutic task. It would tend to make me feel that I need to get my skates on, aware that time is more limited than with a long-term patient, and this will interfere with the possibility of the therapy proceeding at the patient's 'natural' pace. The other consideration is that the vignette is from the beginning of the treatment, when things are generally more uncertain than they would be later on. Those two things together would probably make me want to formulate hypotheses in the way that I have talked about earlier – that is, to put them as very direct interpretations whose aim would be to generate material that might illuminate the psychopathology. Later I would be more focused on working at particular aspects of the pathology.

The first thing that occurs to me is that there is something quite violent in this patient, as in the trashing of the room – conflicts which might link to her becoming depressed and withdrawn. That is, I would hypothesize that this girl's pathology involves internal violence.

Now, to look at this specific session: we don't know why she is late, but it is only two minutes. However, she makes herself twenty minutes late. If it were you, you might come up the stairs and say, 'Have you forgotten about me?' To me it is diagnostically significant that the patient does not. She is a patient who withdraws and sits and waits. This invites the object to treat her badly: one could say that it is a sado-masochistic interchange. It involves cruelty being disowned as something violent and destructive, and being projected into the object. For me, the crucial issue is whether this internal dynamic is fixed or malleable.

When talking to her, I would want to bring this in straightaway, to try to ascertain whether she is perverse (does she have a fixed sadistic internal object to whom she is responding masochistically?) or whether she is more or less ordinary but with a terrible (neurotic) worry about aggression, which is projected into the object.

In terms of interventions, first of all I wouldn't apologize to her as this only undermines things. You have to sit it out and expect to be hated for not apologizing. If she can hate me for this, then it would tilt the balance towards a view that, with a bit of help, her destructiveness can live in her own mind, that it doesn't have to be projected.

That is by way of background and orientation. I would understand the material itself like this: she is telling you in the here-and-now that she feels like walking out because *you* have kept *her* waiting. I would do it that way round, because the impulse to walk out is an aggressive one, so this offers an opportunity to investigate it further, bearing in mind its importance in the psychopathology (in my view). If you could establish that she can know about this wish in her and risk the consequences no matter what, then that would be diagnostic. So my interventions would be based on that; and when she finished her monologue about the computers and so forth, I would say that I think that she feels absolutely furious with me for keeping her waiting. I would take the responsibility for keeping her waiting (even though I am aware that it is not I personally who did it) since that would avoid a split between the receptionist and me. If I wanted to be 'kind' I would link the material with the interpretation, I would say something like, 'I think when you tell me about this incident yesterday and how furious they made you, it is a way of putting on the agenda the fact that by keeping you waiting for eighteen minutes, I have made you feel utterly furious, and that as you sit there your impulse is to walk out and to give me the feeling of how awful it is to sit all primed for this meeting whilst I keep you waiting all the while. That would be my first intervention. If the patient is terrified of her aggression she will most probably deny it and blame the receptionist. Then I would take up with her that she feels frightened of the impact of her hatred and violence toward me (for example, that I might reject her) and therefore she has to protect me by blaming my receptionist. Then I would see if that bit of help allowed her to move closer to her aggression. If it did not, this would tend to strengthen the view that we are dealing with intense destructiveness, for example murderous feelings.

If she could tolerate the idea – if she smiles or squirms or if she says, 'Well, actually it is true, and when I sat down I did think "Should I just bugger off?"', I would feel cheered. Here is a patient who, when she finds an object that can contain her violence, can move into closer contact with it. This would then allow a deeper investigation into her psychopathology. I might suggest (that is, investigate a hypothesis) that the real violence in her is towards me for keeping her at arm's length. That is, am I an unavailable mother in the transference? Does she long to be treated more humanely, to be recognized in a mutual and involved way? – perhaps in a way that a mother is actually involved with her baby, instead of which she finds only a therapist–patient relationship.

Conclusion

The analyst in the above interview has discussed clinical material from an object relations perspective. Although Fakry Davids explained that he felt it was not always meaningful to distinguish between the different psychoanalytic sub-groups, it seems that his description of countertransference in terms of the feelings aroused in him by the patient can be compared to the Kleinian notion of projective identification. However, he has also acknowledged the relevance of his own transference issues as an intermittent disturbing influence in the therapeutic process. In addition, he also refers to 'transference reactions', which he describes as the analyst's characteristic thinking traits, that may either interfere with an ability to think about certain issues or elicit a heightened interest.

As for the case-study vignette presented to him, Davids' central concern and focus have a strong Kleinian ring. His remarks on the client's state of mind in terms of diagnostic categories rely on Klein's developmental model as a useful source of information. He states that his central aim with a short-term project such as this would be to ascertain the extent of the client's need to split off or project her perceptions onto him. He also stated that owing to the short-term nature of the work his understanding of the patient's state of mind would become a matter of some urgency, and would subsequently influence his interpretations. However, in the light of his acceptance of the intrusion of his own transference, it may also have been necessary for him to process the fact that he felt that the case needed to be dealt with on an urgent basis.

Chapter 3

The Communicative Approach to Psychoanalytic Psychotherapy

Thomas Kuhn (1962), writing within the philosophy of science, coined the term 'paradigm' to describe how scientists work from within a determined, unchangeable, fixed perspective. A paradigm provides a framework for thinking (Zukav, 1979), a set of accepted and internalized established assumptions that allow for the formulation of the hypotheses upon which the progress of science depends. Nevertheless, it can be argued that there is also a price to be paid for choosing any limited hypothetical construction upon which to base research and the ensuing practice.

The word science is derived from the Latin 'scientia', meaning knowledge. Those of us who are actively involved in the study of knowledge within the human sciences also approach our work from a specific paradigm. In that sense we are all scientists and philosophers, as we all tend to have fundamental (and often implicit) ideas and beliefs about the basics of human nature. Our affiliation to a particular therapeutic approach can reveal strong personal and professional commitments and motivations that tend to inhibit our ability to consider any paradigm outside our own – the one in which we have made a personal investment. The difficulty of thinking, let alone arguing, across paradigms becomes even more apparent if we think of religious or political beliefs, where individuals may hold to an unquestioned position even when faced with burgeoning contradictory data. In his seminal text, *The Structure of Scientific Revolutions*, Kuhn notes: 'In learning a paradigm, the scientist acquires theory, methods, and standards together, usually in an inextricable mixture' (1962, p. 108).

Current ideas in the physical sciences offer a new world-view, or paradigm shift, in how physical matter, nature, society and individuals interact together and organize themselves. During the past fifty years research in quantum mechanics and systems theory has supported the resultant new hypothesis that all living matter, in both the physical and human worlds, is essentially interdependent. The principle of interdependence is the subject of Fritjof Capra's book *The Web of Life* (1996). The concept is set out in the context of a discussion of ecological systems: 'They derive their essential properties and, in fact, their very existence from their relationships to other things. Interdependence – the mutual dependence of all life processes on one another' (p. 290).

A systems approach represents a paradigm shift in our perception of human nature. It requires us to think holistically – to focus on relationships rather than objects in isolation, and to consider processes and patterns above contents. Such a revolution or paradigm shift in the world of science usually requires a leap of faith and a major alteration in our perception of reality.

In the sixteenth century the astronomer Copernicus discovered that the earth was not the centre of the universe, and for a period of time his ideas and observations were met with incredulity. Such radical ideas were dismissed as heresy, as they were totally antithetical to the religious beliefs of that period. Subsequent developments in science gave support to the Newtonian, mechanistic worldview. The exposition of classical physics developed by Newton showed that the world could be explained by a simple set of empirical rules. This classical paradigm emphasized the fixed, predictable and certain nature of the laws governing the universe.

Whenever scientific discoveries become accepted as significant to the development of knowledge, other disciplines such as psychology, politics and the social sciences inevitably take on board the general implications of these ideas. In the world of classical science other facets of life were therefore also seen as rational, separate and determined. This was an era that took the machine, with its interlocking but separate, individual parts, as a model for its view of human nature. According to the Newtonian picture, in which everything was reducible and separate, simplicity and individuality provided the foundational principles. Thinking was either/or, in an age that sought to reconcile contradiction and avoid ambivalence or paradox.

A radically new and unexpected conception was introduced to the world of physics by Einstein's discovery of the theory of relativity. This new understanding of the relativity of space-time, and the recognition that matter and energy are the same although their appearance manifestly different, paved the way for a very different model of reality. The new physics of the twentieth century emphasized the fundamental interconnectedness of manifestly separate entities. The scientist David Bohm (1980) refers to this idea as 'undivided wholeness'. Heisenberg stated in his *Principle of Uncertainty* (1958) that light can be both a wave and a particle. The idea of the wave–particle duality was in total opposition to the earlier classical position. Observations revealed that neither aspect is more important or fundamental to an account of reality than the other. This has also been described by Danah Zohar and Ian Marshall in their book *The Quantum Society* (1994) as the 'Principle of Complementarity', as both aspects are fundamental and combine together to form a whole. This is a shift in thinking that, as these authors discuss, has also profoundly influenced the social sciences, biology, politics, philosophy, art and literature.

Transference and countertransference

The basic premises of the Communicative model of psychotherapy have also drawn some of their inspiration from relational, holistic Quantum propositions. The communicative approach to psychoanalytic psychotherapy is primarily focused on the here-and-now process of the vicissitudes of the therapeutic interaction. The therapist's task is devoted to addressing the actual rather than transferential elements of the relationship.

In his correspondence with Fliess, prior to his subsequent systematized development of psychoanalysis, Freud documents his conviction that the unconscious is unable to distinguish between truth and fiction (Freud, 1897, p. 260). These infantile, primary-process, pleasure-seeking and non-reality-based characteristics of the unconscious became one of the defining features of psychoanalytic theory and a major consideration influencing the practice of psychoanalysis.

The communicative approach to psychoanalytic psychotherapy was developed in the early nineteen seventies by Robert Langs, partly as a response to some of the major criticisms of methodological inconsistency directed against classical and mainstream psychoanalytic principles and practice (Langs, 1973b, 1976, 1978a, 1978b). In particular it was argued that two of the major concepts employed in the practice of psychoanalysis are open to interpretation and present ambiguities that can be used by the therapist as a means of self-protection. In this sense the therapist is afforded an unrealistic degree of power and control, while the patient is considered the less discerning, and therefore more disadvantaged, member of the dyad. The original definition of transference, including its subsequent reformulation, generally upholds the idea of the distorting influence of the patient's relationship to the therapist and may be considered to encourage an attitude on the part of the therapist as 'the one who knows'. Further, the deconstruction of the patient's defensive strategies, including the defence of transference, as a standard technical psychoanalytic procedure also reinforces this bias.

The theory of transference offers an explanation of how the patient's past enters into the current psychoanalytic relationship. Transference refers to the unconscious inclination to represent present relationships as repetitions of early childhood experiences and relationships. Freud initially considered this distortion to be an impediment to the treatment. From 1909, however, he began to view transference as a vital element in the theory and practice of psychoanalysis. A major modification in the original definition of transference occurred alongside the developments in object relations ideas (Klein, 1932). This reformulation extended the notion to include everything that occurs in the analysis (Joseph, 1985).

A survey of the literature devoted to the psychoanalytic concept of countertransference (see Chapter 1) shows that it is replete with ambiguities, contradictions, reversals and superficial modifications. David Smith, a communicative psychotherapist, in his discussion of the problematical nature of the notion of transference (1991), points to the comparable developments and alterations that occurred in the history of countertransference. He asserts,

> After Freud's death the concept of countertransference gradually became modified, while the Kleinian theory of transference gained considerable ground. Taken together these factors conspired to justify an analytic stance of virtual omniscience and an immunity to the sort of self-disciplined self-criticism that is essential to the growth of any real science. (1991, p. 51)

On the completion of his psychoanalytic training Langs became interested in addressing the lack of empirical psychoanalytic research. The results of his early systematic investigation of psychoanalytic sessions revealed some unexpected and surprising findings. This paved the way for subsequent research and eventually led Langs to the development of the communicative paradigm, as a radical reconstruction of psychoanalytic psychotherapy. Langs's extensive clinical data appeared to indicate that patients are unconsciously, and quite accurately, preoccupied with the immediate interpersonal conditions of the therapeutic encounter. This observation is clearly at odds with the corpus of psychoanalytic writing and the philosophy of human nature that is underlined in the model of psychoanalysis. The notion of unconscious perception would require a very different model of the mind to that according to which the unconscious is incapable of distinguishing what is real from what is not real. Smith highlights the salient differences between these two contrasting and competing views of human nature: 'The paradigm shift from transference to unconscious perception would rule out notions of "the patient's resistance", "the patient's transference" and "the patient's phantasies" ' (ibid., p. 71).

Communicative psychoanalytic psychotherapy has taken a radical leap and dispensed with the two defining psychoanalytic concepts, transference and countertransference. The notion of transference has been replaced by the acceptance of unconscious perception as the guiding principle. Langs has also introduced the unambiguous and unequivocal term 'therapist madness' as a replacement for countertransference. The communicative approach, unlike most, if not all, other models of psychotherapy, sees patient and therapist madness as often intimately linked and intertwined. The approach also asserts that on some occasions the patient's mad behaviour may be instigated, or exacerbated, by the therapist's inability to contain their own madness. These reformulations are considered to place both members of the therapeutic dyad on a more equal and realistic footing, in that both patient and therapist are viewed as being subject to the same existential difficulties and anxieties.

The notion of unconscious perception is also used to support the idea of the patient's natural curative capacity as an integral aspect of the therapeutic process. Indeed, the view is taken that it is the therapist's responsibility to acknowledge the patient's unconscious interpersonal perceptions when he or she, the therapist, has been unable to provide a stable and containing environment. Such a notion of the patient's supervisory capacity to guide the treatment process is in sharp contrast to psychoanalysis, which emphasizes the disparity between the analyst's perceptions (more rational) and the patient's perceptions (often distorted). The communicative relationship and the individual roles within it are therefore seen as less clearly defined, often interchangeable and more complementary, as both therapist and patient are seen as sources and recipients of insight. Communicative psychotherapy is therefore essentially interested in addressing and reinforcing the patient's valid, helpful, and even wise, interpersonal contributions within the therapeutic encounter.

Unconscious perception

Langs's development of communicative psychotherapy eventually led to the replacement of the notion of transference with the concept of unconscious perception. In contrast to the Freudian formulation of transference, which refers to the unconscious pressure to set up false interpersonal connections (connections with their roots in early childhood relationships), unconscious perception refers to a trustworthy and spontaneous ability to perceive interpersonal reality authentically and accurately. The past is considered to enter the present situation as the patient is selectively reminded of the true similarities between early childhood relationships and concerns that are being repeated in the immediate therapeutic interaction. Langs sums this up: 'Communicative Psychotherapy is therefore primarily concerned with the non-transference interpersonal meanings of the patient's unconscious perceptions' (1982, p. 210).

Unconscious perception is expressed primarily through the mechanisms of displacement and disguise, and can be recognized as stories, or narratives, that relate to the behaviour of people and situations that are manifestly unrelated to the clinical arena but considered to represent valid unconscious insights of the patient's perceptions of the therapist. The notion of the need to process reflections of others outside of awareness through the defensive mechanisms of displacement and disguise as a means of reducing anxiety has its origins in Freud's major work, *The Interpretation of Dreams* (1900). Langs's thesis similarly concentrates on the automatic unconscious need to conceal our accurate (albeit disturbing) perceptions of others through the mechanism of encoded narrative in everyday life. What is claimed to be an innate human trait is seen as a protective means of reducing the anxiety that is likely to emerge should we become aware of the potentially harmful or hurtful aspects of other people's underlying motivations and behaviour.

Storytelling is often used creatively as a symbolic medium of expression in plays and films when one character wants to impart a crucial but disturbing truth to another. The recipient of the intended message is also unlikely to decode or overtly comment on the message as this could be tantamount to an admission of blame regarding an issue of which both parties would consciously wish to remain unaware. In this way the communicator and the recipient remain protected from something uncomfortable or painful. Communicative psychotherapy attests to the significance of this form of expression, which at one and the same time conceals and reveals important, emotionally-laden interpersonal truths, especially with respect to concerns relating to inappropriate interpersonal boundaries.

Therapist madness

As we have seen, Langs' communicative psychotherapy has substituted the term 'therapist madness' in place of the concept of counter-transference. As we have also seen, looking at the history of the concept, countertransference is now defined in at least two, contra-dictory, ways. In *The Power of Countertransference* (1991), a text which examines the concept from a mainstream psychoanalytic per-spective, Karen Maroda underlines how the arbitrariness of the notion can encourage practitioners to use it in an undemocratic and defensive way in the clinical setting. Maroda explains:

> However, in practice there are enormous difficulties in making distinctions between the 'real' and the 'imagined', projected, dis-placed or distorted. Traditionally making such distinctions has been a major part of the therapist's role. It is the therapist who decides what is transference and what is not. It is the therapist who decides what is countertransference and what is not. The therapist assumes this power based on the belief that the patient is not in a position to make these distinctions himself. (1991, p. 98)

Unlike Langs, Maroda argues for some modifications in technique from within the standard psychoanalytic paradigm. Her thesis is essentially a request for psychoanalysis to relinquish its rigid stance and instead to adopt a more flexible attitude towards the therapist's disclosure of their countertransference issues to the patient.

Communicative psychotherapy, by contrast, tenders an alternative model of psychoanalysis and human interaction. It would seem that the preferred term 'therapist madness' has been used in order to place the responsibility firmly in the therapist's lap. There is an explicit emphasis on the therapist's obligations. In his discussion of this notion Smith underscores its egalitarian characteristics:

Here, at last, was a true democracy of madness with no built in assumptions about the craziness of the patient and the sanity of the therapist. Communicative psychotherapists must be ready and willing to confront their own madness in every session that they conduct, because patients unconsciously hold up a mirror in which this madness is starkly reflected back to them. (1991, pp. 162–163)

Unconscious communication

Langs asserts that models of the mind and model making in psychotherapy research is an important area that has tended to be neglected in the practice of this discipline. Model making is considered to encourage creativity and new ideas. It enables researchers to test out empirically the hypotheses that are generated from the model, which in turn leads to the development of new models. The communicative model of the mind has been likened to Freud's topographical model, as it is comprised of two basic and separate systems, the conscious and unconscious. The conscious system processes information in a logical and sequential manner in contrast to the unconscious system, which processes its perceptions in a totally different way. While conscious system-functioning recognizes difference and communicates directly, the unconscious is focused on similarity and synthesizes its perceptions in an oblique, indirect way. From a communicative perspective, one of the major attributes of the unconscious is its ability to comprehend interpersonal reality via rapid and perceptive judgements about other people. In *The Interpretation of Dreams* (1900), Freud put forward the view that the unconscious could only express its ideas by connecting to a preconscious idea, thus rendering these ideas less harmful. According to the communicative model, the expression of unconscious perceptions is displayed in a similarly encoded, or derivative, way in everyday communication).

In communicative terms the expression of a derivative, narrative, or unconscious, communication is always connected thematically to an unconscious idea. A dream is symbolically represented and disguised in order to protect the dreamer from unconscious anxiety-provoking concerns. The communicative position focuses on the idea that we also experience deep unconscious perceptions of others in our everyday lives and will communicate these threatening and disturbing interpersonal ideas in convoluted and camouflaged ways. Langs's thesis on the significance of unconscious communication is also to some extent supported by research in cognitive psychology (Haskell, 1987, 1990, 1999), and in experimental psychology (Dixon, 1971).

The communicative concept of an unconscious wisdom carries the idea that we have the ability to recognize inappropriate and unacceptable infringements between ourselves and others that are contributing to a basic sense of mistrust. This is the component of the mind that is viewed as being responsible for interpersonal narratives. These stories are considered to reveal, here and now, hidden truths and concerns related to the interpersonal, in particular concerning boundaries regulating intimacy and separateness.

One of the basic tenets of the communicative approach to psychotherapy is the need for the therapist to scrutinize the patient's narrative reflections that relate to disturbances and discrepancies prompted by the therapist's management of the encounter and setting. The underlying premise is that unconscious communication is essentially interpersonal. Communicative technique requires the practitioner initially to describe the patient's stories (overtly unrelated to the therapy) and subsequently to link the themes to a here-and-now stimulus that relates to the patient's valid experience of the therapist's behaviour.

Communicative model of the mind

As far as the author is aware, her own interest in and interpretation of the communicative approach to psychoanalytic psychotherapy have been fuelled and sustained by its strong interpersonal focus and its commitment to a more egalitarian philosophy of human engagement and communication. The concept of unconscious perception is, as has been emphasized, central to the model and replaces the notion of transference as the principle therapeutic tool. The approach considers the significance of boundaries and limits as one of the most prominent human concerns. From a communicative perspective, the patient is fully able to discern, and will communicate, their interpersonal perceptions of the therapist's ability to manage the framework of the relationship. The communicative therapist is thus obliged consistently to focus on the patterns and themes that underlie the patient's narratives, which are considered to reflect the latter's perceptions of the therapist's management of the boundaries of the therapeutic system. The therapist is then required to feed back the patient's authentic perceptions of the interaction and subsequently to follow the patient's encoded advice.

Although the communicative method depends on a commitment to a holistic interpersonal paradigm, which means that each member of the system can only be undersood in relation to the parts that comprise the whole system, it is also very clear in identifying the practitioner's inherent dilemma, which may indeed impede their capacity to respond in accordance with this paradigm. This is related to the conscious mind's denial of the significance of interpersonal boundaries. This paradox is considered to arise on account of the opposing forces of the unconscious mind's acceptance of, and need for, boundaries and limits and the conscious mind's denial, and need to negate, the meaning of our limitations – limitations that are cogently underscored in the human condition.

The communicative therapist is obliged to attend to and affirm what are known as the patient's 'selective' impressions of the therapist's difficulties in establishing and maintaining a secure therapeutic frame. The term 'selective' used by Langs contrasts with the classical notion of transference in so far as it denotes the genuine perception of an aspect of the patient's experience in respect of the therapist, which is also a reminder of a concern related to a similarly accurately registered relational experience from the patient's past. The communicative model also recognizes the essentially arduous nature of the work and the general reluctance to acknowledge and deal with interpersonal limits. The formulation of this obstacle is based on Langs's two-tiered 'contradictory' model of the mind. The conscious system is considered to be generally insensitive and attempts to obliterate issues and concerns that relate to interpersonal boundaries. It is more focused on personal survival, is self-protective and built for defence. By contrast, the unconscious is viewed as primarily concerned with deeper meanings, exceedingly alert to inappropriate forms of relating and able to endure painful traumatic truths that tend to be denied consciously.

Death anxiety

Communicative technique is focused almost exclusively on the here-and-now of the therapeutic interaction and consistently addresses the need for order and regularity, on the one hand, and, on the other hand, the concerns and anxieties that are felt when either member of the dyad is confronted with the inevitable restrictions imposed on the relationship. This focus on the paradox of the boundaries in therapy can also be seen as a microcosm of human existence. The ultimate limiting situation is death, and Langs would want to say that a sense of our own finite physical existence is what underlies our struggle to accept limitation in all situations. Such is the persistent dilemma of communicative work:

> Secured-frame death anxieties strongly linked to the recognition of the inevitability of personal demise, render these frames difficult to endure – despite their very positive effects. Basically, secured frames are linked unconsciously to the realization that we are all trapped in a living space from which we depart or escape only through death. (1998, p. 75; see also Langs, 1979, 1997)

The notion of death anxiety is well documented by researchers in the field of philosophy and psychotherapy and is considered to be a fundamental human concern (Klein, 1946; Searles, 1961; Heidegger, 1962; Jaspers, 1969; Yalom, 1980) and a major contributory factor in emotional disturbance.

Freud had little to say specifically on the subject of death anxiety; he did, however, assert: 'But the unconscious seems to contain nothing that could give any content to our concept of the annihilation of life' (1926, p. 129). He also considered that the death instinct was primarily at the service of the life instinct and generally externalized as aggression (Freud, 1930, 1933). However, the concept of death anxiety has been explored in depth within a neo-Freudian tradition in Klein's developmental model, which stresses death anxiety and vulnerability as a major and ongoing cause of human distress. Subsequently, we see this emphasis in the work of Harold Searles (1961). The recognition of death requires an awareness of the vulnerability of our position in the world, and Searles considers the cornerstone of an understanding of the source of schizophrenic symptoms to be the unconscious attempt to defend against the realization of one's mortality.

The theme of death has been a prominent feature in Existential philosophy. According to Heidegger, an acceptance of the certainty of death frees the individual to live more realistically in the world, and for Jaspers, the limits of existence point to the importance of human transcendence; this also endorsed by Rollo May and Irvin Yalom in their paper 'Existential Psychotherapy' (1984).

Langs writes: 'It is the specific contribution of the Communicative approach to identify death anxiety as a central source of emotional danger and, in particular, as a major factor in the unconscious meaning of madness' (1987, p. 182). Even the safety of a secure, reliable, consistent environment is not enough to hold at bay affects and profound concerns that relate to survival, referred to as 'existential death anxiety'. 'The palpable contradiction that arises under secure frame conditions is that the secure frame is felt to be a significantly containing experience, but at the same it arouses intense existential fears' (Holmes, 1998b, pp. 61–62). Langs reinforces the tension of this dilemma when he states: 'This sense of confinement is linked to the entrapping qualities of human existence itself – the gift of life that must end in death' (Langs, 1998, p. 7).

At the same time, 'predatory death anxiety' is connected to fears that arise under framework conditions that are unstable and unreliable. The notion of predatory death anxiety may be defined as the warning of danger and threats to the individual's sense of personal safety and survival. Although clients often respond in an overtly favourable and agreeable light to alterations to the ground rules, whether at their own behest or instigated by the therapist, their subsequent narratives tend to negate these conscious responses and usually contain covert references to the persecutory and precarious nature of the modification. For example, in the case-study vignette, following the therapist's suggestion that the client should attend therapy twice a week instead of her normal once a week sessions, which the client agreed was a good idea, the client went on to talk about her manager at work, who, she said, had been pressurizing her to work overtime in a different department for no extra pay. The client continued her story by describing her boss as selfish, greedy and self-serving and concluded by saying that she thought she should look for a new job and try to find an employer who would be more respectful and caring towards his staff.

Boundaries

The term boundary is defined as 'something that indicates the farthest limit, as of an area; border' (*Collins English Dictionary*, p. 95). A boundary line may be overt, or implied; fencing or walling off is a common observable feature of most private properties and is an unequivocal, visible and conclusive sign that determines the cut-off point between one person's personal dwelling space and that of their neighbours. It is interesting to note that of the domestic disputes documented, boundary disagreements about the ownership of land are by far the most numerous. This same issue has also been a major source of ongoing conflict, war and bloodshed on a wider scale between nations, as witnessed in Europe, Ireland, and notably in the present day between Israel and Palestine.

Criminal behaviour by definition entails the unlawful infringement of a person's private boundaries. Crimes such as theft, incest, rape, as well as murder, are all boundary breeches as they transgress and violate an individual's personal space in one way or another. Sins are also referred to as transgressions and trespasses, both of which latter terms clearly capture the sense of going beyond accepted limits, wrongfully entering and intrusion. The strict penalties imposed on those who contravene these limits generally ensure co-operation and acceptance with respect to individual and social boundaries. We are aware that under certain conditions the flouting of boundaries can result in a prison sentence. Prison is the enforced curtailment and restriction of the culprit's freedom, a compulsory boundary that is legally imposed where a person is not prepared to maintain their own boundaries and infringes the personal boundaries of others.

The importance of autonomy and self-control may be summarized as the importance of the capacity to acknowledge and accept the essential limitations and disappointments of life, which include an awareness and understanding of the limits of engagement between ourselves and others. The notable paediatrician and analyst D. W. Winnicott underlined the primacy of maternal containment in his theory of emotional development. From a Winnicottian perspective, the 'good enough mother' (Winnicott, 1960) supplies her infant with a safe, relaxed space, which by necessity includes the provision of clear boundaries. The boundary defines the potential space that enables the tiny infant to create, to be spontaneous, to think and to symbolize. The mother's ability to offer the baby a tranquil space undisturbed by her own anxieties also represents the creation of a boundary space between me and not-me, and the opportunity for the infant to internalize the mother's ability to contain rather than act out its anxieties. A good enough internalized environment, which leads to the secure development of a capacity for internal control or inner management, subsequently decreases the need for control from the external environment. Health, for Winnicott, equals containment, or control. The cornerstone of Winnicott's theory of emotional development is his emphasis on the importance of the boundaries of the setting, which provide the infant with a space to experience and manage unintegrated, disturbing primitive feelings and anxieties (Davis and Wallbridge, 1981).

Clarifying the underlying significance of interpersonal boundary issues as they unfold within the therapeutic interaction is the raison d'être of communicative psychotherapy. Communicative theory and research concurs with Winnicott's developmental premise, which emphasizes boundaries and the primacy of containment. However, the communicative model further asserts that the therapeutic containing function of clear limits and boundaries is inevitably offset and confounded by the arousal of traumatic and incessant dread, as boundaries also equal, represent or symbolize the limits of human existence. This contradiction is the leitmotif of communicative psychotherapy: the need for clear interpersonal boundaries, which provide the internal stability and balance that is required to live co-operatively in the world with other people and which enables the individual to acknowledge and *bear the unbearable* idea of the limits of human existence.

The frame

There is some lack of agreement across the schools of psychotherapy, as well as among practitioners who work from an agreed model, in relation both to the components that constitute the therapeutic frame and to its significance. However, it is safe to say that most, if not all, models of psychotherapy consider the frame as enhancing and contributing to the therapy, but as a backdrop, separate from the actual substance of the therapeutic task. Communicative psychotherapy, by contrast, considers the ongoing quality and vicissitudes of the therapist's management of the frame as the most cogent and meaningful aspect of the work. The therapeutic frame has been compared to the frame that surrounds and defines a painting (Milner, 1952). It is the frame, or the ground rules of psychotherapy, that characterizes and distinguishes it from other kinds of environments and relationships.

By observing people's behaviour together, we are usually able to make quite accurate predictions about the type of relationship that exists between them. For example, an employer would be expected to behave more formally toward an employee than towards a friend. The formalities that accompany any given role are more than just mere conventions: they define both what is expected of the person and the limits of the person's position. The interpersonal disturbances and anxieties that arise when the boundaries between people become muddled or blurred attest to the importance and need for consistency. Langs's clinical research (Langs, 1983) strongly suggests that patients prefer a stable, regular therapeutic frame, and that it is these rules of interpersonal engagement that are their primary unconscious concerns.

Fundamental ground-rule issues that often appear in patients' narrative communications seem to centre around core interpersonal concerns. Similar spontaneous interactive communications that pertain to boundary issues have also been shown to occur naturally in encounters between people outside of the therapeutic relationship (Langs, 1983, 1992). Langs believes that the following framework components provide the most appropriate conditions for a maximally therapeutic environment.

1 Confidentiality

Confidentiality is closely aligned to issues that relate to trust and privacy. The verb to confide refers to private, secret and intimate disclosures that one person entrusts to another. Trust is therefore an indispensable and ongoing requirement for the patient in psychotherapy. The patient is by definition the vulnerable party in the encounter, the person who is unilaterally expected to reveal exceedingly personal and sensitive information about themselves to a relatively unknown therapist who potentially has the power to divulge and abuse their trusted position. Communicative psychotherapy considers the theme of confidentiality to be an ongoing significant interpersonal issue. The detrimental effect of infringements to the ground rule of confidentiality is supported by the unconscious emphasis placed on it by patients in their narrative communications. A communicative psychotherapist will therefore be expected where possible to decline from any activity that could potentially lead to breeches in confidentiality, such as taking notes, taping a session, or liaising with a third party.

2 Privacy

A private therapeutic environment is an essential requirement that enables the patient to feel secure enough to divulge their anxieties and concerns. Ideally sessions should be held in a private office, without the possibility of being interrupted, overheard or overlooked. One of the rationales for the convention of the 'fifty minute hour' is to allow enough time for one patient to leave the consulting room without encountering another patient who is arriving for their session. These provisions manifestly demonstrate the therapist's respect, care and concern for the patient. Such therapeutic precautions are a further indication of the therapist's trustworthiness, commitment to a patient-centred attitude and awareness of patients' acute and realistic sensitivities to the quality of the therapeutic setting.

3 Fees

The patient is expected to pay a single set fee, which should remain the same throughout the sessions. It is not unusual for a patient at the initial session openly to request a lower fee than the one offered by the therapist. However, a communicative therapist would not agree to any alteration unless the patient's narratives were in accord with their consciously expressed requirements. Paradoxically, as previously stated, our consciously expressed needs are often negated by and in direct opposition to our unconscious perceptions. Issues that centre on money and payments for professional services tend to show that the recipient of a reduced fee or the wavering of a fee will often experience the provider with suspicion and may view the therapy as inferior.

Research results have indicated that in the absence of a fee, or when the fee is paid by a third party, patients are more likely to arrive late or miss sessions (Cheifetz, 1984). It would appear that people unconsciously generally appreciate and respond appropriately to the rules of reciprocity. Reducing a fee places the relationship on an unequal footing; one person is then beholden and indebted to the other, which accentuates the power imbalance in the relationship. The obligation to pay also encourages and endorses the payer's responsibility, autonomy and independence.

4 Gifts

The issue of gifts in psychotherapy needs to be considered from both a symbolic and material perspective. Decreasing or waiving the fee is likely to be experienced by the patient as a gift from the therapist, which may then prompt the patient to reciprocate and return the favour with an actual gift for the therapist. When a patient presents the therapist with a gift, the communicative practitioner is therefore obliged to consider the way in which his or her own behaviour has influenced the offer.

As a rule of thumb, gifts offered or accepted by either party are viewed as inappropriate as they disturb and distort the professional boundaries of the relationship. Further, a therapist who offers the gift of an extra session or who prolongs the normal session time is likely to be experienced unconsciously by the patient as highly seductive.

5 Regularity and timing of sessions

The way in which the therapist manages the boundaries of time is a cogent indication of their ability to contain their own anxieties in the presence of a situation of limit. The capacity for time management is the bedrock on which the patient should be able to depend, as it is a powerful source of communication of the therapist's reliability and trustworthiness. The length of the sessions should be agreed at the first meeting and maintained throughout the therapy. If the patient arrives late for a session, the therapist should still conclude the session at the specified time. Issues that link to time constraints will inevitably remain a constant source of difficulty for both members of the therapeutic dyad, as they are potent reminders of the limits of human mortality. It is, however, the therapist's responsibility consistently to acknowledge how their own timekeeping difficulties detrimentally reflect on and influence their ability to contain the patient and to assist them with their own timekeeping concerns and their existential anxieties.

Sessions should take place on the same day each week; the timing and duration of sessions should remain fixed.

6 Neutrality and anonymity

The state of being neutral refers to a lack of distinction and the absence and avoidance of bias. Neutrality may also be defined as harmonious, moderate, balanced and impartial. The idea that a neutral stance implies an attitude that requires the person to be cold and aloof is a common misconception of the term. The therapist's neutrality endorses their professional commitment to the client and tacitly communicates the therapist's care and respect for the client's material. The relative anonymity of the therapist reinforces the notion of neutrality and encourages the conditions that constitute a patient-centered approach. The rule of neutrality is also viewed as supporting, acknowledging and furthering the patient's capacity for autonomy and independence.

7 Referrals

From a communicative perspective, the inclusion of a third party in a one-to-one therapeutic relationship constitutes a risk for the patient and is linked to concerns that relate to confidentiality and sometimes to coercion. Patients are often referred by various sources, such as a GP, social worker, employer, spouse, parent or friend. A communicative therapist will endeavour to be alert to the latent themes in the patient's narratives that allude to grievances, sensitivities and interferences that emerge from any recommendation or information received from a third party. In order to establish and maintain an intimate and trusting relationship, the therapist should as a rule refrain from liaising or corresponding with any person other than her client.

8 The suspension of physical contact

A psychotherapist is by definition a professional person who attends to the emotional disturbances conveyed by the patient. This imperative not only places the latter in the vulnerable position but also characterizes the therapist's essentially onerous and responsible role in the encounter. It is therefore not surprising to find that patients are often acutely sensitive to every nuance communicated by their therapists, even though this may be denied consciously. These sensitivities are especially pertinent and meaningful with respect to the subject of physical contact between therapist and patient. Narrative communications from patients appear to confirm that touching, of whatever kind, by the therapist is experienced as highly seductive. Communicative therapists are therefore expected to abstain from touching their patients, except for a handshake at the first and final meeting.

9 Consistency and the physical setting

Neutrality and consistency are criteria that should also be applied to the physical therapeutic environment. Ideally, the therapy should always take place in the same room, in a professional office that is primarily designated for the purpose of therapy. As indicated above, the therapist should make every attempt to provide the patient with an environment that offers an appropriate degree of privacy. The latter is entitled to a space that is relatively soundproof and reasonably protected from outside intrusion. The room should be neutrally decorated and generally devoid of any of the therapist's personal items that may distract, interfere with or impinge upon the patient's legitimate therapeutic space. Consistent attention to the basic ground rules and to the physical setting is considered to be a confirmation of the therapist's stability and of their ability to offer the necessary containment and sensitivity that sound therapeutic practice requires.

Communicative technique

The communicative approach is unique in terms of both its theoretical and practical focus. Practitioners are expected to devote themselves to scanning the patient's material for disguised references that allude to their own inability to maintain a secure therapeutic frame. Communicative interventions are therefore specifically organized around the therapist's continuous recognition and acknowledgement of their own framework disturbances. The technique is reciprocal: both parties in the dyad give and receive interpersonal insights.

The communicative method is essentially systemic and draws on principles derived from chaos and complexity theory. Dynamical systems have been shown to be extremely sensitive to even minor disturbances because they are subject to different kinds of feedback. Positive feedback can suddenly produce turbulent activity in an orderly system, while negative feedback in a chaotic system can enable the system to adjust and revert to a stable state. It is through the mechanism of feedback loops that a system is able to regulate and organize itself. Negative feedback is not only responsible for rebalancing a system but also the cause of new and creative forms of behaviour (Holmes, 1999a).

There is an intimate link between chaos and order embodied in the systems approach. The application of these ideas has been shown to be relevant to all kinds of dynamic systems and organizations, including individual psychotherapy. Systemic principles indicate that a system's ability to sustain itself through chaotic periods can lead to the development of new forms of stability. This process of emerging order out of chaos is referred to as 'self-organization'. Time is also cited as a crucial factor in the process of self-organization. From a systems perspective, self-organization only occurs in the present (Butz, 1997; Slife and Lanyon, 1991).

Concentration on the immediate therapeutic interaction can enable the client to recognize and experience in the moment how the present and past converge in the here-and-now. It is the therapist's validation of the patient's perception of *something similar happening yet again* that can contribute to the patient's capacity to influence and change their future interactions in the outside world. It is further asserted that in order to promote the capacity for self-organization it is necessary to have an environment of sufficient consistency; only then can the ongoing paradox of chaos in order and order in chaos be addressed. These ideas have also been linked to the basic principles underlying a particular tradition of European Existentialism (Holmes, 2001).

The aforementioned ideas have been included to help to explain the communicative focus on the here-and-now process between patient and therapist in the consulting room. The linking of communicative psychotherapy to chaos theory and Existential philosophy reflects the author's specific contributions to this area. The principles implied in all three, apparently diverse, areas endorse the primacy of the immediate relational nature of being in-the-world with others. Systems theory and Existential philosophy, of Buber (1922) and Sartre (1943, 1946) in particular, offer explanatory support for the communicative axiom, which places the fluctuations of the immediate relational encounter at its helm.

Discussion of case-study vignette

A communicative therapist would be expected to focus on how the client experienced the delays and disturbances that occurred in the waiting room prior to the session in the light of their narrative, rather than of their overt communications. The therapist would then formulate their intervention on the basis of the themes of the client's stories and the link to any alteration of the framework or boundary issue. All other verbal interventions would be deemed as therapist-focused and unsound, including the therapist's initial apology. Although the client's initial overt response to the therapist's apology was 'It's all right', her subsequent narratives suggested something quite different.

Therapist: 'You have talked about how angry and miserable you feel with what has happened at work this week. Perhaps you are also feeling angry and sad about what has happened here today. Although you accepted my apology for keeping you waiting for twenty minutes, it also seems to have reminded you of your difficult week at work. You talked of how angry you felt about your workmates who couldn't even remember your name and do not even bother to pronounce it correctly. I am also aware that I didn't bother to check to see if you were waiting.'

Client remains silent.

Therapist: 'You mentioned that you walked out of your office without turning off your computer. I wonder if you also felt like walking away today without telling anyone. You also mentioned your concern about losing a day's wages. It seems you may also be worried about the lost time here and the payment for this session. Because of the time that you have lost due to my negligence, it seems appropriate that you should only pay for half of this session.'

The client's concern about money at work is viewed as a covert indication of her concern about whether she should be liable to pay for the missed portion of her session. Langs (1998) describes these messages as 'models of rectification'. On this occasion the therapist decided to alter the normal fee arrangement in response to the client's unconscious rumination about money. Models of rectification are embedded in clients' narrative messages as a form of guidance for the therapist. They are the client's attempts to help and supervise the therapist, to inform the therapist about what he or she really needs and to prompt the therapist to act accordingly. Of course, the therapist's sudden decision to reduce the fee may also be related to her own anxiety about the missing time.

Client: 'Thank you. That sounds fair.' [Pause.] 'When my mother rang me – I told you that she rings me regularly once a week, mostly at the weekend. I never know what to say to her. She talks, it's always been like that. I just let her talk. I stand with the phone away from my ear and she just continues. It's hard. Sometimes I pretend I am not at home. I know she doesn't want to listen to me talking.'

These comments from the client may allude to the therapist's inability to contain her anxiety and to her need to 'fix' the problem prematurely due to the foreshortened session. The therapist's concerns in this session may well have been exacerbated by the fact that the contract is also time limited.

Therapist: 'Perhaps you are also saying something about how difficult it is to talk here too. I wonder if these regular sessions remind you of your mother's regular phone calls – if you are also telling me how hard it is for you to come here and talk and your concerns about whether I want to listen to you talk, which may be similar to the struggle you have with your mother.'

Client: 'Yes, I like, well, I am close to, my sister. I like being with her, she talks more than me but she does listen to me. She understands about our mother. My mother wants me home, she doesn't like me being over here. I don't want to go home, but I have to because my visa runs out in September. She wants to run my life ... [pause]. There are things that happened [pause]. I can't say [pause]. Things she said.'

Therapist: 'It is time to finish now.'

The communicative therapist would see the client's final positive story about her relationship with her sister as a partial validation of her preceding intervention. The client's positive narrative would be silently noted but not overtly addressed. Nevertheless, the client's associations overall, including her final comments, are suffused with anger and other negative emotions and contain themes related to interference and the lack of sensitivity.

Communicative technique is characterized by a set of exceedingly explicit and prescribed rules for listening and intervening. As I understand it, Langs's rationale for this rigidity is closely related to his philosophy and model of human nature, which views people as excessively reluctant to attend to either boundary issues or encoded messages from others that contain criticisms linked to these issues. In other words, at a conscious level human beings are generally all over the place and predisposed to incestuous and unbounded modes of interaction. This way of being militates against the unpalatable awareness and anxiety of our essential isolation, and reinforces the omnipotent idea that if we can manipulate the ground rules that normally govern our interpersonal interactions, then we may also be able to control and influence the boundary of life itself. The therapist's responses in the preceding continuation of the vignette may be viewed as either supporting evidence for this hypothesis and/or a consequence of the anxiety that can ensue from the exacting technical demands of communicative practice.

Langs also formulated these meticulous and exact technical procedures in response to his dissatisfaction with the field of psychoanalysis and psychotherapy in general, which he views as sorely lacking in scientific rigour. Presumably, these technical injunctions are intended in the first place to contain therapists and keep them on track, while also providing a technique that is based on the scientific criteria of conjectures and refutations. The method is considered to be more neutral than other approaches as the patient's perceptions of the interaction take pride of place and as it is the patient, and not the practitioner, who gauges the accuracy of the therapist's interventions, this gauging being encoded in their subsequent unconscious comments – although the final decision as to whether the patient's ensuing narrative is positively toned still rests with the therapist. The fact that self-deception is viewed as a prevailing human trait suggests, however, that it will continue to be a patient-centered concern with respect to the therapist. Nevertheless, Langs's uncompromising focus on technique encourages the idea that it may be possible, with practice, to provide a therapeutic environment that is generally free of mistakes or boundary disturbances.

Some of the synonyms listed under the heading of 'mistakes' include misunderstanding, misleading, deceptive, imperfect and bias (*Roget's Thesaurus*, 2000, p. 495). By contrast, words that denote a lack of error include terms such as infallible, virtuous, irreproachable and faultless (ibid., p. 494). Yet, the ubiquitous theme of dissatisfaction and disappointment in our relations with others, and its concomitant conflict and strife, are psychotherapy's stock in trade. Emotions such as anger, shame and anxiety contribute to both the communicator's inability to express their disappointment appropriately and the recipient's reluctance to acknowledge or accept such criticism. Misunderstandings and mistakes frequently lead to interpersonal impasses and are recurrent, perhaps inevitable, features of human interchange.

The elevated reliance on technical procedures, one of the emblems of communicative psychotherapy, has in this author's considered opinion eclipsed and concealed the true hallmark of the model, which is its interpersonal axioms. Furthermore, what one might call this lack of embodiment and disunity appears, paradoxically, to have led to the technique being applied in a mechanistic, uniform way, resulting in a lack of interpersonal engagement. It is the author's view that by shining some light on philosophies such as Existentialism and Dynamical Systems theory, which respectively stress the haunting issue of 'bad faith' and its opposite, the universality of interconnectedness, some gain may be made in tempering this imbalance. Sartre coined the term 'bad faith' to express the interminable human struggle to be truthful either with others or with ourselves: it is a struggle in which we constantly fail. The Existential tradition and Dynamical Systems theory draw attention to the omnipresence of paradox in the human condition and in nature. Both these positions also maintain that a deep-seated opposition to accommodating the polarities of existence is a typical property of humankind.

In this respect these tenets are in accord with the prevailing challenge of unconscious perception and the conscious opposition to receive interpersonal truths that tends to hold sway. From this perspective, the therapist's vigilance in respect of recognizing and acknowledging the patient's interpersonal concerns is of paramount importance. Anecdotal evidence from victim support projects which provide victims with the opportunity to confront their perpetrators shows that this opportunity for contact is beneficial, in as much as the victims have experienced a reduction in their conscious expression of hostility and need for revenge. Further, although the primary purpose of such programmes is to assist the victim, reports indicate that it is also of some benefit to the attitude of the perpetrator, despite there being no expectation made of them to apologize. Admittedly, the data are scanty and superficial; nevertheless, the fact that Langs's model of rectification, which asserts that the therapist needs to heed the patient's supervisory advice, must, by definition, refer to something that takes place after the event suggests that it may be not only irrelevant but also untimely. Rectification may therefore be viewed as a means of *avoiding the patient's disappointment* and as a way of *circumventing the ongoing vicissitudes and paradoxes of the encounter*, which seem to be pivotal in all interpersonal interactions.

Conclusion

The philosophy and theory that informs communicative psycho-analytic psychotherapy does not employ the concept of counter-transference, as both members of the dyad are considered to be subject to similar kinds of ongoing existential anxieties. Furthermore, both parties are seen as having natural therapeutic abilities. Langs's model can be said to have reversed the usual roles and rules that tend to define client and therapist.

The therapist (as well as the client) suffers from interpersonal difficulties and concerns around intimacy and separateness, which are expected to be an intrinsic and continuous element of the work. The client (as well as the therapist) imparts insights and attempts to help, or heal, the therapist.

The work is primarily focused around the client's perceptive impressions of the here-and-now encounter. The past is relevant in so far as these perceptions are selective, realistic reminders of the past being repeated in the here-and-now. Therefore, as the concept of transference is inapplicable to this approach, it would appear by extrapolation that its countertransference counterpart is also. Yet it would also be reasonable to say that the whole of the approach is in fact focused almost exclusively on issues related to countertransference. It may also be argued that the approach is in fact centered around both definitions of the concept. However, Langs's curious revolutionary slant generally designates the aptitude for insight the possession of the patient, and the tendency for misrepresentation the attribute of the therapist. At the same time, the technique expects the therapist not only to own up to their mistakes but also to remedy the situation.

Chapter 4

Countertransference Mavericks

This chapter discusses the work of three men who began their professional careers as respected analysts in the traditional world of psychoanalysis but went on to extend the boundaries or re-classify some of the fundamental, defining principles of Freud's work in quite radical ways. What they did resulted in their being distanced, if not isolated, from the psychoanalytic establishment.

The word 'maverick' recalls the Texan rancher William Maverick, who reared unbranded cattle. *Collins Dictionary* defines a maverick as 'a stray calf, especially a person of independent or unorthodox views' (1986, p. 523). Other terms such as 'individualist', 'free spirit', 'renegade' or 'go-it-alone' have been used as synonyms for maverick. Each of the analysts discussed in this chapter is clearly recognizable as a maverick and may even take, or have taken, pride in his position outside of the psychoanalytic orthodoxy. In a recent article in the *Observer* newspaper, 'How to work with a maverick', Neasa MacErlean (2001) writes: 'They would feel uncomfortable in a company tie and have enough self-confidence to stand outside the crowd and follow their own beliefs.' She also notes: 'Their individual style turns some people against them.' These comments seem especially apt in the case of Sándor Ferenczi, the first psychoanalytic countertransference dissident to be considered here.

Sándor Ferenczi (1873–1933)

During the past twenty years a number of publications have appeared that examine Ferenczi's unorthodox contributions to psychoanalytic theory and practice, his intimate relationship with Freud and his unconventional and troubled personal relationships. In all of these accounts Ferenczi emerges as a forthright, candid man, prepared to tilt at windmills and tell what he saw as the unvarnished truth. Ferenczi's own case-study material, recorded in his *Clinical Diary* (Dupont, 1988), reveals him to be a man who was committed to admitting and exploring his interpersonal difficulties and his motivations in his work with patients even when those admissions painted him in an unflattering light.

From the beginning of his career as a medical practitioner in 1900, Ferenczi showed a proclivity to treat the outer reaches of society, choosing to work with patients who were either socially or economically disadvantaged; he also worked in the area of sexually transmitted diseases. Ferenczi appeared to share an affinity with outsiders – with those who are reviled, ignored, or condemned by others. In her introduction to a selection of his work Julia Borossa notes: 'He took up his first appointment at a pauper's hospital, St Rokus, and then, later, at another comparable institution, St Erzsebet, where he specialized in treating prostitutes. He gained a wide-ranging experience of disease, from genital disorders to cancer and alcohol poisoning' (1999, p. xvi).

Borossa also emphasizes Ferenczi's devotion to humanitarian causes: 'From the outset a dedicated clinician with an interest in the world around him, he is committed to exploring the ties that bind people and societies together' (ibid., p. xxi). Later on, as a psychoanalyst, Ferenczi wrote on the subject of sexuality from a heterosexual and a homosexual perspective. He became a fierce public opponent of those who supported the view that homosexuality should be punishable as a criminal offence. He was also interested in esoteric subjects, including clairvoyance, to which he referred on several occasions in his *Clinical Diary*, where he noted: 'Really mastering anxiety, or rather overcoming it, might make us quite clairvoyant, and might help humanity to solve apparently insoluble problems' (Dupont, 1988, p. 13).

Ferenczi and Freud

Ferenczi first met Freud in 1908. Their encounter rapidly developed into a close professional and personal relationship that lasted almost until Ferenczi's premature death from pernicious anemia in 1933, at the age of fifty-nine. Throughout this time the two men communicated by letter, and between them penned more than a thousand letters which revealed a great deal of information about both themselves personally and the relationship between them – what Piers Myers (2000a) has described as 'a multi-faceted intimacy' (p. 78), as in addition to being friends, Ferenczi and Freud were also colleagues, pupil and teacher, and, during at least three brief but intense periods, patient and psychoanalyst.

The correspondence between Ferenczi and Freud also reveals a private life characterized by a lack of conformity. Ferenczi became involved in an intimate relationship with a married woman named Gizella Pálos, who had two daughters, Elma and Magda. At first he took Elma under his wing, then became her analyst and finally fell in love with her. This entanglement with a young woman fifteen years his junior led to further convolutions when, at Ferenczi's urgent request, Freud consented to conduct an analysis with Elma. The analysis spanned the first four months of 1912, after which Ferenczi renewed his own analytic treatment of her until August the same year, when he brought both his professional and personal relationship with her to an end. In the following years Gizella Pálos obtained her divorce, and in 1919 she and Ferenczi were married. In his biography of Ferenczi, Martin Stanton suggests that these events were for Ferenczi an enduring source of torment, and in effect blighted the remaining years of his life. In particular, Ferenczi was aware that during the time of Elma's psychoanalytic treatment, both he and Freud had consistently betrayed her private confidences (see Myers, 2000a, p. 82).

Psychoanalytic contributions

As a Hungarian, Ferenczi was eager to introduce psychoanalysis to his country of origin and make an established place for it there. He not only founded the Budapest Psychoanalytic Society, in 1913, but he also achieved the distinction of becoming the first professor of psychoanalysis at the University of Budapest, in 1918. These developments alone placed Ferenczi at the forefront of the psychoanalytic movement; nevertheless, some of his other original contributions were not met with same degree of enthusiasm by Freud or by his other psychoanalytic colleagues.

In the final years of his life, Ferenczi's attitude towards psychoanalytic theory and practice began to diverge radically from Freud's traditional model. He made a number of innovative, controversial theoretical reformulations, and in addition placed a new, distinctively interpersonal emphasis on the analytic interaction, which ultimately damaged irreparably his reputation with Freud and others in the psychoanalytic movement. In 1932, in a public address to the 12th International Psycho-Analytical Congress, in Wiesbaden, he set out these controversial reformulations; but this was met with dismay on the part of Freud and Freud's colleagues, who intimated that Ferenczi's rejection of the psychoanalytic doctrine must be due to some form of mental illness.

Ferenczi died not long after the presentation of his paper 'Confusion of Tongues between Adults and the Child' (1933). With this work and the contents of his *Clinical Diary*, Ferenczi has bequeathed to psychoanalysis and the whole of psychotherapy a legacy that has only recently begun to be recognized as having significant value.

Countertransference

Although Ferenczi furthered the cause of psychoanalysis by redefining some of its basic tenets, including Freud's original theory of impotence, his name is generally associated with some of his more eccentric and non-conformist psychoanalytic beliefs and aspects of practice. Recent interest in Ferenczi's work appears to be related to the outspoken nature of his contributions and his emphasis, in particular, on counter-transference issues.

In 1932 Ferenczi began to set out in his *Clinical Diary* the advantages and disadvantages of a method of reciprocal analysis. Ferenczi attributes the innovation of this highly unusual procedure to a patient identified as 'R.N'. It is apparent from these diary entries that Ferenczi's agreement to experiment with the technique of mutual analysis was not based on whim but on what he considered to be the serious introspective obligations inherent in the analyst's role. Ferenczi is in fact painstakingly open in expressing his hesitation, and some-times his anguish, about joining in with his patient in this mutual endeavour. At first he writes: 'Confession of artificiality in the analyst's behavior; admission in principle of emotions such as annoyance, unpleasure, fatigue, "to hell with it", finally also libidinal and play fantasies. Result: patient becomes more natural, more affable, and more sincere' (Dupont, 1988, p. 11). Further on, however, he ques-tions these early remarks: 'Can and should the analyst, analysed in this way, be completely open, right from the beginning? Should he not take into account the patient's reliability, capacity to tolerate, and understanding?' (ibid.).

Time and again Ferenczi returns to his own self-reflective process, to the inequality of the analytic encounter and to the importance of the analyst's self-introspection. 'The motives for reversing the pro-cess (the analyst being analysed) was an awareness of an emotional resistance, more accurately, of the obtuseness of the analyst' (ibid., p. 85). Nevertheless, by the early summer of 1932 Ferenczi had con-cluded that mutual analysis should be used only as a 'last resort'. He also expressed concerns about the training and supervision of analysts. Patients, he felt, were often analysed better than their analysts, and as far as supervision was concerned, he felt that analysts should be supervised by their patients: 'No attempt to defend oneself' (ibid., p. 115).

The report Ferenczi gives of the technique of mutual analysis is a passionate account of an analyst's sincere attempt to grapple with, and admit to, his own countertransference difficulties. Unfortunately, and alarmingly, Ferenczi's difficulties are as pertinent today as they were seventy years ago. His journey into the uncharted and dangerous waters of mutual analysis also reinforced his determination to address the imbalance of power between analyst and patient, and the undermining influence this can have on the latter. The issue of the analyst's dominance and attributed perceptive capabilities as contrasted with the patient's lack of power and attributed inability to perceive reality became for him a central theme that continued to pre-occupy him, and that also contributed to his downfall within the psychoanalytic community.

One of the most profound influences on psychoanalytic thought and practice was Freud's revision of his theory of seduction. His early view that reports of sexual experience in childhood referred to actual events was replaced by him by the view that these apparent memories were in fact rooted in the child's fantasy life. However, Ferenczi's final paper, delivered to the International Psychoanalytical Association in 1932, and ironically in honour of Freud's seventy-fifth birthday, addressed the subject of childhood sexual experience as a reality. Ferenczi had begun to notice that some of his patients expressed covert criticism of him, and that contained in their associations were disguised affects of fury and hatred towards him, which he encouraged them to reveal. He became acutely alert to his patients' ability to know implicitly how he, as their analyst, felt about them. Again he experimented by acknowledging to them the reality of their perceptions about him. Asking himself what was behind this perceptiveness on the part of his patients, he commented: 'Something had been left unsaid in the relation between physician and patient, something insincere, and its frank discussion freed, so to speak, the tongue-tied patient; the admission of the analyst's error produced confidence in his patient' (1933, p. 296). Ferenczi then made the important and creative (albeit to the orthodox psychoanalytical mind, outrageous) link between the analyst's hypocrisy and the insincere, abusive parent. He asserted that not only is incest not an uncommon occurrence but it is an expression of a powerful parent's denied hatred towards the child, producing within the child feelings of helplessness and a subsequent identification with their aggressor. Furthermore, the powerful and sometimes insincere analyst then repeats the patient's trauma from the past, on which the patient is again unable to comment owing to their relatively powerless position within the therapeutic interaction:

> The analytical situation – i.e. the restrained coolness, the professional hypocrisy and – hidden behind it but never revealed – a dislike of the patient, which, nevertheless, he felt in all his being – … such a situation was not essentially different from that which in his childhood had led to the illness. (ibid.)

Although there is now a thriving Ferenczi society in the United Kingdom, as well as one in Budapest, it is certainly safe to say that his ideas have never taken root or become assimilated in any overt way into the mainstream of psychoanalytic thought. Ferenczi's writings are rarely included or discussed on psychoanalytic training programmes, and although his name may be familiar to people involved in the field, the substance of his work remains generally unknown or unacknowledged. His name is mentioned in various places in Joseph Schwartz's history of psychoanalysis (1999) but mainly in terms of his part as a founding member of the psychoanalytic movement. By contrast, Julia Borossa (1999) suggests that there are echoes of Ferenczi's ideas to be found within the Independent tradition – though it would seem to me that these echoes are very faint in, for example, Eric Rayner's very thorough survey of this tradition (Rayner, 1991), where Ferenczi's name is mentioned principally in relation to the work of Michael Balint, his English-language translator. Be that as it may, given that Ferenczi's most innovative and controversial work is steeped in relational principles, it is not surprising to find that his clearest influence is to be seen within the American Interpersonal School of psychoanalysis.

Ferenczi is commemorated for his iconoclasm, remembered for his struggle with the intellectual, technical, emotional and ethical considerations that underlie psychoanalytic work and applauded for his sustained investigation and questioning of psychoanalytic doctrine. He was certainly a man before his time and, it seems, guaranteed to fail, since he was grappling with relational issues that belong to a systemic, participatory and holistic paradigm while being ensconced within the framework of an intrapsychic model. Ferenczi was particularly concerned with iatrogenic traumas and repetitions that were liable to be induced in the patient as a consequence of the undue power afforded to the analyst. He viewed the analytic encounter as a co-operative venture, and as conjointly created. It appears from his clumsy yet sincere egalitarian attempt at 'mutual analysis' with R.N. that when he took the role of the patient and wrestled with his mistrust and hatred of women, this was an acknowledgement of his transference issues with this patient. Furthermore, his rationale for introducing an experiential procedure of this kind was based on the belief that his patient was in any case aware of these interpersonal difficulties between them and would therefore gain some relief from his admissions. This recognition could also be seen as curative, in the sense that it stands in direct contrast to the abusive parent's denial of their maltreatment towards the child. Instead of repeating this 'hypocrisy', the analyst supports the patient's incisive perceptions and criticisms, which reinforces the latter's sense of reality.

Ferenczi showed the intimate link that exists between power and abuse, and in this he was prepared to face the unpalatable and for the most part unacceptable idea that we are all capable of abuse, and that the powerful parent and the powerful analyst are always at risk of abusing their position by hiding behind their role. He dealt with this dilemma by resolutely incorporating it into the analytic process, albeit in an awkward way. His attitude of responsibility has a distinct flavour of Existential philosophy in action, as he appears to endorse the reciprocal influence of the analyst's behaviour on the patient. His confessions imply that if the analyst is prepared to confront his or her own unbearable truths within the relationship, this will provide the patient with a more positive, honest and hopeful introject.

The interpersonal character of Ferenczi's ideas and their practical application flies in the face of received psychoanalytic wisdom. His writings, especially his *Diary*, show him to be an honourable, fair-minded person, respectful of his patients and more than willing to account openly for his professional behaviour. Nevertheless, until recently his work was viewed as heresy, generally unappreciated or ignored. The theme of Ferenczi's seminal ideas and his indomitable attitude are also vividly apparent in and throughout the work of the second of this chapter's countertransference mavericks.

Harold Searles (1918–)

I have avidly consumed Harold Searles's refreshing and innovative theoretical and clinical psychoanalytic contributions with continued surprise and admiration since my introduction to his work some years ago. The only direct communication I have had with him was via a letter to ask if he would agree to be interviewed for this chapter in my book. He declined my request owing to his age (then 83) and what he referred to as his 'physical infirmities'. I became aware, after my initial disappointment, that his courteous but forthright response corroborated my enthusiasm for his work and my impression of him through my reading as an honest and straightforward man, whose dealings with others are strikingly transparent, modest and essentially compassionate.

Searles and the significant pioneering achievements of his psycho-analytic work cannot be separated. He has been interviewed on at least two occasions (Langs and Searles, 1980; Stanton, 1992), when he has talked in an unusually candid manner about his family background, its links to his own 'psychopathology' and its relationship to the focus of his work. Searles was born in 1918. He sets out the influence of his upbringing in a small backwater town in the Catskill Mountains in upstate New York, a place with a population of only fifteen hundred people which he describes as 'very anti-Semitic'. He speaks fondly of hometown and parents, yet describes his father as a 'prejudiced, paranoid man' and his mother as a 'schizoid character type of a person' (Langs and Searles, 1980, p. 9). He surmises that his father's intoler-ance may have contributed to his own apparent lack of prejudice, and that his mother's 'bluntness' may have rubbed off on him. He also recounts his isolation and confusion while studying to be a doctor, when he felt that he 'narrowly avoided a schizophrenic breakdown' (ibid., p. 12).

Searles is noted among other things for his trailblazing psycho-analytic work with schizophrenic patients. After training as a psychoanalyst, he took up a post in 1949 at Chestnut Lodge, an insti-tution that housed and treated patients with chronic mental illness. He practised there for nearly fifteen years. Interviewed in September 1991 (Stanton, 1992), Searles told of his work with one patient who was able to leave Chestnut Lodge and live on her own, and of his continuing work with her (both in and outside the institution), which spanned thirty-nine years. His interest in schizophrenia culminated in his groundbreaking volume of collected papers (1965) on the subject, in which he argued, contrary to the classical view, that psychoanalysis was an appropriate tool for the treatment of psychotic illness. In this collection Searles also acknowledges the significance of the principles underlying Klein's work and the contribution she made to the management and understanding of the origins of schizophrenia.

Although in this interview Searles refers to his publication on schizophrenia as his finest work, he is at pains to point out the close connection between his own psychopathology and his professional motivations:

It came from my life's blood really, from my own pretty damn close brush with schizophrenia back in undergraduate college. I never had professional help. I continued working, studying, and doing well, but I had a goddam close brush with it. It came from that, and it came from working with very interesting patients at Chestnut Lodge in an extremely stimulating setting. (ibid., p. 330)

Searles is one of a rare breed of psychoanalysts who have made it their business to examine the precepts of psychoanalysis in the light of egalitarian principles, which is to say in terms of how they apply not only to the patient but also to the analyst, and ultimately to the vicissitudes of the relationship. In his paper 'The Dedicated Physician' (1967) Searles discusses the ambivalence that is often associated with the therapist's role – a role which normally requires and entails a considerable degree of dedication but which may also be used to defend against the therapist's unconscious sadistic and depressed feelings and as protection from the patient's experience of hopelessness and malicious impulses towards the therapist. Reaction formation is generally regarded as an obsessional defence, evoked as a defence against an unacceptable impulse. For example, if a person is unable to acknowledge consciously their own cruelty or animosity towards another, they may be compelled to exaggerate an opposing tendency. Searles therefore cautions therapists to be aware of the likelihood that where they sense a noticeable degree of dedication, care and concern for a patient, there are also likely to be unconscious countertransference issues that relate to hate and active neglect. Indeed, Searles often emphasizes the significant paradoxical quality involved in caring for others and maintains that a strong desire to cure the patient is in itself anti-therapeutic 'The therapist functioning in the spirit of dedication, which is the norm among physicians in other branches of medicine, represents here, in the practice of psychotherapy and psychoanalysis, an unconscious defence against his seeing clearly many crucial aspects of both the patient and himself' (ibid., p. 74).

One of the dangers in a sense of needing to rescue the patient resides in the assumption that the patient wishes to be cured, and, furthermore, that the therapist is the only member of the dyad that is capable of effecting this cure. However, as Searles sets out in his illuminating and distinguished paper on the causes of schizophrenia, gloriously and ironically entitled 'The Patient as Therapist to the Analyst' (1975a), the patient also has an innate propensity to treat the analyst, and both patient and analyst are ambivalent about change. The patient, too, has concerns about the therapeutic endeavour in which they are engaged, and expects the therapist to fail them in the same way that their own dedication, self-sacrifice and therapeutically-minded strivings towards their parents, in childhood, have earlier failed. For Searles, the major causal factor that has led to the patient's psychosis is then repeated in their relationship with the analyst: the patient wishes to help (cure) the analyst but assumes that these attempts will fail yet again; furthermore, the malicious feelings that the patient continues to harbour towards the parents in the past will be reflected onto the analyst in the present. Finally, the patient feels a reluctance to be helped owing to the sense of safety and protection they have achieved by becoming and remaining ill, and which they are consequently disinclined to give up.

Searles continues this discourse of equivalence by speaking of the therapist's resemblance to the patient: the therapist, too, wishes both to heal and harm:

> In other words, an intensely pressuring, dedicated therapeutic zeal denotes an unconscious determination, on the part of the therapist, to protect and preserve, for reasons of his own psychic economy, the patient's present level of psychotic or neurotic ego functioning. This determination arises from the various narcissistic and infantile gratifications the therapist is receiving from the patient, who represents at one level a transference–mother who is feeding him, as well as from the fact that the patient's illness serves to shield the therapist from seeing clearly his own illness. (ibid., p. 78)

Furthermore, by maintaining the patient's position as the one who is 'ill', the therapist is able to preserve their own omnipotence. If, however, the therapist can acknowledge their own anti-therapeutic impulses as well as the patient's inherent therapeutic attributes, it is likely that they will be more predisposed to fulfil their major therapeutic obligations as therapist. This entails unravelling the circuitous and enduring countertransference issues.

It can be argued that Harold Searles's writing and working life have been entirely dedicated to underscoring the significance of countertransference and to insisting that countertransference constitutes the primary therapeutic tool. Following his critique of the use of drug and electric shock regimes for the treatment of schizophrenia, he states: 'My approach focuses, by contrast, upon the countertransference realm, in the broader sense of that term, as being of the greatest and most reliable research and therapeutic value' (Searles, 1975b, pp. 375–76).

The therapist's meticulous recognition and readiness to observe their own countertransference struggle within the interaction is thus, for Searles, the defining feature of the therapist's task. In this way both patient and therapist have the opportunity to move beyond the entanglement of the necessary early symbiotic stage, and can begin to gain a clearer and more realistic sense of themselves as separate, as well as in relation to one another. Searles asserts that this vital symbiotic phase can only be achieved if the analyst is willing to tolerate their ambivalent affects towards the patient. In particular, he emphasizes that this phase is interrupted by any sense of desperate dedication on the therapist's part, which will arise from the therapist's unacknowledged vulnerability and defensive need to maintain an omnipotent position. Without the experience of merging, Searles is saying, there can be no successful negotiation of the subsequent stage of disentanglement. Finally, for Searles, the stage of therapeutic symbiosis enables the patient to know that they are able to help the therapist to become a whole person, which in turn strengthens their capacity to trust in the therapist's competence to help them.

It is remarkable to what extent Searles has been consistent in his willingness to pursue and examine his own countertransference difficulties in relation to his patients and in his readiness to unveil and pass on these experiences to other practitioners; many of us in the profession would be hard pressed to acknowledge these difficulties even to ourselves. We see in his work a lucid demonstration of the ever-spiralling patterns and connections that form between patient and therapist and the influence of the play of their transference and countertransference on each. By emphasizing the therapist's psychopathology, and its consequences, along with the patient's incisive talents, Searles brings out the parity between them. His work is outstanding in the fields of psychoanalysis and psychotherapy for this persistence in excavating his own covert motivations and their effects on his clinical work. It is demonstrably a commitment carried out in the service of his patients, in a spirit of deep curiosity and with an acceptance of the endurance of personal conflict that this entails. Many of his own personal struggles are used to illustrate a point, and most importantly he seems to discourage dogma and encourage the capacity to doubt. One gets a flavour of his energetic fair-mindedness from the following observation:

> Incidentally, it occurred to me at this juncture that I do not feel at all thoroughly clear, myself, as to the difference between love and hate. This particular matter may best be regarded as an ever-intriguing, basically unknowable or incomprehensible subject in any full and detailed final sense, and the exploration of this subject may be one of the basically fascinating and inspiring aspects of the practice of psychotherapy or psychoanalysis. (Searles, 1987, p. 263)

Both Searles and Ferenczi have been exceptional in their unashamed and unequivocal admissions of the intrinsic correspondence between their work with their patients and their own pathology. It may be conjectured that this openness of attitude towards their own emotional difficulties lies at the heart of what made them both such dedicated, perceptive, unbiased and empathic analysts. It would seem it is this willingness to confront and acknowledge these interpersonal links that relieves the therapist of the need to be the one 'who knows', of the need to control and objectify the patient and that also reduces the risk of the therapist's needing to reproject unrecognized ambivalent, disturbing interactional affects into the patient.

The ability to tolerate ambivalence in one's feelings is significantly related to emotional maturity and the ability to care. As Winnicott (1963) pointed out, it is precisely that capacity which enables the mother/therapist to perform their maternal/therapeutic holding duties in a 'good enough' way. Conflicting emotions are an inevitable aspect of all intimate relationships. It may be argued that the way in which a person manages and expresses their ambivalent feelings is the ultimate influence on the quality of the relationship. Winnicott warned of the inherent danger of 'sentimentality' (Winnicott, 1958) that would impede and thwart the ability to provide the experience of 'good enough mothering', and defined sentimentality as the mother's inability to acknowledge her own aggressive impulses toward her child. As commentators on Winnicott's work have observed, 'The truly responsible people of the world are those who accept the fact of their own hate, nastiness, cruelty, things which coexist with their capacity to love and to construct' (Davis and Wallbridge, 1981, p. 153).

The notion of sentimentality which Winnicott identifies in one kind of maternal interaction may be likened to Ferenczi's concern with the therapist's hypocrisy toward the patient. Both terms capture how the denial of these unwieldy contradictory affects is nevertheless tacitly seen through by the child/patient, which promotes a sense of mistrust and an introject of a person who is unable to contain and manage their ambivalent impulses.

The parallel between Searles and Ferenczi is apparent in the willingness of each consistently to examine and struggle with their own difficulties per se, as well as in relation to their clinical work with their patients, and in their iconoclastic attitudes to the theory and practice of psychoanalysis.

The choice of psychotherapy as a career assumes that the therapist, as well as the patient, has a need to work through their own disturbances. As Searles and Ferenczi suggest, the therapist is unlikely to be able to fulfil their task if they need to suppress this apparently paradoxical fact, and, furthermore, the patient is not only able to discern this, but has a natural tendency to assist the therapist in this.

As detailed above, there are noticeable similarities between the beliefs, ideas and practice of the two analysts discussed so far in this chapter. To some extent these same themes can be detected in the ideas currently promoted by Robert Langs, the final maverick of this chapter. Nevertheless, it may be argued that his technical and scientific focus in relation to the issue of countertransference contrasts sharply with Ferenczi's and Searles's more humanistic, reciprocal and personal orientation.

Robert Joseph Langs (1928–)

Robert Langs was born in New York. He initially trained and graduated as a medical practitioner in 1953 and then went on to specialize in psychiatry. In 1959 he qualified as a psychoanalyst after receiving his training from the Nathan S. Kline Institute in Orangeburg, New York, in the classical tradition. Langs must surely count as one of the most prolific writers on the subject of psychoanalysis; to date he has written over fifty published books in this area, as well as countless journal papers. His seminal ideas on the ubiquitousness of countertransference can be clearly discerned in his early two-volume work, *The Technique of Psychoanalytic Psychotherapy* (Langs, 1973a, 1974).

The first presentation of Langs's fully-fledged competing psychoanalytic model appeared in his book *The Bipersonal Field* (1976), in which he outlined the dynamic and holistic aspects of the therapeutic encounter and the way in which both members of the dyad consistently influence each other. Langs initially described his radical approach as 'adaptational–interactional'; later on he characterized his approach as 'communicative'; in his current work (Langs, 2004) he has reverted to his original designation. His emphasis on the term 'adaptational' is taken from Darwinian ideas, and refers to the evolution of human emotional development, which he views as primarily designed to cope with the environmental domain rather than purely concerned with internal psychic fantasy issues. His empirical research findings reinforced this view and led him to assert that the patient's unconscious narrative communications are invariably stimulated by real, rather than distorted, issues related to the framework of psychotherapy (see above, Chapter 3). Langs further claims that although the meaning the patient places on a particular boundary disturbance will vary owing to idiosyncratic factors in their early background, there are nevertheless grounds for universal support for 'secure frame' psychotherapy as the most powerful healing factor (Langs, 1992).

Langs's assertive claims and his prescribed technique have tended to detract from some of his basic principles and have led to a considerable amount of criticism within the world of psychoanalysis and psychotherapy. In an interview with David Livingstone Smith which took place in 1989 (Smith, 1989), Langs responded to his detractors as follows:

> I'm glad that you mention that particular accusation. To say that a person breathes in oxygen and gives off carbon dioxide isn't rigidity: it's nature. To say that muscles contain myosin, that's nature. To say that people encode images in response to emotionally charged information is nature. To say that when occurring in the therapeutic situation these responses deal primarily with the ground rules of nature. This is not a rigid approach. It is a testable approach which attempts to identify regularities of nature. (ibid., p. 119)

Langs has argued that the only way psychoanalysis and psychotherapy can progress is by alignment with the physical sciences and by finding ways to verify its precepts statistically. He has written extensively on this subject and has carried out a number of research projects with mathematician Anthony Badalamenti, using measures drawn from physics. Langs maintains that the results of his quantified analysis of the clinical dialogue not only highlights specific factors that produce countertransference difficulties but also establishes the communicative approach as a formal science of psychoanalysis (Langs and Badalamenti, 1992a, 1992b).

Yet again Langs's findings were received in a less than favourable light and led to a series of papers which appeared in the British Journal of Psychotherapy decrying his pompous attitude and erroneous assertions as well as refuting the idea that physics is an appropriate tool with which to measure the therapeutic interaction (Burgoyne, 1994; Harris, 1994; Schwartz, 1994) As someone who has not received any formal training in the physical sciences, I am not in a position to comment on some of the finer methodological and theoretical points. I would, however, like to raise a particular issue which, as far as I am aware, and most surprisingly, has not been addressed before in relation to this discourse. As one of the papers points out, the main vehicle used for the studies was 'videotape recordings of psychoanalytic consultations originally prepared for a teaching conference on how analysts work' (Schwartz, 1994, p. 394). From a communicative perspective, the videotaping of sessions constitutes a major boundary 'deviation'. A communicative therapist would therefore predict that the patient's narrative material would contain allusions to infringements and concerns that relate thematically to lack of privacy and confidentiality, as well as indirect references linked to exploitation and voyeurism. This author is therefore at a loss to understand why this fundamental communicative tenet was not included in the variables being measured.

Not only has Langs written a plethora of books on the topic of communicative psychoanalysis but he has also ventured into the realm of playwriting. Although his plays remain unpublished, they have been presented publicly at conferences in both the UK and New York. Of the two that I attended, one, 'The Frog and the Swan', from 1997, dealt with a clandestine meeting between patient and therapist that took place in a cocktail lounge. The second, 'Unholy Trinities', from 1999, explored the life and promiscuous love affairs of Lou Andreas-Salome, a notable (deceased) Freudian psychoanalyst. One of the questions which was put to Langs after the showing of the first of these two plays (and to my mind the most communicatively relevant) was what we were to make of Langs's narrative communication to this small audience, which was encapsulated in the theme of his play. It is to his credit that Langs acknowledged the pertinence of the question, yet he also seemed bemused; and it was left to one or two of the more daring participants to conjecture on the interpersonal communicative aspects of Langs's own narrative that were disguised in his play.

Langs has also turned his attention to the supervisory relationship, and has developed a communicative model of supervision (Langs,

1994). He criticizes the classical and mainstream stance on supervision for placing little emphasis on the boundaries of the supervisory interaction, and argues instead that the importance his model gives to the ground rules of therapy should also be given in a similar way to supervision. Langs considers that the supervisory relationship will be subject to similar concerns and dilemmas to those that arise in the therapeutic interaction. These include issues related to the supervisor's management of the environment (privacy; confidentiality; neutrality; regularity and timing of sessions) but also reflection on the systemic parallels between the supervisory encounter and the therapeutic encounter – parallels which are likely to be contributing to and tacitly endorsing the supervisee's relationship with the patient.

Paradoxically, one of the persistent criticisms that has arisen in the literature relates to the fact that Langs illustrates his work only by presenting clinical vignettes in public and in print drawn from work offered by students of his approach, rather than from his own clinical practice. In their 1980 dialogue (Langs and Searles, 1980), Searles speaks glowingly of Langs's groundbreaking contributions to psychoanalysis; but he also refers to Langs's 'harsh-sounding criticism' of a therapist's work:

> I notice that as time went on, in my reading, your compassion became evident to me. After you have told the therapist a great deal in a harsh sounding way, then your compassion becomes very evident. Now I am sure it has been recommended to you – and that you, for your own good reasons, have elected not to act upon the recommendations – to use material from your own patients. That would make all the difference. It would remove completely any aspect of this book as having been written in terms of your opining from a superior position. If we readers had a chance for you to share with us your own mistakes, then you would no longer be subject to that kind of criticism.

Langs then responds: 'The reason I don't present my own material is related to my commitment to the frame and to my patients' (ibid., p. 133).

The American analyst Merton Gill has critiqued Langs's model from a number of perspectives, even though he is in general agreement with some of Langs's ideas. Gill (1984) takes particular issue with Langs's customized technique regime on the grounds that it 'remains true to the classical tradition in the rigidity of his approach' (p. 411) and encourages a 'blank screen' attitude on the part of the therapist. Like Searles, Gill also takes exception to the fact that Langs is unwilling to display his own clinical work to public scrutiny and comments: 'To some extent Langs is able to maintain the illusion that the good analyst will behave essentially appropriately by using the work of relatively inexperienced trainees for his clinical demonstrations' (ibid., p. 400).

For my own part I have always failed to understand why Langs mostly (to my knowledge) focuses on trainees' clinical material rather than on the narrative elements that emerge in the immediate interactions between himself and a given trainee. This concern seems just as relevant to the supervisory interaction, whether it takes place in the public or the private domain. I have previously addressed this in a paper (Holmes, 1999a) in which I examined the issue of how an underlying pattern can be repeated on many different levels of a given system (a phenomenon known as 'self-similarity'), and signify disorder in that system (see further Chapter 10 below). The following vignette, concerning the supervision of a therapist's work with her client, provides an illustration of this. The presence of a particular theme, or cluster of themes, is vividly recognizable in the behaviour and/or associations of all the persons involved.

A therapist arrived late for a weekly session with her client. Subsequently, in her weekly supervision, the therapist presented an account of this session to her supervisor. The material of the presentation began with the client having talked about her boyfriend and his unreliability, which the client was reported as having found disturbing. The account of the client's material then continued with a story she had told about her flatmate: the flatmate had caused the client to be locked out of their flat by forgetting to leave the key to the door in its usual place. The therapist then reported that several minutes after this, the client recalled a memory from childhood of waiting in an anxious and disturbed frame of mind for her mother to arrive to collect her from school. The mother indeed arrived late. Two final pertinent facts: (1) prior to the supervision session in question, the therapist and supervisor had had some brief contact of a social nature; and (2) at the previous supervision meeting, the supervisor had run over time and finished the session late.

It is clear how the associated themes of lateness, unreliability and disappointment or distress echo and re-echo through this scenario – an uncanny parallel process in the here-and-now of supervision. To my mind, it is the addressing of this process that constitutes the essence of the work that needs to be done. For, it seems to me self-evident that where the supervisor is willing to acknowledge their own influence and countertransference difficulties within the supervisory relationship, the supervisee will be enabled more easily to consider their own input and influence in relation to their patient.

A communicative therapist responds primarily to the 'trigger', the 'adaptive context' or the stimulus that has prompted the patient's narrative, which by definition relates to something that the therapist has either said or done. The communicative model is based on the idea that derivative communication is prompted by actual incidents in the immediate situation. Langs initially adopted the phrase 'adaptive context', and subsequently replaced this with the term 'trigger', to describe a real occurrence that has stimulated an internal reaction. The importance and the implications for the patient of a trigger are then conveyed in their spontaneous, unconscious narrative messages. More often than not, the themes that are embedded in the patient's communications reveal concerns that the patient has about the therapist's behaviour towards them, and the therapist normally formulates their interventions around themes of an adverse or troubling nature. In theory at least, this means that the communicative therapist is resolutely dedicated to struggling with and admitting to their own countertransfence issues disclosed to them by their patients. As far as this author is concerned, this is the crux of the work: not to eliminate countertransference, nor to establish a totally secure frame (were such a thing possible, which is doubtful); but to create and establish a relationship of trust. If the therapist is genuine in this respect, the therapeutic encounter is more likely to contrast with the patient's past and current disappointing and frustrating interpersonal experiences. It is further conjectured that the therapist's acknowledgement of their own vulnerabilities within the interaction (as revealed to them by the patient) can be both empowering and ego-enhancing for the patient.

The integral link between countertransference and communicative practice has been examined in a paper by Eugene Silverstein (1984), in which he concludes:

Countertransference error in technique is more likely to be exposed and analysed through communicative approaches to listening than through approaches that do not begin with the adaptive context. This conclusion follows from the fact that the adaptive context, by definition, focuses on the therapist's interventions, particularly their latent implications. The therapist who listens with an adaptive context in mind is compelled to review his or her actions constantly and to consider the patient's unconscious commentary. (p. 125)

The Langsian approach to psychoanalytic psychotherapy has attempted to counteract the bias that is evident in the tradition of classical psychoanalysis by principally homing in on the therapist's countertransference. This contrasts with the orthodox position, in which transference tends to take pride of place. It is also at odds with the idea that it is the analyst (rather than the patient) who is able to discern and experience the patient's true concerns. I, for one, feel that this is a laudable position, however much this humble and self-effacing stance required of the communicative therapist may also contain conflicting underlying motivations. Some of these motives have been examined in 'Confessions of a Communicative Psychotherapist' (Holmes, 1999b), where I comment: 'When therapists experience heightened levels of guilt they may attempt to moderate their discomfort by focusing on the boundaries per se in a rigid manner, or by resorting to confession as a defensive rather than therapeutic measure' (pp. 48–49). Furthermore, as David Smith has suggested (see Chapter 9), one of the latent reasons for choosing psychotherapy as an occupation may be to gain 'secret knowledge'. If we accept this suggestion, we must assume that this motivation also applies to the communicative practitioner, as it is they who decide which is the most significant theme being offered by the patient, and it is they who decode the patient's message and link it to the relevant trigger.

Although there has been some interest in the communicative approach to psychoanalytic psychotherapy since its introduction in the early nineteen seventies, it has in general attracted little attention or received a hostile reception from the psychotherapy profession. The number of people who belong to the communicative societies in Europe and America has also dwindled in the past decade, which is perhaps an indication that few practitioners are willing to align themselves to this model in any pure or wholehearted way. In part this may be due to a lack of evolution of Langs's original formulation of the model, which is imperative for the survival of any model, in combination with Langs's own zealous promotion, and unyielding certainty, of the model's scientific status. David Smith, one of the few people to have written at length in this area, has now turned his attention to evolutionary psychology (see Chapter 2). There are also a handful of therapists in Italy and a small group in Germany who have continued to research and write on the subject of child psychotherapy from a communicative perspective. In my own research I have examined and linked together some key Existential concepts to do with the notion of 'being-in-the-world', in order to bring out the interpersonal focus of 'being-between' patient and therapist. In this research I have further sought to illustrate and integrate the communicative paradigm with ideas taken from chaos theory (Holmes, 2001).

Langs has made some formidable unique and creative contributions to the theory and practice of psychotherapy. As such, he is one of the prime instigators of the interpersonal paradigm for understanding human communication. It is to be hoped that some of these essentially egalitarian principles will endure and eventually be given some consideration by the profession.

This chapter has presented a synopsis of the ideas and practice of three men of vision whose work has gone against the grain and beyond both the classical and mainstream descriptions and usage of countertransference. Although each of their innovations was developed separately and at different times, the synchronicity between their work is quite apparent in their attempts to dignify and empower the patient and in their common focus on the interpersonal and interdependent qualities of the therapeutic interaction. The essential difference between the three seems to relate to the way in which they have approached the issue of countertransference. Ferenczi's concern with the analyst's hypocrisy led him to dare to experiment with techniques that would be described as exceedingly unconventional and immoderate. Unfortunately, he may be remembered more for these anomalies than for his professional integrity and progressive and active contributions to countertransference, with which he struggled throughout his career. By contrast, Langs's lofty aspirations to develop a science of psychoanalysis and his lack of doubt concerning his model appear to have led either to an outright rejection of his work or to a total acceptance and a generally uncritical stance. As far as this author is concerned, there is something profoundly irreconcilable between Langs's certainty in relation to his bipersonal theoretical postulates, which caution the therapist to doubt and regularly question their interpersonal motivations, and the technical assertiveness of their application. Harold Searles is renowned for his single-minded clinical enthusiasm and for his thorough and detailed analysis of his clinical work. His publications contain much material on the subject of countertransference which repeatedly documents the often unsavoury and unpalatable challenges of his extensive work as a practitioner. These endeavours, his consistent acceptance of his loving (sometimes erotic) as well as hateful emotions towards his patients, as well as his consummate respect for their intransigent suffering, combine to give his work a particularly compelling quality. Searles always remained an outsider, as, unlike most of us in the profession, he did not align himself to any specific model or group. This fact may also have contributed to his ability to question, reason and feel in a more expansive and less inhibitive way with his patients.

Chapter 5

Existential Psychotherapy

The term 'existential' is derived from the Latin *existere*, meaning 'to stand out'. 'Existence' in this sense refers to human beings who have an awareness of their existence in the world of objects and other people as well as of their capacity to stand out, develop, emerge and become through their freely chosen actions. At the same time, human existence is also characterized by its limitations and the existent's recognition that their being in the world is finite.

Although the origins of Existential philosophy have been attributed to the work of the nineteenth-century Danish philosopher Søren Kierkegaard, notably to his *Concept of Anxiety* (1844), many of its seminal ideas can be traced back to axioms and principles that are the hallmark of the Eastern Buddhist tradition. For example, the term 'transcendence', which is central to Existential thought, is closely associated with Buddhist teachings and with the idea that human beings have the freedom to go beyond their habitual ways of experiencing themselves in the world. Other common threads that unite the two philosophies relate to self-awareness, individual experience, impermanence and self-delusion. Likewise, the overarching concern which unites Existentialists and Buddhists is their joint interest in the dilemmas that dog the human condition – the inevitability of change, the yearning for security in an insecure world and the difficulty of living in the present; and yet, the origins of Buddhist philosophy can be dated to as far back as 563 BC (Honderich, 1995).

Existential philosophy is primarily focused on illuminating the tension between the givens, or limits, of human existence and the individual's essential capacity to create themselves through their freely chosen actions. Many Existential writers have been at pains to point out that the tension and anxiety that emerge from our awareness of our inherent freedom to define ourselves tends to make cowards of us all, and, instead, take refuge in different modes of denial. Paul Tillich

(1952) referred to 'the courage to be' oneself even when faced with the anxiety that unavoidably accompanies our exerting our freedom and confronting our mortality. Courage, for Tillich, always entails a going towards, rather than a recoiling from, that anxiety. For, paradoxically, the attempt to avoid anxiety is seen as so weighty that the individual is unable in its presence to pursue any other goal and, instead, becomes caught in a vicious downward spiral of timidity.

Jean-Paul Sartre, the French Existential philosopher, writer, novelist and dramatist, devised a number of trenchant and often cited maxims, including 'existence precedes essence' and 'man is condemned to be free' (1946). Both of these phrases capture the Existential ethos that began to evolve in Continental Europe in the latter half of the nineteenth and early twentieth century. For Sartre, human beings, unlike objects, are composed of nothing but their freedom to make choices: they are therefore forced, compelled, or condemned to be free. Sartre asserts that even when people's choices are severely curtailed, they are still at liberty to choose how they will react to a given situation. Sartre illustrates his central thesis by citing the example of a prisoner whose physical choices may be extremely restricted but who still retains the capacity to decide how he will react under such limiting conditions. In this sense human beings are always able to exert their freedom by the attitudes they choose to adopt, under any conditions with which they are confronted. They are free in so far as they have the capacity to continue to alter, reflect upon and revise their attitudes. The nothingness, or lack of essence, that defines human beings denotes that each individual's biography is generated through their personally chosen, autonomous actions. Existentialists assert that the void that embodies the human condition continues to be a source of anxiety owing to each individual's intrinsic capacity and responsibility to define themselves. The figurative expression that someone is 'full of themselves' is commonly used to describe an arrogant and conceited person and conjures up an overconfident individual with firmly held ideas. Yet this kind of attitude is merely an extreme version of the human urge to hang onto a stable and fixed identity by clinging to one's values at all costs and, as it were, filling oneself up to resemble an object, leaving no space for doubt or change.

Human beings are therefore defined by their freedom and their lack of essence but are often prone to deny this, preferring to believe that they are determined and object-like. That is, on this view we come into existence without any given purpose or definition other than the purposes and definitions that we give ourselves, through the choices we make; and these choices can never be final as we can continue to update them. Human existence can never be determined in the way that objects by their makers can and are; and yet the predisposition remains to take illusory comfort in the notion that we are irrevocably constituted. It is this inclination to relinquish freedom which, though it may reduce anxiety, also inhibits the individual's ability to stand out and to establish meaning in their life from his or her own, necessarily unique standpoint. Existentialists view the human condition in terms of its absence, as a 'nothing' rather than a 'something', which continues to emerge throughout the individual's life. Human beings create themselves and mould their own natures by the values they espouse, as these are disclosed through their actions.

Responsibility and freedom are close allies, and responsibility implies accountability, agency, obligation and decision-making. The responsible person accepts that their choices can only be based on their freely chosen subjective decisions, which includes the choices they make regarding their intentions towards others. The realization that this is so and that one cannot rely on the usual, traditional external decision-making resources, such as religion or common convention, generates a profound sense of anxiety. This awareness, in each individual, of their inherent freedom corroborates the essence of existence, which Kierkegaard (1844) graphically described as the 'dizziness of freedom'. Taking responsibility for one's actions is deeply disturbing for the reason that, first, human beings lack recourse to any outside authority to prescribe how they should act and live; and, secondly, any personal decision requires the individual to choose from different courses of action without knowing what consequences their choices will have in the future.

The German philosopher Martin Heidegger wrote extensively on the nature of being and is regarded as one of the originators of the Existential movement. Heidegger (1927) used the German term *'Dasein'* to describe existence; this is commonly translated as 'being there'. For Heidegger, 'being there' encapsulates the meaning of being: being-there-in-the-world as a constituent part of the world. Human existence is thus not only intrinsically inseparable from the world in which it is but also inextricably connected to other people. Finally, 'being there' describes the unique characteristic of existence, which is to be aware of itself in the world and to reflect on this awareness with the certain knowledge that its being-in-the-world is transient.

Meaning

Human beings have been described as meaning-seeking creatures, possessing a profound need to make sense of their existence (Frankl, 1946). If we must die, and if we must accept the fact that no outside authority such as the principle of a given religion can provide an explanation of the meaning of our existence and the purpose of our life, then what is the point of existence? If, as Neitzsche (1883) proclaimed, 'God is dead', then how is it possible to know what to value: how is it possible to live a fulfilling and satisfactory life without any externally-derived guiding principles to follow?

The human tendency to question and to act in response to a reason is entrenched in the quest to establish a purpose to our everyday activities and, on a wider scale, ultimately to give meaning to our very existence. Nevertheless, the tasks we set out to achieve, be it to swim the Channel or fight for a particular cause, do not in themselves have any intrinsic meaning other than the personal value that is placed on them by the individual who takes them up. This distinctive style of philosophizing, which strips existence down to its bare bones by declaring that each existent must determine his or her own meaning and make sense of his or her own existence, is experienced as ridiculous if the world itself is impervious to reason. The sense of disorder and feeling of insignificance that emerges from the awareness of the inescapable contingency of existence is often too hard to bear. Human beings tend to deal with this anxiety by denying this immensely disappointing and unpalatable realization: far preferable, instead, to shore up one's belief in the importance of existence by immersing oneself in the everyday trivia of life rather than confront the knowledge of one's gratuitous and finite position in the world.

Meaninglessness

It is not surprising that human existence has been described by some authors as 'absurd', given the view that human beings are thrown into a world that does not provide them with any clear meaning, purpose, or function, and that existence inevitably includes suffering and must finally culminate in death. The concept of absurdity was consistently addressed by the Algerian writer Albert Camus in his fictional works. In the parable of the human condition, the *Myth of Sisyphus* (1942), Camus describes Sisyphus' ongoing existential project as a repetitive and tedious task. Sisyphus is committed to rolling a stone up a hill, knowing that it will continue to elude him by rolling back down time and time again. It is this incessant laborious toil carried out by Sisyphus which symbolically affirms the essential absurdity of the human condition. Yet Camus represents him as a happy and dignified man who consolidates his own meaning through his chosen pursuit whatever the outcome.

The Viennese writer Victor Frankl founded a school of psychotherapy which focused on the importance of meaning and the possibility of establishing meaning even in the presence of great frustration and suffering. The school of 'logotherapy' developed by Frankl derived its name from the Greek word for meaning, '*logos*'. Frankl also coined the term 'existential vacuum' to describe the emptiness experienced by people who are bereft of internal, subjective meaning. The purpose of logotherapy, Frankl explained, is that it 'tries to elicit [man's] striving for a meaning to life, and it tries also to elucidate the meaning of his existence' (1967, p. 35). For Frankl, meaning can also be found 'by the stand we take toward the world, that is to say, by the attitude we choose toward suffering' (ibid., p. 37).

Anxiety

For the sake of brevity and simplicity, it may be said that the classical psychoanalytic view conceptualizes anxiety as a defence against the conscious realization of forbidden instinctual wishes. Nevertheless, by 1926 Freud had revised his ideas on anxiety and considered its emergence as an indication of approaching or imminent unknown psychic danger. The various strands of psychoanalytic thinking are also in general agreement that the reduction of the patient's neurotic anxiety (as defined above) is one of the main purposes of the psychoanalytic process. In contrast, and speaking generally, existential psychotherapy is interested in enabling the client to acknowledge and accept the reality that life is fraught with anxiety. From this perspective, neurotic anxiety is seen as camouflage, or denial, of the actual, unavoidable anxieties of the human condition.

The term anxiety, which is the English translation of the German *Angst*, is a subject of considerable interest and importance to Existential philosophy. Anxiety verifies and affirms the fundamental uncertainty that is built into human existence. Anxiety is related to freedom – to the necessity to choose and the dread of choosing, as well as to the ontic and ontological restrictions that inevitably accompany human freedom: as we have seen, the human condition is epitomized by a lack, by nothing rather than something; death is an inescapable part of human existence. Anxiety is thus an affect that cannot be sidestepped but is, on the contrary, a human given, that needs to be confronted and endured.

Authenticity

The problematical and frustrating aspects of being-in-the-world with others (being-with-others) have been explored in relation to the difficulties that constantly arise in our interactions with other people. The Existential viewpoint suggests that authenticity, which is identified with authorship, is linked to the dilemma of making choices from an individual, rather than collective, standpoint. The person who relinquishes their individual responsibility by making choices based on convention or commonplace values and assumptions is not, by definition, authentic, as these decisions have originated from an external rather than internal or truly personal source. Human existence is distinguished by the existent's inherent freedom to make choices. To choose in accordance with standards that have been laid down by others, as a mere reflection of the values of the group, is therefore inauthentic and not an expression of individual self. Heidegger (1927) referred to this mode of being as 'Das Man', usually translated as 'the they'. Nietzsche described this general or neutral way of being as 'the Herd'. Thus authenticity, for Heidegger, is an acknowledgement of the way we actively interpret our experience of being-in-the-world, and enables us to construe our attitude towards others in a spirit of equivalence and mutual respect. By contrast, inauthenticity emphasizes the difference between self and others and drives an attitude of competitiveness between individuals. At the same time, however, Heidegger argues that an awareness of the ongoing tension between these two modes of being-with-others can in fact give force to a person's willingness to express their individuality and thus encourage them to embrace the full potentiality of their existence.

Sartre described inauthenticity as 'bad faith', and emphasized how strongly human beings are predisposed to refute their essential freedom. This is the same as saying we have a strong predisposition towards self-deception. Likewise, for Sartre, the notion of self-deception is intimately linked to our relationships with other people. The propensity to take flight into 'bad faith' is a mechanism that separates the individual both from themselves and from others, leading to ways of interaction with others which are sterile and stereotypical. In his well-known vignette of the desperately over-acting waiter

Sartre graphically illustrates people's tendency to take refuge in their professional role as a means of denying both their own freedom and the freedom of others. The stereotypical actions, or 'dance', of the waiter reduces him to an object or thing, and in this way he safely detaches and isolates himself from the diners he serves (cf. Holmes, 1998a, p. 125). The brilliance of Sartre's account is that it is an instantly recognizable deceptive and self-deceptive ploy that reveals the need to find security by representing ourselves in a one-dimensional way. Bad faith, for Sartre, is the primary ruse that human beings employ in order to deny their unique position in the world and to dissociate self from other. This inauthentic mode of being has been well summed up by Mary Warnock: 'The conclusion of the argument from the general to the particular is that human beings are capable of very specific kinds of self-deception, and that their general relationship with the world makes it inevitable that they should practise it' (1970, p. 100). Thus, if bad faith underlines the incessant challenge of being with others in an open and engaged way, then it is to be expected that this struggle would be at the forefront of the therapeutic encounter, or at least be present to serve as a professional caution; yet, at the same time, Sartre's (and Warnock's) point is the indefatigable and chronic quality of this defence.

Death

It is a certainty that all living things will at some point in time cease to exist. However, it seems that human beings are the only living creatures to have the capacity to recognize their finite position in the world. Existential philosophy does not merely view death as the end of life but emphasizes the significance and profound influence that the fact of death has throughout the life of each individual. Human existence is characterized by two, apparently opposite, poles. Human beings are defined by their freedom, on the one hand, yet they are also intrinsically marked and limited by their mortality, on the other. The ability to exert one's freedom authentically is therefore considered to be dependent on the ability to acknowledge that one is limited by one's mortality. Recognition of death then comes to be seen as the spur that urges and activates the exercise of a person's freedom and potential in the present (Heidegger, 1927).

There are many everyday expressions, notable sayings or quotations and famous verses that allude to the terror of death and our awareness of the fleeting nature of time and the essentially time-limited character of human existence. Expressions such as 'Time waits for no man', 'No time like the present', 'Time is of the essence', 'In the midst of life we are in death', 'Procrastination is the thief of time' and the Latin phrase *'tempus fugit'* (time runs away) are common phrases that point to the tension and anxiety that are an inescapable part of human existence. We struggle in vain to evade the truth these express. As Herbert Spencer put it: 'Time: that which man is always trying to kill, but which ends in killing him' (*Penguin Book of Quotations*, 1960, p. 371).

From beginning to end, we find ways of constantly evading the existentially unavoidable fact that life must culminate in death. What Existential philosophy then does is draw out the implications of this: although death may be viewed as the opposite to life, both poles are inextricably entwined. Paradoxically, the personal attitude that individuals take in relation to their death will radically influence and impinge upon their life.

Isolation

Existentialists regard the development of the self as the responsibility of the individual. Through their actions, persons create their own distinctive identity. Existential isolation arises from an awareness that this task can only be carried out single-handedly and autonomously. The experience of originality and uniqueness that accompanies what we could think of as the 'self-project' of each is counterbalanced by the solitary character of that experience – the sense that it can never be fully expressed between one individual and another. Therefore, Existentialists emphasize, there is always a gap, or hiatus, between people, however intimate their relationship. Human beings tend to find this realization too distressing to endure, and are prone instead to deny this state of affairs by immersing themselves in the illusory belief that their intimate relationships can protect them from knowing about the isolation that is firmly anchored to human existence.

Phenomenology

The term 'phenomenology' comes from the Greek verb 'to appear, to bring to light'. It is used to describe a specific philosophical method – a way for the individual to philosophize about and explore their mental acts, in order to illuminate aspects of their experience that would otherwise go unnoticed. The Existential school of psychotherapy uses the phenomenological method developed by Heidegger to enable clients to examine particular areas of their existence from different perspectives. As Ernesto Spinelli explains: '. . . It is less important what we believe than the manner in which we believe. These arguments play a central role in the ideas of existential phenomenology' (1989, p. 107). Existential phenomenology allows us to explore an attitude or concern in different lights, in order to uncover how we restrict our freedom to make choices by attaching that freedom to a meaning which we assume to be predetermined.

Phenomenology is the study of phenomena, or the appearance of things, or how things appear; it is a method that examines primarily by describing. As John Macquarrie has observed:

> The point about phenomenology is that it offers a description in depth, so to speak, causing us to notice, removing hindrances that stand in the way of our seeing, exhibiting the essential rather than accidental, showing interrelations that may lead to a quite different view from the one that we get when a phenomenon is considered in isolation. (1973, p. 21)

The phenomenological method is concerned with the process of immediate experience and aims to access and reveal the essential nature of experience. The method uses the rule of *epoche*, a term derived from the Greek, meaning 'suspension of belief'. The rule of *epoche* is the attempt to bracket one's usual assumptions and prejudices and follow the rule of description rather than analysis, or explanation. This cardinal guideline is employed in order to discourage our proclivity to perceive always from a particular perspective, and to reduce our usual susceptibilities, biases and assumptions.

The rule of *epoche* is used by Existential phenomenology to underscore the relativity of our experiences. The subjective dimension of experience is central to Heidegger's Existential phenomenological method, unlike Husserl's original formulation (Husserl, 1925), which was primarily concerned with the essence of experience. The application of the Existential method highlights individuals' awareness of the intentional, active nature of their experience.

Existential psychotherapy

The role of the Existential therapist is to act as a guide to assist the client to explore and re-examine the assumptions, prejudices and partial views that are limiting their capacity to make choices. Spinelli states:

> If there is an ultimate aim to phenomenological therapy it is to offer the means for individuals to examine, confront, clarify and reassess their understanding of life, the problems encountered throughout their life, and the limits imposed upon the possibilities inherent in being-in-the-world. (1989, p. 127)

The Existential process assumes that the therapeutic interaction is based on a real relationship between client and therapist and offers the client the opportunity to engage in a dialogue that is focused at the level of description rather than analysis, aimed at uncovering the client's fundamental view of themselves and the world.

Existential psychotherapy, grounded in and informed by the philosophy of Existentialism and the phenomenological method, is principally concerned with addressing and illuminating the client's subjective experience. The client's conscious impressions are therefore the dominant focus of the therapeutic work and take precedence over any other considerations. Existential therapist Hans Cohn explains:

> Immediate experience has priority over theoretical assumptions, and what 'appears' – the phenomenon – always has to be taken seriously. Thus in Existential psychotherapy it is important for the therapist to remain open to whatever the patient brings, verbally and non-verbally, and not to impose theoretical assumptions on the phenomena. (1994, p. 700)

Cohn also emphasizes the authentic nature of Existential anxiety that inevitably accompanies the commitment to freedom, the acceptance of choice and uncertainty and the need for fortitude. This is in direct opposition to neurotic anxiety, which Existentialists consider emerges from the attempt to evade the freedom that is ingrained in the human condition.

Existential interview

Emmy van Deurzen is an Existential psychotherapist and supervisor, a chartered counselling psychologist and fellow of the British Psychological Society and British Association for Counselling and Psychotherapy. She directs the New School of Psychotherapy and

Counselling in London, where she is a professor with the Schiller International University. She also co-directs the Centre for the Study of Conflict and Reconciliation at the University of Sheffield and is a partner in the organization Dilemma Consultancy in Human Relations. Van Deurzen founded the Society for Existential Analysis in 1988, the year her book *Existential Counselling and Psychotherapy in Practice* was published (second edition, 2002). Other books of van Deurzen's are *Paradox and Passion in Psychotherapy* (1998) and *Everyday Mysteries* (Van Deurzen-Smith, 1997).

As one of the leading exponents of Existential psychotherapy in this country, van Deurzen is well placed to comment on how she views this tradition. In the following comments she explains what Existentialism means to her.

The Existential approach is a philosophical approach; it does not focus on the intrapsychic process but rather on the interpersonal, interactional, contextual aspects of being a person. What that means is that in the therapeutic relationship you will be focusing on understanding how a person is in the world in lots of different ways. You would look at how they are in relation to the world of objects, things in the material world. You would also observe how they are in relation to other people; but also how they are in relation to themselves, and how they are in relation to ideas and in relation to life itself.

So, you would find out what the person's position is, what their perspective is, what their point of view is, and how they enact that in their everyday existence. Of course the objective is not just to get an overview of how they live and how they experience the world and what their attitude is but rather to understand where that becomes problematic to them. Then the objective becomes to try to understand the problems that they are having in relation to their particular stance in the world, and also in relation to the human condition itself. This requires us to understand the human condition and its predictable problems and challenges, as well as to have some grasp of how those particular individuals get caught up in those particular problems and how and why they feel overwhelmed by the challenges.

The Existential approach goes back to Classical Western philosophers, and it also bases itself in some Eastern philosophers who have investigated what good human living is. These philosophers have come up with theories of how you can help people to improve their way of living. These are old resources which we can use in the present to work with people to clarify their own way of life. But of course the tradition of Existentialism, or Existential philosophy, as I like to call it, is really a lot shorter than that. It goes back to Kierkegaard in the early nineteenth century, Nietzsche in the late nineteenth century, and then to the movement of phenomenology.

The term 'phenomenology' is generally associated with Existentialism. Asked how this method would be employed by the Existential practitioner, van Deurzen explained that it was a systematic method, which offers a particular and unique way of suspending one's usual judgements and assumptions and therefore enables a person to reconsider a problem from a number of different perspectives. This does not mean that a person's usual perspective is dispensed with but that it is put in context with a number of other possible perspectives in order to get a better overall picture. Van Deurzen believes that this is the primary task for the Existential therapist: to throw light on and illuminate an issue for the client from a different perspective.

The practice of Existential therapy

My own understanding of Existential therapy is that it tends to eschew the idea of technique. What I wanted to know was how Existential philosophy and phenomenology translated into practice. The issue of trust was the first necessity raised by van Deurzen: so that the client can begin to tell you how they really are in the world.

What you sometimes find is that for a very long time people hide from you (I don't consider this as a defence but rather as an essential survival strategy), and they hide from themselves, too. They hide essentially from the issues they are struggling with. So your first task is to engage with the person in a way that allows them to increasingly come out of hiding and to begin to look at how they themselves experience the world, together with you. First of all you need to help them establish how they do perceive the world. This is done as a joint enquiry, a journey of discovery of how they are generally in the world, how they feel things, how they experience themselves as a person. In that process you usually find that they come to their lives from a particular direction, which makes them get stuck, or feel blocked. The objective is to help them move around so that they can get other perspectives – have a broader overview rather than being stuck in one position.

But in that process you find that their particular perspective is generated or determined by, or composed of, a number of factors.

We all come to the world in a biased way. As the therapist you come to the world in a biased way as well. Sometimes your bias and the client's bias will be the same, sometimes they will be diametrically opposed. It is easier to find out that they have a bias when their view is dissimilar to your own. If you both have a similar bias it makes for agreement between you but not for good understanding of the client's bias. You need to be flexible enough as a therapist to have a good sense of what your own bias is, whilst being able to appreciate what other people's biases might be; which means you need to know quite a bit about the human condition, about how we get stuck and how we become biased.

Of course it isn't easy to know one's own prejudices and bias. We have so many presumptions and we are biased on many different levels. Our views are most often skewed and we have biases that we don't even know we have. To start with, our biological and genetic make-up provides us with a particular sense of who we are, which induces a particular perspective on the world. For instance, if you are thin or robust, if you are tall or small, this will give you a completely different experience of the world. Your cultural, racial, social, family background will all give you a particular perspective on life and other people. The particular events of your childhood predispose you to look at the world in a specific way. We are made up of various angles on the world, specific biases. I would argue that this is what the self is – a number of specific and different ways in which we refract the human experience and things that we encounter in the world.

Clearly the process of being a person is incredibly complex, so it is nonsense to speak of getting rid of bias. This is like saying: get rid of self. We need these biases, these specific perceptions and points of view, to be able to usefully interact with each other. Our biases, when encountering and touching each other, either reflect each other, or clash with each other. This is how we make alliances with each other or oppose each other. It is what human relationships are made of. What you can do is get some grasp of them, some awareness of how it works. When someone is caught in a negative reaction to another person you can help them to understand how they can move away from that. People can learn to use different facets of their personality in different ways. They can engage with the world more openly or they can learn to relate to others with different facets of their per-sonality. They can learn to overcome obstacles and to understand the ways in which they catch on other people in the world. This is the task of the Existential therapist: to help people to understand how they engage with the world and to find new ways of doing so. Sometimes the task is very complex and sometimes it is difficult to accomplish. If you work in a primary care setting and can only offer eight sessions the task is much too vast and you have to limit the work; but you can ask: 'What small aspect of this person's experience is problematic now, and how can I realistically help them to loosen that up a bit and move slightly from that position so that they can do something more productive for themselves?'

Van Deurzen's assertion that the self is merely a conglomeration of all our biases, and the implication that we can never be rid of them, may also be of interest for the way we think about the ongoing influence of countertransference. She does, however, seem to offer some hope that we can become more aware of them and that the client in Existential therapy can have the opportunity of exploring their biases. But what of the therapist? Does the therapist reflect on his or her biases, and is there a link between bias and countertransference?

Well, countertransference, as such, I find to be an unnecessary and inappropriate term. It comes from the bias of the biological enterprise of psychoanalysis, which is only one small facet of the therapeutic interaction. Even though it has been elaborated on and contradicted and looked at in many different ways by psychoanalytic authors it is still largely associated with that particular field and that particular way of looking at things. What is useful about it is to be reminded of the importance of considering the therapist's input into the relationship. I think the term as such has become unhelpful, since, like transference, it conjures up ideas about displacement of past material onto a present situation. I prefer the term 'therapist bias' because it allows me to look at a whole range of things. Of course therapists have many biases, as clients do. We all have our biases; we need them; we need to work with them; and the therapist's bias is crucial in the therapist's understanding of the client. It is the therapist's bias that actually allows the therapist to see the client at all. It is also what enables the client to become aware of their bias. It is the therapist's bias that will push at the client and that provides a new angle on the client's problems. It is also, together with the client's bias, what will make client and therapist disagree, and thus it becomes the vehicle of unhooking the client from the place that they are stuck at. *The therapist's bias is a therapeutic instrument* – providing the therapist has awareness of its effect on the client. However, it could become a destructive tool, in the way that much therapeutic bias is dogmatic and often undeclared, or not reflected on.

As I understand her, van Deurzen is saying that she prefers the term bias to countertransference partly because it is not a technical term associated with one school, or with one person (the therapist). Bias is a general term that applies to everyone, whatever his or her position. Furthermore, if bias is a fundamental element of the human condition, then it must also be a major theme that powers our relationships. With this in mind, I asked how the therapist might formulate an intervention that would address this issue:

Any approach, including the Existential approach, comes with a particular theory, a particular way in which explanations will happen. I will allow myself my theory and apply it to the client, gently at first, sometimes more forcefully so, in order to provoke their own response to it. I do not use it in a dogmatic way but in a positive, constructive, creative way, allowing clients to come up against it when it obstructs them. During a session I find myself constantly using my own bias with the client in a very direct way. I might for instance point out to them that they like certain things or assume certain things about their life. When I describe this to them quite bluntly, my bias is expressed, since I implicitly voice my perspective on their predicament. Rather than putting this view on their life forward as an interpretation or a truth, I will invite them to use it as a starting point for their own exploration, perhaps by disagreeing with it. The message is: 'This is how I see you and your current pre-dicament, although I know it is different from how you have told me about it, but that is what it looks like to me.' If the relationship has become a trusting one, my client will know what I am setting out to do and rise to the invitation. They may then say, 'No, that is not quite it, for me it is like this.' The blunt edge of my awareness and my point of view has set them off having to formulate their own and they become more aware of how they look at the world. So, together we start puzzling out what they believe and how they experience the world.

My bias, or the light that I throw on their issues, is stimulating them to look for a slightly different stance on their issue, which is not the original way they presented it but it is not what I said either. As the client is starting the work of exploration, they are able to begin to reveal things that have been hidden to them. I can't elicit such a search for truth, if I go into the therapeutic situation thinking I have got to be the divine interventionist, who can give the final statement about something. What I *can* do is to be engaged with the exploration and help the client to formulate their own position by being aware of my own bias. What I can do is put my bias at the service of the client; and what I certainly can do is help them to explore and diversify and get a better picture – not the true picture, but a better picture.

Bias, rather than countertransference is therefore central to the Existential approach and can been seen as a gift rather than an obstacle. We use the term 'bias' because this is what we are. We are limited, we are perspective, we are representation, we are partial truth; we are constantly in a process of renaming things, reorganizing things, reunderstanding things. This is what human beings do: they create meaning, change meaning and undo meaning. As a therapist, this is what I help my client to get better at doing. Rather than assuming that they are stuck, or doomed to a particular perspective, because they had a particular childhood, the idea is that they become more open to reflecting on things in alternative ways. It is important to stand back, to intervene in a minimal way, to let the client emerge in their own way.

The use of countertransference where it is defined as an impediment or interference related to the therapist's past seems to be in opposition to van Deurzen's notion of bias. Biases are the therapist's feelings and beliefs, which are conveyed to the client as reflections of what the therapist has understood about the client's dilemmas. In this sense the therapist's bias is used to encourage clients to widen their own sphere of self-understanding by consciously reflecting on and readjusting their own biases towards dilemmas that have hitherto been considered only from one particular perspective.

In my next question I asked about the link between phenomenology and Existentialism, and for examples of interventions that would typify this way of working.

Things that I would find myself saying a lot are: 'But it's not just that is it? It's also like this,' or 'This is how you see that now, but do you remember last year when this or that happened and you looked at it like this?' Or: 'There is another way of viewing that isn't there? Which is to see it like this.' Or: 'Some people might say this or that about it, now how does that relate to what you were saying?' These are the kinds of interventions – trying things out and exploring things a bit further, questioning things, helping the client to rediscover their adventurous spirit so that they can look at things differently and realize that they are not doomed to look at things from only one perspective. From a Heideggerian perspective it would probably be called being their voice of conscience, and encouraging them towards the experience of the moment of vision.

I would tend to use the phenomenological method to question my own perspective on the client's issues. This happens very often after the fact, rather than in the therapeutic relationship in the room. It is just not possible to do all of that self-questioning at the same time as focusing on the client's bias. Often when I am in the room with the person I get too drawn into the actual situation of that person's experience, which can reduce the clarity about oneself.

In the ten minutes after the session is over, when you write your notes, or in supervision, I think it is then that the phenomenological method comes into its own: when you describe to yourself what actually happened and how you can then consider that in a much more objective way – stepping back and reflecting on the session, wondering why I came to it the way that I did and asking myself what it says about where I am at the moment with that particular issue. Then what you start to see is that when you have different sequences of clients in a day you come up with different interventions and your own bias get shifted accordingly to how you have made yourself available to that person's particular perspective.

The rule of *epoche* is part of the phenomenological method, and the practitioner is expected to bracket their assumptions and biases. It sounds as if van Deurzen is, by contrast, suggesting that the practitioner should express their biases to the client rather than attempt to put them to one side.

The notion of bracketing one's assumptions, which is integral to the phenomenological method, is a very artificial one, because it gives people the erroneous belief that you can get rid of your biases, which is a completely foolish idea. I often remind students or supervisees that what Husserl (who was a mathematician) said about it was to put things in brackets, which means setting them aside from the rest of the equation, which means dealing with certain things first but then bringing things back into play. What you are *not* doing is sweeping things to one side and pretending that you have removed them from the equation. Your bias remains part of the equation, and you have deal with it.

I think phenomenology is very misunderstood by a lot of people. It is much more profound and intense than people give it credit for. It is not something that one can just do; it requires commitment constantly to investigate how you are coming to something. Husserl set great stock by the concept of verification. Gendlin, who developed the therapeutic method of focusing, has really understood something about phenomenology and has written many wonderful papers on the subject. He really understands the idea of *Befindlichkeit*, which is Heidegger's concept of how you find yourself in the world – meaning, how you are experiencing things inside of you, how I am resonating with the things I encounter. Phenomenology would invite a person, client or therapist to become increasingly aware of their own disposition and state of mind and use their *Befindlichkeit* to make sense of the world.

The experiential activity of *Befindlichkeit* is clearly salient in the phenomenological method. As van Deurzen states, it is a tool, which she employs after the session to improve her own self-understanding and, I would add, presumably also to reconsider the relationship between her own biases and her clinical work, as a form of Existential self-analysis, as it were. Nevertheless, the difficulty of this remit is brought home to me when I think about my own therapeutic prejudices and the durable nature of bias, no matter how mutable in principle. For if it is bias which (as I believe) is a major contributory factor to misunderstanding and discord between people, why would it not also be considered as a salient component of Existential practice?

Discussion of the case-study vignette

Van Deurzen commented on the case-study vignette as follows:

I would begin by saying: 'And this has happened today as well hasn't it? You have also found yourself being as if you were invisible with the receptionist, and presumably with me as well, since I had not managed to find out that you were here for twenty minutes. You didn't find a way to get to me and I didn't find a way to get to you. So how did that happen? What is that saying about how you experience yourself?' Then just wait and see what comes and explore her experience in the world. My hypothesis would be that she does do something that encourages people to treat her like that, that she is easily overlooked. She is – as one is when one moves a long way away from one's roots and one's identity, which she has done in multiple ways. She has moved away from her country, from her national identity, moved away from her job, and probably there are other similar aspects that she has lost. What I would immediately assume is that she has not been able to recreate safety or confidence in her own environment and so feels empty inside and depleted, which does actually make her feel empty and not just invisible to other people, but to herself as well. I would say that what I need to help this client with is enable her to reclaim all the multiple facets of her experience, including reclaiming her voice and her existence. I would wish to help her to get a sense of what she was after in the first place and what has stopped her from going for it. I would explore ideas with her rather than pathologize her, seeing it instead as a momentary hitch, which has taken her on a very difficult path.

It is important to stay with the client's emotions, to resonate and go into her world with her. So one way might be to say: 'That is incredibly upsetting isn't it? They overlooked you;' and then wait and perhaps repeat her experience in a slightly more dramatic way than she has presented it so that she gets a sense of her suffering and she can then start to express different emotions, such as anger or sadness, for instance. Then perhaps I might focus on the anger by saying: 'This is not good enough, you can't let yourself be treated like this! Is that what you are saying?' To get her to formulate her desire, her need for something else – to find her entitlement to something of her own again.

If I found myself feeling outraged about her situation, I would trust that and I would think, why is she not more outraged? So if she came to my office after being kept waiting for twenty minutes, I would not apologize, as it was not my fault; but I might say, 'Well you have lost twenty minutes of the session and I feel pretty angry about this too. It shouldn't be happening. Why is this happening? What are you doing to let this happen to you?' To get her to think about it, I might use provocation but always staying on the client's side. Obviously I am making a value judgement here by believing that people should speak up for themselves, and she might argue with this, which could be very interesting, as sometimes you end up having a project for a client and they don't agree with it. So one might say: 'Shouldn't you speak up for yourself? What is it like to never speak up for yourself? Is that how you want to be?' And they might say: 'I think that is all I can manage at the moment.' And then you have to take that seriously – to say, for instance: 'Yes, I can see that this is OK for you at the moment. When would you know when you could manage a bit more?' And then you would continue to explore the issue with them until they felt they had been able to throw some light on it and felt heartened at the thought that there might be a new way through.

Conclusion

Existential psychotherapy encourages the client to reflect on their partial way of being-in-the-world in order to illuminate the other choices available to them. Existential psychotherapy has adopted the principal tenets of a philosophy which examines, enquires and investigates the possibilities and limits of human existence through cognitive dialogue between client and therapist. It is this conscious interactive approach which is clearly antagonistic to the principles of psychoanalysis and its fundamental concepts.

Existential psychotherapy is distinguished by its focus on the dilemmas, possibilities and limits of human existence and its concern with description rather than analysis. The philosophical underpinnings of the approach are therefore generally opposed to hypothetical explanations or theoretical and conceptual constructions concerning an account of 'human nature'. In this sense, Existentialism is clearly antagonistic to a theory of human nature constructed around the existence of unconscious processes which are brought together as psychoanalytic principles and boldly illustrated in the notion of countertransference. Emmy van Deurzen prefers the term bias, to which she compares unfavourably the concept of countertransference. She suggests that not only are we are made up of biases but that biases are the embodiment of the self. In this sense our biases enable us to describe ourselves as they unmask our points of view and reveal our personal commitments and idiosyncratic positions in relation to the world and other people.

Emotional turmoil and suffering arise from these individual tendencies or biases as they restrict our ability to consider other options. Existential psychotherapy accepts that the therapeutic encounter is based on a real relationship and that the client's biases are valid reflections of their current world-view. The therapist's remit is to involve the client in an exploratory, philosophical dialogue which will stimulate and develop their ability to understand and entertain the contingent nature of their conflicts and so give them the opportunity to consider other alternatives which have hitherto only been implied. By contrast, the lack of objectivity implied by the concept of countertransference refers to bias in a way that suggests a lack of choice.

This definition of the concept is also synonymous with terms such as distortion, misrepresentation and misinterpretation of reality. Countertransference also contravenes the rules of the phenomenological method, as it is a construct based on Freudian meta-psychology and not therefore directly observable.

Nevertheless, a few authors have wished to point to the complementary factors that exist between Existential principles and the unconscious. The fact that Existentialism is rooted in a philosophical standpoint and attitude in relation to other people, rather than a particular school of thought, suggests that practitioners from other theoretical persuasions, including psychoanalysis, might choose to assimilate this approach into their interactions with their clients (Sabbadini, 1990; Holmes, 1998a, 2001).

The communicative approach to psychotherapy is in agreement with the Existential premise that the relationship is rooted in reality. It is also phenomenological in as much as the therapist only describes and feeds back the patient's narrative material. This stance is, however, rapidly discarded as soon as the therapist interprets the client's associations, as the former's intervention now includes assumptions about the unconscious that are based in the realm of metapsychology and not, therefore, directly observable. Nevertheless, the model itself reinforces the authenticity of the client's material. In spite of these noticeable incongruities, this author contends that it is worthwhile to forge links with some of the principles subsumed under the heading of Existentialism in order to accentuate the relevance of an interpersonal here-and-now stance.

Chapter 6

Client-Centered Psychotherapy

The American psychologist Carl Rogers is renowned for his initiation and cultivation of client-centered psychotherapy. Rogers developed his ideas in the early nineteen forties in the United States. From the nineteen sixties his work in the humanistic tradition was to become internationally recognized as a significant force in the field of psychotherapy, counselling and education. Rogers (1961) paid tribute to the influence of European Existential philosophy, in particular to Kierkegaard's assertion of the innate human tendency toward growth and account of the human condition. However, the notion at the centre of Rogers' work, the impulse towards self-actualization, was far more in keeping with the New World ethos – in particular with the upbeat, optimistic culture of post-war America – than with the Angst-ridden Zeitgeist of European Existentialism.

Theory of the self

Rogers believed that human beings are inherently capable of self-understanding and will naturally advance towards personal growth if they are provided with the appropriate conditions. Rogers (1980) cited the now famous 'potato story', an observation from his youth, to reinforce this notion of a spontaneous tendency towards growth in all living organisms. He noted that even potatoes when placed in unsuitable conditions, without necessary light, will nevertheless develop shoots by utilizing whatever light is available to them.

From a Rogerian perspective, the essential, or 'organismic', self is innately trustworthy. By contrast, the individual's 'self-concept' tends to develop from the attitudes and values of early significant figures in their life. Just as the potato needs light to develop, human beings have a need more than anything for positive regard. If this support is not forthcoming, the individual will adapt their behaviour in the hope of gaining some esteem. Rogers explains that conditions of worth and the basic need to gain positive regard can lead to a hiatus between the person's self-concept and the organismic self.

Client-centered therapy and its core conditions

The principles of Rogerian therapy rest on the assumption that the client knows best about their own difficulties. The therapy is therefore non-directive, with the emphasis placed on the quality of the relationship between client and therapist above and beyond any technique. Although Rogers originally described his approach as client-centered, the term 'person-centered', adopted some years later, has also come to represent the same fundamental principles, which could then be employed in many other contexts outside psychotherapy.

The client-centered therapist is expected to provide three 'necessary and sufficient conditions' (Rogers, 1959) which will enable clients to feel safe enough to explore and discover their own values. Rogers believed that the therapist's ability to offer the appropriate client-centered attitude would inevitably facilitate the client's capacity to integrate their beliefs with their self-concept. The core condition of 'unconditional-positive-regard' refers to an attitude on the part of the therapist towards the client of total acceptance. An acceptance of other people requires the therapist first and foremost to have attained an adequate degree of self-acceptance. The second requirement, of congruence, relates to the therapist's ability to communicate their genuineness to the client. Such authenticity necessarily entails the therapist's moment-to-moment awareness of his or her own fluctuating thoughts and feelings. The third requirement is empathy. This in turn requires a commitment on the part of the therapist to understand the client's worldview. All three conditions are seen as essential and interrelated, and rely on subtle and complex modes of verbal and non-verbal modes of communication.

Interview

Mary Harris is an experienced therapist, lecturer and clinical supervisor with a training background in the humanistic tradition. Dr Harris was born in America but has for many years taught and practised psychotherapy in Germany and in the United Kingdom. She has also been responsible for setting up and managing a number of clinical consultation centres in Europe. Harris emphasized that although her approach to psychotherapy is grounded in client-centred beliefs and concepts, it also incorporates Gestalt work and some aspects of Existentialism, and is psychodynamically informed. In the following passage from our interview, she explains what is meant by the client-centered approach to psychotherapy.

The basic philosophy is humanism. By that I mean I agree with Carl Rogers' basic tenet, which is that every human being has the potential to grow and to self-actualize – to move in a positive direction – and it is that belief and that faith in human nature that informs my work with people. That is not to say that I think that everyone will choose to move in a positive direction, or choose to self-actualize, because my theory is also informed by Existential principles, which means I believe in the idea that we do have choices in how we act and respond to situations.

At the same time, I am also influenced somewhat by psychodynamic theory because I believe that who we are is a product of our environment, and when I am with clients one of the questions that is in my mind, especially at the beginning of the therapy, is in what way this person is repeating what I call 'the family dance'. So if she, or he, is having problems with their boss in the present, then I might be thinking about whether the boss represents a mother or father figure, and how they might be re-enacting that family drama with people in their current life. But when it comes to working with clients I tend to be more humanistic. In other words, I don't use a blank screen and I believe that in order for change to take place, one of the things that the client needs is unconditional positive regard and a sense of warmth and caring on the part of the therapist. So, when I am working with clients I am interested in helping them explore what is in their current awareness (which is humanistic and also Gestalt), and then in the back of my mind I am thinking about how this represents some aspect of who they were as a child, or the events that have happened to them.

The main thing which I was grounded in when I was doing my training is the humanistic concept and practice of active listening and basic attending skills. When I use these it means that I am essentially reflecting feelings and content and summarizing, with the idea that if I can do that accurately I will help establish trust and convey empathy but that I will also help the client clarify in their own mind what is important for them and what is present – without leading them. If I can give them an accurate summation of what is important to them that they are presenting, that will take them deeper into their own work, which is to my understanding very humanistic and client centered.

At the same time, Gestalt principles also inform my practice, and that means I am interested in what is happening in the room, in the here-and-now – the feelings that the client is experiencing and how that affects what is happening between the two of us. I would say things to the client, if it seemed appropriate to bring them into their awareness, such as, 'What are you experiencing right now as we talk about this?'

Although Harris clearly acknowledges her humanistic position, she also explains the rationale for integrating elements from other schools of thought, including the psychoanalytic and Existential, while still maintaining a client-centered perspective. With this in mind, I was interested to know her ideas about the concept of countertransference and whether she viewed it as a useful tool in her work with clients. She continued:

Before I talk about countertransference, I do need to talk initially about transference, at least my understanding of it, and then tie that into countertransference. As I am not primarily psychoanalytic, I don't use these concepts as the main focus of my work. I don't believe that transference and countertransference always occur with clients but I do believe that there are times when they are very potent and it can become a very essential part of the work; and I think that if it is ignored, that the work with the client will suffer.

My understanding and the way I use transference and counter-transference have more to do with the Gestalt theory of projection. As far as I know Gestalt doesn't talk about transference; but if you read what has been written on projection then it appears to be something very similar. The difference, though, is that transference is usually seen as initially created from people in the client's child-hood, and I have a broader view of it than that. To me it's not so important to analyse and figure out where it came from as it is to understand how it is affecting the person in the present tense. So if someone is working with me and they say things like 'You think I'm irresponsible', that is what my psychoanalytic colleagues might call transference, but I would call it projection, and I would be interested in working with it in the present tense. For example, one intervention I might use is to ask them to tell me more about what they think I think about them. They might then say, 'Well I know you're judging me. You really think I'm irresponsible and lazy.' I would then ask them to expand on these feelings but in a Gestalt way, because for me this might be the basis for polarity work, which means that there is a Gestalt that is forming, and reflecting it, using a Rogerian technique, and intensifying it perhaps brings it to the foreground for the client, to make them more aware of it.

In making the comparison between the notion of a Gestalt and transference, Harris is endorsing the sufficiency of the therapeutic interaction, which does not require an exploration and analysis of the client's early familial dilemmas in order to create a therapeutic shift. I asked her about the polarity work she referred to, and whether it was similar to the Existential focus on paradox. Harris replied she was not interested in doing it as an exercise. Rather,

I am interested in doing it to become aware of the values in the person's mind in the present tense, and also to give them a way of talking about that, so that they might be able to say to me at some point, 'I think you're judging me and I'm angry at you'. Then that, to me, would be a way of working directly with the transference, in a way that is very powerful, very emotive, as opposed to a cognitive exercise.

The accent here is on the potency of what is being expressed between client and therapist in the immediate encounter, rather than either the Existential examination of paradox or the analysis of transference, both of which are suggested to be rather more abstract and less close to the bone.

Harris continued by talking about what she understood by countertransference and how she would use it in the clinical context. She said that at the same time that her clients were becoming aware of how they were feeling in the here-and-now, she was also aware that with some clients her own issues would come to the fore, which is what she would describe as countertransference:

My litmus test for that is when I am waiting for a client, and the doorbell rings and I feel, Oh damn they are here. That tells me that my countertransference is active, in other words I'm having negative feelings and secretly hoping that the client won't turn up; and when I experience that then I know that I need to dig deeper into what is going on inside me and what that person has triggered, perhaps who they remind me of from my childhood. I then need to take it to my therapy, my clinical supervision, so that whatever experiences I'm having don't impinge on my work with the client. It is sometimes hard to separate what my issues are from what the client's issues are; that's where it gets tricky. I need to be very aware of how I am feeling inside and open to looking at how much of it is my stuff that I'm projecting onto the client and how much of it is the client's stuff that they are projecting onto me.

The ideas expressed by Harris about countertransference are not dissimilar to those of some practitioners who see countertransference is something highly inappropriate which needs to be deliberately avoided at all costs, and addressed outside the therapy rather than in the consulting room between client and therapist. This position is in keeping with Freud's original definition.

The idea of working in the here-and-now is grounded in the humanistic tradition. Harris elaborated on the significance of this focus.

One theory of Gestalt therapy, which is also connected to Existential ideas, is the I–thou relationship, when you get to the point of being able to talk in the present tense, that is a very deep level of therapy. Gestalt comes under the umbrella of humanistic theory but it is more focused and directive than a purely Rogerian, client-centered way of working. I think that the more directive way of working, if it is used responsibly and sparingly, can further the work. One of the criticisms of client-centered therapy is that it sometimes leaves the client floundering and not feeling held, and without a sense of direction in the therapy. What I find useful in combination with the client-centered approach, philosophy and technique is to use the Gestalt approach as well, which can create a holding and focus but is still non-directive. I see a big difference between helping a client find focus – in other words, what is most important to them in what they are talking about – and direction – which on a bad day would be saying something like, 'I think you need to look at such and such', which to me is therapist led as opposed to client led.

The expressions 'client-centered' and 'person-centered' suggest that there may be some nuances that separate the two terms. I asked Harris if she would clarify the difference from her perspective.

Historically, I think the first term that Rogers used was 'client-centered'. What he meant by that was (which is hard to believe now but at the time was a revolutionary theory) that each of us has within ourselves the ability to grow and to understand as opposed to an expert coming in from the outside to do it for us – and that's the basic premise. If I can create that atmosphere of trust and understanding, then the client will find their own direction. 'Person-centered' versus 'client-centered' has to do with the idea of separating out the idea of a client from a patient (which means someone who is ill) from a person who is my equal and the idea that we are exploring and making a journey together. 'Client-centered' and 'person-centered' both come under the heading of humanism; but there are also other branches of that. Gestalt is one branch that I am interested in. Something that I have discovered since I have been here from the States is that an Existential approach is also one of the branches that comes under the heading of humanism. Existentialism certainly informs my work with clients in a humanistic way, whereas in this country it is seen as separate field, unlike in America where it is seen as a facet of the humanistic approach.

My next question was concerned with whether client-centered therapy had a concept that could be viewed as in any way comparable with the notion of countertransference. Harris explained that although Rogers did not incorporate the term into his model, he did talk a lot about knowing oneself and of the need for the therapist to be genuine and congruent. She said she understood this to mean that the therapist needed to have ongoing therapy and supervision in order to remain aware of their own issues as these arose in the clinical situation.

The thing about actualizing and growing is that it is never completed. I am always in the process of becoming and growing, and when there are things that I become aware of in the room, it is important not just to blurt it out; but when it is a consistent feeling that I am having toward the client, then I must go away and do my own work on it, to try to understand what it is that is affecting me. I must then come back and use it therapeutically to work with the client.

I think that one of the primary differences between psycho-analysis and the humanistic approach is that I will use myself as an instrument by using my own reactions; and Rogers talked about appropriate self-disclosure, which is something that I use, I hope, to a positive effect. An example of this might be when I see a client struggling with a feeling which they seem unable to express. Then at some point I may find myself feeling sad for the client. It is very important that I understand that it is not my own sadness that has been triggered but that it is informed by what Rogers and many other people refer to as empathy. It might then, sometimes, be appropriate for me to say something like, 'I'm finding myself feeling sad, and I wonder if part of what I'm feeling is your sadness'. When I do that, and it is accurate, then clients say that is very helpful.

This led to some discussion about empathy and whether or not it should be placed under the umbrella of countertransference affects.

What makes empathy different from sympathy is that empathy includes a non-possessive kind of caring and hopefully an ability to put myself in the other person's place and to understand their feelings in the situation. This is maybe very different from how I might be feeling in this situation. This is what makes the work so difficult. It makes it very hard if I am thinking that a client is feeling very hurt or angry and I also need to stop and think: Is this how I am feeling, and what is it that makes me think that this is truly what the client is feeling, or is it a feeling of my own that I am projecting onto them? To me, the ongoing work of staying aware of who I am and how this impinges on the client and what I bring never stops – it continues in my work with clients. Rogers talks about self-disclosure being a part of the therapy only if and when the therapist is sure it is something that will be useful to the client, as opposed to something that the therapist needs.

Rogers, of course, doesn't use the term countertransference; but what he does talk about in great depth is the necessity for the therapist to know themselves and to continue doing their own work and to be aware of how they, the therapist, will affect the client. So although he doesn't use psychoanalytic terms, I think what he is talking about is very similar; but it is worked on outside the session not during the session.

Although Harris asserts that working with countertransference does not take place in the consulting room with the client, she does, however, state that she finds it can sometimes be very useful to disclose her immediate feelings, especially when the client is able to resonate with these affects. For some psychoanalytic practitioners, this kind of humanistic intervention, which is an appropriate expression of empathy, congruence and genuineness, may also be considered a countertransference response. It is in the theoretical realm and in the axioms that underlie their assumptions about human nature that these approaches are distinguished and clearly separated from each other.

The existential and humanistic therapist is also likely to take issue with terminology that is common psychoanalytic parlance, such as 'pathology' owing to its symptomatic and medical connotations. He or she will prefer instead to think of problems arising from the inevitable difficulties of the human condition, the suggestion being that we are all, by virtue of being human, 'in the same boat', which means we all suffer in similar ways. Yet, to some degree, this same assumption is unlikely to be disputed by a psychoanalytic practitioner. In the language of psychoanalysis 'normal' and 'pathological' occur along a continuum, which means that none of us is immune to personal and interpersonal difficulties and to the dilemmas of human existence. Where psychoanalysis differs is in the significance that is placed on the term psychopathology (the area of medicine concerned with the cause and effect of disease), where the continuum from neurosis to psychosis is viewed as determined by the individual's more insular early family setting.

Harris expounded on the type of interventions that she felt would be described as typically client centered:

Clients often come to therapy and spend the first fifteen minutes of the session talking about how angry they are toward their boss, spouse or children. They may say things like, 'I just can't trust them, and you can't trust anybody'. Some time during this process I may be thinking, how does this relate to what is happening in here? At some point I would probably say, 'I wonder if you ever feel that way about me?' What I would be interested in is to give them an opportunity to bring this into the room and to talk in an affective way about how they are feeling about the work that we are doing and how they are feeling about me. I would encourage them to say something about what happens to them now, as they talk about what is going on in the room, and how that is affecting them right now.

An example of an empathic intervention might be when a client is talking about something painful, and I try to get a sense of what the primary feelings are so that I can stay focused and not get lost in the general verbiage of their communications – which helps me in my own mind to create a kind of a map. I might then say, 'It sounds like you feel hurt by what your partner has done to you' – the hurt would be the reflection of feeling, and the issue to do with the partner would be the reflection of content. If I have done that accurately, then I am showing the client that I am empathizing and understanding what the experience is like for them, which will hopefully give them a springboard for them to go forward. If I have got it wrong, that need not matter because, in Rogerian terms, if some trust has developed, then the client will feel safe enough to say 'No, that's not it, I meant this', and that will still take us further.

This, to me, is a humanistic way of working with clients – trying to understand how they feel within their frame of reference, and with what Egan calls the proper degree of tentativeness, instead of imposing things on them, which gives the client the space to correct me rather like a dance. I need to keep listening and keep correcting from their feedback. Then I do believe that this will take the work further; this to me is a very client-centred way of working.

The feedback that Harris talks of here also sounds similar to the application of the therapist's bias described by Emmy van Deurzen.

As she mentioned earlier in the interview, Harris considers the Existential school as part of the humanistic tradition. This explains why, as she sets out in her following comment, she uses aspects of Gestalt therapy, which is underpinned by the phenomenological method.

Something else I do that is humanistic but informed by Gestalt ideas is polarity work. At the same time as I am with a client I am listening for the psychic conflict; and usually what emerges after about fifteen minutes for the client are some sort of conflicting feelings. On the one hand, they are very angry towards their parents and, on the other hand, they usually feel very guilty. The problem, as far as I am concerned, is not their parents; the problem is what they are doing in the present with those conflicting feelings. What I would firstly do is reflect and say: 'Is that right, you feel both of these emotions?'; and if that resonates for them I might ask them to do some Gestalt work with those conflicting polarities, to see if, from a Gestalt perspective, one is in the foreground. This might be a voice that the client experiences in their mind, which I may then ask them to play out loud, and the voice may say something like: 'Oh you should be grateful, remember all the things they have done for you. How could you possibly be angry at them!' I will suggest that they stay with those thoughts and feelings, and at some point the other polarity will assume the foreground by saying: 'But wait a minute, I'm angry about this!' This can be a very powerful and intense experience for the client.

I asked if it was a realistic to expect the therapist consistently to provide the core humanistic conditions. Harris went on to describe how she has integrated Rogers' ideas into her clinical practice:

One of the criticisms of client-centered therapy is that on the surface it sounds very difficult to be both genuine and to give unconditional positive regard. If, for example, I feel angry toward the client and I want to give them positive regard, then I have a conflict. My understanding is that this is an opportunity for growth. If I feel annoyed with the client because they have arrived rather late for the last three sessions in a row, and I don't consider it and I am feeling some discomfort about it, then I am not being genuine. If I say to the client: 'You know you are supposed to be here at ten o'clock. It is now fifteen minutes past and you are not taking the therapy seriously', then perhaps I am being congruent but my acceptance has slipped.

A way of working which would allow the therapist to remain true to both principles would be to say something like, 'I'm not feeling comfortable with what has been happening'. If I express my feelings directly, but respectfully, then it is to be hoped that this will not be perceived by the client as an attack but will open up the possibility for a very open dialogue. If I talk about how I feel about their lateness but in a non-judgemental way, and take the ownership for my feelings rather than saying 'I feel you should etc.' (which would be a judgement), then this often enables the client to talk about it openly, without feeling judged or attacked. By directly saying how it affects me I am able to remain truly congruent, which invites the clients to talk about their own experience. This can be a way to combine both the acceptance and the genuineness in a way that is very therapeutic for the client.

Many people have not experienced in their childhoods a way of being honest without being attacked. This model, it is hoped, provides both. Congruence, then, is about what I am thinking and feeling and finding a way of expressing it without attacking the other person.

Discussion of case-study vignette

There are two things that strike me immediately about what is happening with the client. I think the main thing I would want to clarify when we arrived in the consulting room is her experience of what happened for her in the waiting room. I would comment on the fact that she had been waiting and although she was a couple of minutes late she had registered with the receptionist, then waited for about fifteen minutes and registered again at the desk. I would also apologize to her for the misunderstanding, which is an important point, and I would be very interested to know what it felt like for her to be sitting in that room and to be ignored and invisible. Then, as she talked about her experiences during the week of feeling invisible, ignored and not being treated as a person, this would reveal a theme from her own life that was beginning to emerge. Something specific that I would do when she says, 'That is not my name, they can't even call me by my name', would be to say: 'It's really important to you to be called by your proper name. I want to make sure that I have got it right. ... – is that correct? It seems that to be called ... and not ... is a way of not seeing you, of your not being recognized for who you are. You have told me how it felt for you today and your distress at work this week, and I'm wondering if your experience today feels like a continuation, feeling invisible in the waiting room. Perhaps if you had come in here today and we had not talked about this, you would feel invisible yet again. I wonder what it is like to talk about this experience now? I also wonder if there have been other times in our sessions when you have felt unheard and invisible – and if that is true, I wonder if you can tell me about that?'

Sometimes an intervention is made without the expectation of an immediate response. So in the case of this rather silent client, if she had been sitting away from me and saying no with her body but had then turned toward me with a few moments of eye contact, that might be an acknowledgement of what I have been saying. If, however, she keeps turning away and shakes her head, then that clearly suggests that I have got it wrong. I wouldn't sit in silence and wait for thirty minutes because I don't find that therapeutic. I would, somewhere in between that time, do some gentle probing. So if she remained silent, I might say: 'That doesn't seem important to you. Is there something else you would like to talk about?' I would then just remain silent. If that continued with a lot of silence and body language, like sighs, which are most expressive, then I might comment on the sigh. I might also say: 'We have been here for thirty minutes and you haven't said anything. I get the impression (although I may not be right) that it is difficult for you to sit with me. I also think that there may be a lot going on in your mind that you are not saying and I want you to know that I am interested in that but I'm not going to push you, as it is your time and you can use it in the way that you choose.' Then I would just sit with that and wait.

In response to my question about countertransference, Harris said:

My countertransference would be the part of me that was thinking as I was waiting for the client, 'How rude! I have been waiting for fifteen minutes, she doesn't respect me!' and projecting my own feelings about her. Such an example would be so very clearly related to my issues that I would, I hope, be able to recognize this and keep it in abeyance, and then be able to find out what really happened from the client's perspective. To me, countertransference is present when I notice the feelings attached to my thoughts about the client.

Conclusion

The particular version of humanistic theory and practice presented in the interview with Mary Harris clearly shows her interest and commitment to addressing how the therapist's behaviour impinges on the client and the therapeutic process. She also acknowledges how her own affects can influence the encounter in either a positive or a negative way. The term countertransference is not a notion that is associated with the humanistic or client-centered school of thought. This client-centered therapist does, however, suggest that in order to provide the core condition of empathy the practitioner is required to consider that her experience of the client may also be coloured by her own feelings. The concept of countertransference does not feature in the person-centered texts cited at the beginning of this chapter. Both these texts also posit that if the therapist is prepared to be self-reflective, then an attitude that embodies the core conditions can be achieved. This contrasts with the idiosyncratic position expressed by Harris here.

From a psychoanalytic perspective, countertransference is seen as an essential part of the therapeutic process, however the practitioner chooses to define it. The analyst would be expected to consider their countertransference feelings in the room with the patient as these feelings emerged. By contrast, the client-centered approach is more likely to see countertransference as separate from the actual encounter but relevant to address after the session in supervision and their personal therapy. At the same time, Harris stated that the importance of congruence would on some occasions lead her to share her thoughts and feelings with the client. More importantly, as the definition of countertransference implies, countertransference issues often remain elusive and unavailable for immediate conscious reflection.

Chapter 7
Integrative Psychotherapy

There are now a number of training establishments that offer professional accredited training in Integrative psychotherapy. It has become apparent from my discussions with colleagues who teach in this area and from the literature that is available on this topic that there are also various types of Integrative trainings. Not only do the trainings vary in terms of what is integrated but also the term itself seems to mean different things to different organizations.

The verb 'to integrate' is defined as 'to make or be made into a whole; to incorporate or be incorporated, to amalgamate or mix and made up of parts' (*Collins English Dictionary*, 1986, p. 442). 'Integration' is linked in *Roget's Thesaurus* to the word grouping 'entire–complete–indivisible–total–solid', where other synonyms are given as 'synthesis', 'combination', 'unification', 'unity' and 'blend' (ibid., p. 50). Further, the noun 'integrity' comes from the Latin *integritas*, meaning 'completeness', 'uprightness' or 'having the quality of being unimpaired' (*Hodder & Stoughton Latin Dictionary*, 1965).

In the preface to her book *The Therapeutic Relationship*, Petruska Clarkson (1995) explains that her focus on the dynamics of the therapeutic interaction has developed out of her own trainings and now longstanding experience of working with five diverse therapeutic traditions. Furthermore, given the plural and provisional nature of available theories of the human condition, Clarkson considers it important and valuable to cultivate a post-modern integrative model, which she sees as based on the interpersonal components of these competing therapeutic views. Her model also emphasizes the therapist's distinctive qualities in relation to personal integration, which she considers to be a life-long process:

I have not yet succeeded in integrating these strands in myself, in my practice as a clinician and supervisor, nor in theory. I may never do so. For me, integration is more vital, alive and interesting in its

verb form *integrating*. I hope that it is as an integrating psychotherapist that I will continue to learn and develop. (1995, p. xi)

Clarkson's integrative approach to psychotherapy contains five
modalities of client–therapist relationship. These are: the working
alliance; the transference/countertransference relationship; the repara-
tive/developmentally-needed relationship; the person-to-person relationship; and the transpersonal relationship. The associated training
framework explores the similarities and differences between the
modalities.

All five relational modalities are considered to be useful and valid,
and it is assumed that they can be integrated. Therapists are expected
to be able to make informed choices as to how they will make use of
these relational alternatives, and will do so according to their assessment of the individual client's needs at the time. Clarkson states that
only one of the five modes of relating will be at the forefront of work
with a client at any given time.

The transference/countertransference interaction is one element of
the relational framework. Clarkson differentiates between 'reactive'
and 'proactive' countertransference. The first is consistent with the
projective identification definition of countertransference, where the
therapist's feelings are viewed as an aid to understanding the patient:
'Reactive countertransference describes those responses of the psychotherapist which are elicited by or induced in the psychoanalyst by
the patient, and which specifically resemble the intrapsychic object
relations patterns of the patient's historical or fantasised past' (Clarkson, 1995, p. 90). The second refers to reactions introduced into the
relationship by the therapist and which may be either useful or damag-
ing. The term 'complementary reactive countertransference' devised
by Clarkson refers to the therapist's inner, felt and presumably conscious, and incisive, experiences of the client's emotions. An example
of Clarkson's integrative inclusion can be seen in the link that is
made to 'complementary reactive countertransference', which is classi-
fied under the heading of 'phenomenological or countertransference
indications'.

A second approach has been put forward in the book *Integrative
Psychotherapy*, by Maja O'Brien and Gaie Houston (2000), in which
psychoanalytic, humanistic/Existential and cognitive/behaviourist
schools of psychotherapy are compared and contrasted. Although
the work of these authors is focused on the importance of understanding how different theoretical models are applied in practice, they

leave the reader with the choice of which models to integrate and which integrative attitude to adopt. As for their own ideas on integration, they write: 'We offer a different model, the Open System, which suggests the interdependence and possible mutual enhancement of the legion of psychological therapies' (p. 9). These authors include an eclectic grouping of orientations under the general umbrella of 'integrative', presumably because of the emphasis they place on the practical aspects of the therapist's role: 'We emphasise that an integrative therapist is guided by the experience of being with the client first and theory second' (p. 18). It thus appears that this particular integrative framework is based more on *doing* therapy, and also that their model relies heavily on what is done at the assessment stage and on the therapist's ability to match a given approach to a given client.

Although O'Brien and Houston take into consideration the dynamics of the therapeutic relationship and offer the reader a brief summary of the history and problems associated with the concepts of transference and countertransference, their work overall is more goal oriented and aimed at sharpening the therapist's integrative skills. Clarkson's relational framework, by contrast, is clearly far more committed to exploring the process of the transference/countertransference interaction as an ongoing therapeutic issue.

The following interview features a third integrative model and also highlights the different ways in which Integrative psychotherapy is defined, taught and practised within the various Integrative training establishments.

Integrative interview

Helen Davis is the head of the Minster Centre, where Integrative psychotherapy is practised and taught, and where Davis has developed an original model and professional training programme over a long (nearly thirty years) period of time. Davis has also played an instrumental role in the standardization of professional guidelines and accreditation for Integrative psychotherapy within the Humanistic and Integrative section of the main validating body (UKCP).

To my first question about the type of training offered at the Minster Centre, Davis replied:

We consider that most organizations that call themselves integrative are actually eclectic. They try to mix one theoretical model with another. It could be Object Relations with Gestalt, it could be a Rogerian viewpoint with Transactional Analysis, and so on. They see themselves as integrative because they integrate two methods of theory and practice. This is not our central focus. Integration requires that we define all relevant elements that need taking into account. We are made up of multiple intelligences, each predominating in a necessary aspect of humanness. These are physical, emotional, mental, psychic and spiritual intelligences. Each one has direct links into, and in various ways permeates, each area. Each state of being uses time, space, grounding (reality base), boundaries, charge (energy) and weight (density). These six phenomena are present at all times in different forms, depending on whether we regress, progress, process or disintegrate. These aspects of life encompass the universal (the Earth and all galaxies function equally through these phenomena, as quantum physics shows) and the personal. We map out all these aspects and study how they link, influence and interact with each other to make up each unique human being. The individual has all these aspects, and each aspect has an individual focus and history.

Each person has their own individual life experience, the inherited influences of parents and others close to them and their life experiences, and those of generations further back. This also means we need to think about the reality of inherited DNA and the effect of that on the individual.

The person inhabits their own skin within a given nuclear family, within a larger family, and in the context of a particular community, village, town, country, hemisphere, religion, language and so forth. In order to progress through our life we need to acknowledge that a state of integration is a momentary snapshot in time. Moving on means dismantling the status quo and finding a new state that allows us to accommodate new experiences and situations. This means constantly dealing with polarities of different forces and intensities.

We at the Minster Centre are interested in many different approaches and see them as many different points of view that have their own value. In our training we include the theory, skills and practice of humanistic psychologies, psychoanalysis and object relations, Existentialism and phenomenology, bodywork (neo-Reichian and others) and transpersonal and Jungian approaches. Each one is explored as a different way of looking at human behaviour. What we have noticed is that most bodies of thought are focused on a different aspect of the person as a starting point and that they radiate out in principle to include the whole from their own viewpoint.

We live and function in a physical body that reflects and encompasses whatever is going on emotionally, mentally, physically and spiritually. We cannot remove ourselves from the body and make an assumption about the psyche independently. The body and the psyche are part of a multi-structured system – each aspect of that system connecting to each other.

If we are looking at transference, we are looking at one system meeting another system: the therapist has intellectual knowledge, a particular personal life and unique experiences; that is what you have to offer the client. The client is dependent on the extent of the therapist's knowledge and on the therapist's capacity to relate to them. The therapist who has had a psychoanalytic training will be inclined to think in analytic terms, the Existentialist will do so in Existential terms, and so forth. We feel it is important to recognize this and then to open up the possibilities of creating our own individual language emerging from our own life experience, which then includes the viewpoint of the various theorists that have gone before. If you have integration then you must also have its counterpart of disintegration – balance and imbalance. Until you have looked at the link between the two and grappled with them you cannot go very far.

Generally I get a sense in the outside world that integration is putting things together so they are manageable. The inside world is led by two major factors. These two factors are the response to negative experiences, which take two basic forms – a reaching forward for, and towards, life and an effort to maintain life; or, if the experience is bad enough, a withdrawal from life and a longing and reaching for death. Distress, threat to existence or life, damage and pain to any aspect of the person must be taken into account if the organism continues to survive.

The need for well being, if life is chosen, is a natural movement forward, fraught with dangers of potential loss of well being. What we really have to do is to mention that things are not always manageable and then, how do we manage the unmanageable? I think the core of this dilemma is related to terror. Our students spend three to four years being presented with all kinds of theories and styles of facilitation and then enter the integrative year. They go through a process that involves the experiences of pre-birth (pregnancy) and birth, pre-genital character-structure development, evolving sexuality, adolescence, the family, death, the transpersonal and transformation. This requires the student to explore all these areas through their own personal life experience.

The model that Davis presents is rather unusual as it is an approach which not only integrates different theoretical traditions but also encourages the student to address the personal dilemmas, contradictions and struggles that generally arise in the process of integration. Furthermore, as she implies, the principles that govern a systems approach can be useful in elaborating the dynamics of this type of an integrative perspective. She continued by talking about the importance of the personal and interpersonal aspects of the training, which are considered to be crucial to students' subsequent ability to engage appropriately with their clients. The experiential component is a crucial aspect of the training as it furthers an exploration of the student's own life experiences in relation to the diverse theoretical traditions and concepts presented on the course. This student-centered approach enables the student to consider and gain a better understanding of how these ideas have influenced their own life and behaviour, how, in particular, as Davis said, 'all these different inputs have moulded them, contributed to their development and their defences and made them less malleable'; this at the same time brings into sharp relief the existential similarities between their clients' and their own dilemmas. This is all done in a group situation, which by necessity entails engagement and is a core base of therapeutic practice:

It is to be hoped that this kind of very personal sharing and engagement ensures that therapists will not then see themselves in a knowing light or as knowing more about the client than the client themselves. Engagement with another and the recognition of problems associated with engagement are the essence of what psychotherapy is about. Transference provokes the countertransference because it is a mutual process; it can never be anything other than mutual. It is an avoidance of countertransference to use theoretical concepts to come between the pure responses of two people. However, to take a step back for both of you, and look at the meaning of the process, does involve language and ideas which have their uses; but as soon as you use ideas in place of engagement you are not experiencing it fully if it remains an intellectual exercise. My experience of another is, in a way, controlled by my relationship to another, as is the other's experience of me. This is a mutual process, which is unavoidable under any circumstances, unless one of us is literally dead.

Countertransference is therefore totally fundamental to therapeutic practice. We incorporate it into our approach by engagement in the interaction and by making it present and conscious and ongoing, and in supporting the client to say what is going on for them. It is a risky business, as I believe there are conscious and unconscious elements in our sharing, so that however you engage with another, and whatever your translation of the experience is, or however perceptive you might be, there is a huge gap between that and who you are and who the other is. Your knowledge is always limited. It is therefore quite likely that the more you engage and share, the more you are dealing with unknowns and therefore gain knowledge. In Maurice Merleau-Ponty's terms, all experience is potent and pregnant with potential.

This is where responsibility comes in, by which I mean the ability to respond and be conscious and engaged. I believe that if the therapist has engaged on a level that is appropriate for the client, then the client will also start engaging more and more fully with the therapist. That seems to be a natural process: because you recognize the other, they will feel recognized and can then begin to expand. But if you do not, they will tend to cut you out. That is a very typical example of seeing if something is happening or not, because if you have really engaged and have acknowledged what you have seen in another person, it is this recognition that enables them to change. One notices the changes in clients' breathing, in their perception and in their emotional response to the therapist. The therapist is also energized when they see change. That is a part of the human condition; but we are still unable to measure this process in any quantitative way, or to know how or why it works.

It is clear from Davis's description of the use of countertransference that she views countertransference as a pivotal tool. As I understand from what she says, countertransference is always present, and it is the therapist's responsibility to communicate to the client those affects that are consciously available to him or her. It would also appear that this is how Davis would define engagement in the therapeutic process – as the therapist's agreement to respond systemically to his or her own here-and-now experiences in relation to the client's material. This in turn presents to the client a demonstration of an experience of trusting and implicitly encourages them to respond in a reciprocal manner by engaging more openly with the therapist. The ability to engender some hope, motivation, optimism and belief in one's capacity to relate may even be posited as a major therapeutic achievement.

Discussion of case-study vignette

What I would want to know about this case-study vignette is what happened when client and therapist first met. This feels like an important missing element. Did the therapist interview the client, take notes on why the client was there and what the client was looking for from the therapy? If so, this is vital information in terms of their initial meeting. It is the first meeting between client and therapist that is more powerful than any further meetings that they will have. I don't know what happened at that stage. I would expect at the first session to know about the client's history and their family background. I would want to know at the outset, from the client, as much factual information about them as possible, which I would write down. I would want to know as much as I could about the client's life and I would also note down my responses to their answers.

I notice from the vignette that this is a very silent client and that silence has predominated during the first few sessions. There are dozens of different kinds of silences. There are bored silences, terrified silences and so forth. Why isn't the therapist filling some of those silences to meet what they are getting? If the silence is a terrified silence, then this is tantamount to freezing the client to death.

The client is depleted in some way to start with, otherwise they wouldn't be there. It is the therapist's duty to energize and take responsibility for the situation until the client has got enough energy to take over. This is one thing that Alexander Lowen said and that I really agree with: 'When the client comes into the room they are undercharged, they can't manage their lives, things are difficult for them.' So, to leave them in that silence is repetitive punishment. The therapist must use their energy to help charge them. As their energy and awareness rises and their selves come into focus, they take over and the therapist withdraws the energy they have been using to stimulate the process. But if the therapist just sits there, saying they have to do it by themselves, it's like leaving a child by itself and saying, 'They are going to have to find out how to feed themselves'. Maybe they were never taught to feed themselves, they won't know how. There are many forms of starvation.

People want to do things but we don't tell them how, we don't show them how and we don't give them the information to find out. There is an instant that then reflects what is going on in the whole system. The therapist is ignoring her; the organization the therapy takes place in is ignoring her; and the working environment is ignoring her; which brings to the surface the misery about being ignored and how badly she feels about it.

I think it would be really appropriate to go with her to the receptionist and say, 'You have really let her down. I'm sorry I did it badly by not phoning down to find out what was going on.' I would later explore if this is common in her life: 'Is this something that you have recognized that has happened before for you?'

The things that have been happening that are not to do with the client creating them means that it is very unconscious material. Mismanagement or mistakes made by either the therapist or the institution in which the therapist works are not the responsibility or the creation of the client. I only know what has happened in this session, that she has had a bad enough time this week to begin to talk about it. What I don't know is how different this session is from the first two. Perhaps this situation was the final straw that provoked her to talk in this session. I would then want to acknowledge and look at how I had also behaved in a similar way and ignored her like everyone else. Let's find out how I am doing this and what it is between us that we are doing together. She is my client and I should have taken responsibility for finding out why she had not appeared for the session.

I take a very different position today than I would have twenty-five years ago when I first started practising. If the client wasn't here on time I would have seen it as their problem and they would have lost the time. We live in a very different world now, and there are many different practical problems that make it difficult, even with the best intentions, always to arrive on time. I would rather share this with the client, and when possible I will give them the extra time.

Conclusion

We have seen that Petruska Clarkson has developed an integrative approach assembled from the relational elements of a number of similar and competing models of therapy, including the transference/countertransference interchange. Countertransference is then subdivided in two opposing ways. 'Reactive countertransference' refers to reactions in the therapist which are assumed to belong to the client, whereas responses that come solely from the therapist are labelled 'proactive'. In this author's opinion, the model places an undue degree of responsibility and power on the therapist's shoulders as he or she is the one who decides which relational theory should take precedence and determines which form of countertransference is present at any given time. The fact that Clarkson offers guidelines on how to make these onerous unilateral decisions also tends to undermine and contradict the essence and complexity of the interdependence which is underlined in the term 'relational'.

The second model, put forward by Maja O'Brien and Gaie Houston, is more in keeping with the pragmatic and cautious philosophy that is often associated with an integrative attitude. This orientation suggests that a willingness to embrace one particular approach may be problematic in that it encourages a form of theoretical blindness to anything other than the 'truth' of one's chosen position: 'Integrative counselling is not tied to any single therapy since its practitioners take the view that no one, single, approach works for every client in every situation' (O'Brien and Houston, 2000, p. 113). Sceptics question the idea that any one explanatory model has a monopoly on the truth and challenge the idea that there is even a truth to be found. However, the possibility of upholding such a position has been questioned: 'It might be that these sceptical doubts are unnatural or improper, that the legitimacy of our beliefs is not affected by ignoring them' (Honderich, 1995, p. 795). Pragmatism, which evolved from the sceptical movement, maintains that practical considerations should always take precedence over rule-based theory. It can be argued that the kind of pragmatic integration that provides the practitioner with a range of alternative strategies is less likely to consider the significance of the unconscious or the importance of the therapist's subjective experience, which in turn suggests that it is also more likely to downgrade the role of countertransference, especially if emphasis is placed on the therapist's need to acquire a stockpile of therapeutic tools. The approach also expects the therapist to be able to discriminate between approaches in terms of the client's needs.

The integrative approach outlined by Helen Davis examines a range of therapeutic paradigms from within a systemic framework, which is an allegance to the view that the therapist and the client constitute a system, and can only be considered in relation to how they influence each other (see Chapter 8 for a more detailed explanation). The application of such a holistic infrastructure, which is then employed to act as a counterpoint for the examining and experiencing of a broader spectrum of ideas, seems to be scientifically rigourous and also in accord with the notion of integration. In true systemic mode this approach also confronts the contrary but crucial issue of disintegration and the personal and professional dilemmas that inevitably arise when integration fails. This desire to be inclusive is continued in relation to transference and countertransference, which are viewed as the bedrock of the encounter, as a mutual and repetitive process that also involves inextricable elements of both members' past relationships. It is further to be noted that Davis indicates that it is often difficult for the therapist to know which aspect of the transference/countertransference matrix he or she is experiencing.

An integrative stance generally requires the practitioner to integrate ideas and traditions that can otherwise be polarized. However, psychoanalytic principles and Dynamical Systems theory have many points in common. It was therefore somewhat surprising to hear Davis state that she would also take pragmatic steps to deal with the issue of the clinical delay by discussing the issue with the receptionist and the client rather than also consider the possible underlying systemic dynamics and motivations that might have contributed to this disturbance.

All of the practitioners cited in this chapter agree on the feasibility of combining ideas and methods taken from contrasting therapeutic models. However, a comparable, and indeed key, issue that links the integrative proposals made by Clarkson and O'Brien and Houston is the stated reliance on therapists' (objectively assessable) competence to distinguish between approaches and to select among them on the basis of their knowledge of their clients' needs. Further, the core value of attending to the therapeutic process is highlighted and given emphasis in both Clarkson's and Davis's integrative models. Both practitioners also agree on the challenging nature that integration poses, although Davis, in contrast to Clarkson and O'Brien and Houston, brings out the extent of the struggle between the opposing forces that face the practitioner who chooses the integrative path.

Chapter 8

Systems Therapy

Dynamical Systems theory developed out of research in the field of quantum physics, although, as has been widely noted, its basic premises are also remarkably in tune with ancient Eastern philosophy. While these discoveries have had far-reaching effects in many significant areas of everyday life, their paradoxical suppositions remain difficult to grasp as they rely on a lateral, or non-linear, way of thinking.

Systems theory is chiefly concerned with the interaction between the elements that compose a given system. The scientist James Lovelock formulated the Gaia hypothesis (Lovelock, 1979) as a way of thinking about the planet: his model views the world as a complex holistic system in which the entire living world cannot be separated from the complex processes of geology, meteorology and atmospheric physics. The physicist David Bohm developed the term 'holomovement' to describe this process in the physical world; he also coined the phrase 'implicate order' (Bohm, 1980), which is the arrangement of the whole inferred in each individual part and in the relations between the individual parts. These ideas have been taken up and employed in a number of diverse disciplines, including psychology, economics and medicine.

Ludwig von Bertalanffy was one of the first researchers to examine the scientific principles of General Systems theory in relation to biology: he described this theory as a general science of organization and wholeness. In *General Systems Theory* (1968) Bertalanffy pioneered the systemic approach in the field of psychology and psychiatry. Salvador Minuchin (1974) was at the forefront of the coalition between Systems theory and family therapy; and Michael Crowe and Jane Ridley (1990) combined a Systems approach with couples' therapy. More recently Michael Butz (1997) and Robin Robertson and Allan Combs (1995) examined the relationship between Chaos and Complexity theory, psychology and various approaches to psychotherapy.

The term 'Chaos theory' can be viewed as a misnomer, as its name suggests extreme disorder and confusion rather than an essential element that is intimately linked to its opposite. During the past thirty years scientists have focused their interest on the chaotic aspects of systems and on the paradoxes that emerge when a system is disturbed. Their findings have shown that even when a system appears to be erratic, unstable or chaotic, there is nevertheless a hidden order that underlies the chaos, which is an inseparable element that is linked to both the onset and decline of the disturbance. As Butz explains: 'It should be mentioned here that the philosophical concept of chaos has long been regarded as a useful mythological tool to describe the unsettling experience of change' (1997, p. 4). The relevance of these opposites is applicable to almost every area of life; for example, it would be impossible to know what it meant to be healthy if we had no knowledge of what it meant to be ill. It is only our awareness of being unhealthy that alerts us to the fact that we need to attend to our system.

The principles that govern Dynamical Systems theory are therefore not focused at the level of 'either/or' nor even 'why'; instead attention is centered upon the process and activity of the system – that is, the way in which all the elements in the system interact with each other. The interdependent perspective of Systems theory has shown that what appears to be the easiest way out of a disturbance often creates further difficulties. The tenets of Systems thinking also suggest that the most appropriate responses will often feel counterintuitive, as Systems thinking entails the ability to perceive on a number of different levels at the same time: 'A good systems thinker, particularly in an organizational setting, is someone who can see four levels operating simultaneously: events, patterns of behaviour, systems and mental models' (Senge, 1990, p. 97).

Systems thinking is about seeing influences in a circular fashion and requires the ability to alter and reframe our usual linear worldview. It is about seeing the relationship between opposites rather than opposites in isolation from one another. Even though we may be able to accept the fact that order and disorder are inherently linked, there are many examples that indicate our inability to embody and apply these ideas in our everyday lives. Though we may tacitly know that in order to re-establish the position of a skidding car we must drive into, rather than away from, the skid, nevertheless the anxiety generated under these chaotic conditions as well as our habitual way of being generally compel us to ignore this knowledge. Paradoxically, by attempting to evade the disturbance, we are likely to encounter further disruption. This same principle applies to the swimmer who is caught in a current. Under these crisis conditions the hardest thing to do is to 'go with the flow', as it requires a deep understanding, acceptance and integration of the patterns and cyclical activity (ebb and flow) which typify and accompany all systems. The expression 'swimming against the tide' captures the swimmer's struggle and attempts to get back to the shore; yet staying with, rather than going against, the natural structure of the tide eventually ensures the swimmer's return, as the tide will spontaneously repeat its enduring cyclical route. The truth behind the aphorism 'it takes a thief to catch a thief' is readily apparent to the person confronted by a forest fire. Although from a straight-forward, commonsense, linear perspective it would seem appropriate to tackle the fire at its source, this strategy is often ineffective owing to the rapid way that fires usually spread. If we approach the problem from a unified perspective and consider the way in which fire is shaped and energetically inclined to proliferate and scorch the environment, it will make sense to create further small fires on the outskirts. This ensures that when the fire reaches these places it will automatically extinguish, as there will be nothing left to power the flames. In certain areas of Australia that are susceptible to fires, it is now mandatory periodically to kindle small controlled fires (referred to as fire breaks) in order, paradoxically to, protect one's land from fire.

The interest and developments in Dynamical Systems theory have emerged primarily from discoveries that have occurred in Western science. Yet these cutting edge ideas are also to be seen in ancient Chinese and Japanese philosophies. The principle of yin–yang (249BC; see Fung Yu-Lan, 1958) is used in Chinese philosophy to classify everything in the universe, and refers to the interplay between opposite forces in terms of their complementarity. The Tai Chi symbol is a gestalt, like the picture that is both a face and a vase: one needs to adjust and enlarge one's vision, to allow oneself effortlessly to re-focus and accept the pattern and order that is concealed within the first-noted chaos. Similar parallels are readily available between non-linear ideas and the 'try softer' dictum that is emphasized in the Japanese philosophy of Zen. This contradictory instruction is consistent with a Systems focus, as it reinforces the significance of staying with the process, and underlines the need to suspend and restrain our usual, driven ways of being in the world.

In Western culture parallels have been drawn between these examples and the pauses in musical compositions, which are considered not to be a lack of music but rather an integral aspect of the melody. In fact, the composer Debussy is said to have made the statement, 'Music is actually the space between the notes'. The Alexander technique, which can be described as a form of physical and psychological re-education, enables people to become aware of themselves as material beings in relation to their breathing and posture. The importance of inhibiting one's habitual, automatic reactions is a crucial component of the Alexander method – 'saying no' to our customary way of doing things and instead observing how we sit, move and breathe. The founder of the method, Samuel Alexander, coined the expression 'end-gaining' to describe the anxiety and frustration that forces people to continue to behave in ways that have tended to produce discomfort and frustration. The philosophy that informs the Alexander technique is therefore related to undoing or unlearning: through becoming aware of how we do things in habitual and automatic ways, we are enabled to experience with great immediacy how this lack of awareness contributes to the faulty functioning of our person in a systemic and holistic way.

The focus on the whole system and the significance of complementarity or interdependency is clearly depicted in the simplicity of Zen art. These Japanese ink paintings consist of empty backgrounds, which are seen as exceedingly important, overlaid with a circle, which is considered to represent symbolically among other things a continuous pattern of unity.

All these examples illustrate the fundamental difference between a linear and a lateral way of thinking. Linear modes of thought require one to separate and exclude in order to analyse sequentially. Lateral thinking, by contrast, is concerned with inclusion and the relationship between objects, nature and people. It therefore seems fitting to suggest that musicians, martial-arts experts as well as therapists should all be interested in the significance of pause, silence and non-action as a way of seeing the movement and pattern of the whole system.

Feedback

Feedback is a distinguishing feature of dynamical systems. Research has shown that positive feedback can suddenly produce turbulent activity in an ordered system, while negative feedback in a chaotic system can enable the system to adjust and just as abruptly return to a stable state. Ilya Prigogene was awarded the Nobel Prize in 1977 for his theory of dissipative structures, which helped to explain how change could occur in both physics and the natural world. His work

(Prigogene, 1980) illustrates how non-linear systems are able not only to sustain themselves through chaotic periods without collapsing but also to develop new forms of stability. The process of the emergence of order out of chaos is referred to as 'self-organization'. Prigogene's work further suggests that chaotic periods in themselves are necessary in order to allow for the emergence of new order. The theory of dissipative structures may also throw some light on how change can occur in individual as well as family therapy. Research has shown that the way in which the system deals with the tension between chaos and order is critical, as it can either propel the system towards possible catastrophe, maintain stability or lead to profound change.

All systems have the capacity to regulate themselves through feedback. This feature of all systems was recognized and illustrated by Norbert Wiener in his major text on cybernetics (Wiener, 1948), which had considerable impact on our understanding of how systems function. The term 'cybernetics' is derived from the Greek *kybernetes*, meaning a steersperson or someone who guides, navigates or takes the reins. Cybernetics has been defined as the science of communication and control in both living and mechanical systems (O'Conner and McDermott, 1977). A thermostat is a prime example of cybernetics in action. When the room reaches a certain temperature, an automatic mechanism comes into play and ensures that the temperature in the room remains stable. This same homeostatic principle also applies to our body temperature; the autonomic system generally enables us to maintain a stable temperature through the unconscious use of feedback. The development of second-order cybernetics in the nineteen sixties took into account the notion that the observer was also integral to the system under observation and could not be separated from it.

Systems theory and family therapy

Positive feedback is also referred to as 'reinforcing feedback', and like the self-fulfilling prophecy means that things will either keep getting worse or better; in this way positive feedback amplifies change in the same direction, for better or worse. Negative feedback, also known as balancing feedback, is brought about to limit change and can either create stability or can indicate resistance to change. For example, in a family situation one of the children may habitually create a distraction whenever a disturbing issue is raised between the parents. In this way the child ensures that when things start 'overheating', his or her feedback, or 'symptom', is unconsciously activated to prevent the system from getting out of control. If, however, the whole family could bear to stay with the chaos and not dampen down the disturbance, there is a chance that when it reached its zenith, the family might be able to rearrange itself in a more creative way. One of the ways a systemic therapist might begin to work with this example would be to slow down the process and point out the rigidity of the family's pattern of interaction, of which they are probable unaware. It is expected that highlighting and exploring the family's cycle of automatic feedback reactions and responses will contribute to breaking the unconscious chain of events that has maintained the system's stuck position.

The applications of a Systems approach and the principles that control the mechanism of homeostasis have been used now for many years to describe and understand family interactions. In this light the family is seen as a homeostatic system that maintains its balance through rules that tacitly regulate the ongoing emotional interactions of its members. This can ensure that when a given encounter feels 'too hot to handle', again an unconscious balancing operation will automatically come into play to stop the family system from 'over-heating' or even destroying itself. Family Systems therapy emphasizes the unconscious role that symptoms can play in keeping an individual stuck in a perverse family dynamic but which, paradoxically, also satisfies certain unconscious needs of the other members of the family. As Rudi Dallos states: 'The view of symptoms as a communication of unconscious feelings can be seen to have played a central part in the development of sys-tems theory' (1997, p. 21). Thus a person suffering from agoraphobia would be likely to need considerable support from their partner and other family members, and this apparent helplessness may serve as an unconscious means for the symptom-bearer to gain some power. This can also be a way for the sufferer to divert attention away from the essential relational difficulties within the family system.

The origins of these ideas are also clearly traceable to the principles that inform psychoanalysis. As Dallos has pointed out, the difference between the psychoanalytic and Systems models is that the former tenders a causal, individualistic explanation of the person's symptoms, based on intrapsychic factors, unlike the systemic, non-linear paradigm, which emphasizes the interpersonal dynamics between family members that are contributing to and helping to sustain the ongoing pattern of family interaction: 'Systems theory, in its emphasis on the intimate interconnection of the parts of a system, reveals that choice is inevitably contingent. Each person's actions have an influence on others', which in turn shapes their subsequent actions' (Dallos, 1997, pp. 28–29).

Family therapists have employed some of the principles of Systems theory in different ways during the last thirty years as a means of understanding and working with the family system. During this time there have been various shifts and fashions in the application of systemic ideas to the practice of family therapy. It seems fair to say that family therapists do not have a unified theory of the way in which a Systems approach should be applied to family therapy. The advent of second-order cybernetics did, however, prompt some therapists to shift their attention away from questioning, clarifying and focusing to a more narrative/conversational approach. In this way it was hoped that the power inherent in the therapist's position would be reduced and the therapist's lack of objectivity within the system would at the same time be acknowledged. Some family therapists (Skynner, 1987; Gibney, 1996) have argued that the therapist's primary role is to provide the family with a containing space in which to express their recurring patterns of disorder. These same practitioners draw on ideas taken from psychoanalytic theory and practice, especially the countertransference emotions experienced by the therapist, which are considered to contain important information about the therapist's input and his or her links to the family.

Family narratives and myths

Family therapists are interested in the interacting and competing stories that members of a family tell about their experiences within the family. Dallos defines a narrative as 'an account or story about how the current situation has arisen, what events/experiences in the past have moulded individual personalities, ways of relating and so on' (1997, p. 125). The focus on narrative is a relatively modern influence and has been described as a 'third wave' in family therapy (O'Hanlon, 1994). The work of the Australian psychotherapist Michael White (1986; White and Epston, 1990) has been a primary influence in the development and establishment of narrative therapy. The narratives that people relate are considered to be a significant element of family systems therapy as they hold important information about how narrators see themselves and also clarify how they view their relationships with others. The stories people tell about their dilemmas and relationships often contrast with the way in which the therapist hears some of the latent and non-verbal messages contained in the narrator's commentary. It is the therapist's task to point this out and help the individual or family to unravel these contradictory messages. From an

Existential as well as a client-centered perspective, people often confuse their assumptions with their personal values, and their stories are therefore likely to contain attitudes and feelings that are related more to how they think they should feel and behave rather than what they truly believe. A classic and unfortunately common example of this discrepancy concerns the area of physical or sexual abuse. Under these taboo conditions some family members feel compelled to tell their story in a defensive and distorted way, which then influences other members of the family, to put pressure on themselves to comply with the misrepresentation.

The secrets that are embedded in the family's complicit governing narrative are referred to as 'family myths' as they are an agreed but false version of the reality of the family situation. From a systemic perspective a family myth can be understood in terms of the way in which it can keep the family system intact; 'the function' of homeostasis was to protect a family from disintegration, which might occur if the unconscious conflicts surfaced. The concept of the 'family myth' captures this notion of families as engaged in unconscious processes of distortion. One common example of such a 'myth' has been seen to be the common belief held by two parents that their child has a problem that is largely unrelated to their relationship. (Dallos, 1997, p. 177)

The tradition of family systems therapy seems to have developed in a rather piecemeal way, which has resulted in a lack of conciseness in the model itself, which in turn has given the family therapist a certain amount of leeway and freedom with which to apply its diffuse principles. The brief account presented above has outlined a few of the major areas subsumed under this umbrella. It is hoped that the following interview will help to clarify how some of these systemic ideas can be put into practice when working with family dynamics.

Interview

John Byng-Hall is a consultant child and adolescent psychiatrist, semi-retired, at the Tavistock Clinic who trained at Cambridge University, the Maudsley Hospital and the Tavistock Clinic. He is a past chair of the Institute of Family Therapy in London. He has for many years been one of the leading lights of the family systems approach to psycho-therapy in this country. He has written and lectured widely on the subject for over thirty years and still retains a keen interest and critical eye on the up-and-coming ideas and practice that are the currency of family systems therapy at the present time. In my interview with him, Dr Byng-Hall started by describing the basic principles that he considers inform the family systems tradition:

Family therapy started mainly in the United States in the nineteen fifties and sixties. Many family therapy pioneers came from a dominant psychoanalytic tradition from which they rebelled and turned to systems theorists such as Bertalanffy and Bateson. It was a time of tremendous creativity. The basic idea behind systems theory is that of mutual influence: each aspect of what happens in family life influences, and is influenced by, all other aspects. Family therapists involve family members in changing the way they relate, which they then take home with them, and their mutual influences can support the change. My overall aim is to help the family find ways of resolving their own problems. An individual in therapy goes home to an unchanged family, so it often needs longer.

As Byng-Hall went on to comment, what was interesting in Britain was that John Bowlby at the Tavistock Clinic wrote one of the earliest papers on family therapy in 1949, and some of his ideas filtered across to the United States and played a role in the origins of family therapy in America. Bowlby explored systems theory at its very start in the nineteen fifties and used it in his theorizing about attachment relationships while still keeping his links to psychoanalysis. These early ideas influenced Byng-Hall's work, and his interest in systems ideas also included insights from psychoanalysis. As a member of the staff of the Tavistock Clinic for 28 years, he said he had recently noticed a renewed interest in psychoanalytic ideas in family therapy.

I asked Byng-Hall about the influence of this systemic revolution in relation to the notion of countertransference. This was his reply:

Well it is interesting because I think that family systems therapy was originally preoccupied with the power of transference and counter-transference phenomena in family groups; but we would not use these terms because they were not part of the new terminology. The way in which families make therapists feel and respond to them can be so strong that a number of strategies were developed to help therapists who are drawn into the family interaction – something to help them to stay connected without being recruited into a family role. One example was the use of one-way screens, which enables the therapist to come out of a session to obtain another view of the family from the observing group. There is also the use of video, which allows therapists to observe themselves working from outside the immediate emotional pull of the family. These remain as valuable assets, especially for training, but there has been an increasing interest in how therapists can reflect on their own responses and use that information.

My next question was related to the range of therapeutic strategies mentioned above. Might they have a detrimental influence on the family and the ensuing interaction? Although Byng-Hall thought this could be so and might work to prevent some things from coming to light, it nevertheless seemed from his experience that once the interaction was underway all participants seemed to forget about the taping as long as confidentiality was maintained.

As I understood it, Byng-Hall's description of the function of the observing group behind the screen appeared to be related to counter-transference issues. I wondered if he thought that these liaisons might also contribute to the families' lack of trust and power within the therapy? Byng-Hall agreed that occasionally families did object to people eavesdropping on them but by and large they seemed quickly to accept the situation. He further stated that he saw transference and countertransference as mutually influencing each other. He conceptualized this process in terms of family scripts, in which the family comes to expect roles in family life to be played out in particular ways within various contexts. As he explained, if a family member stops performing the expected role, there will be pressure on them to resume the role. If that does not work, another member will be recruited to the role. Within the context of family difficulties, the family 'transfers' its expectations of how conflict is to be tackled onto the therapist, based on their family script, and pressure is duly exerted on the therapist to do it their, the family's, way, at the same time as the family probably consciously hopes for the expert to do it his or her way. In relation to countertransference Byng-Hall remarked:

The therapist needs to be aware that they can be drawn back into one of the roles played in their own family of origin, as, say, a peace-keeper. For example, the family may set up an argument, and the usual peacekeepers, who might be the children, hold back, and the therapist may feel so anxious or enraged, or whatever the impulse is, which is the countertransference response that can precipitate your action, say, to protect, or oppose, one or other family member. When you do this then you are immediately drawn into a family role. The pressure to adopt this role is greater when the family's way resonates with your own family script in which you were allocated a similar role. Family therapists can use self-reflective ways in which they ask themselves questions about how much it is me. How much is it the family? And, what are the implications of what I do or say now?

Byng-Hall explained that in talking about a systemic family approach, countertransference meant that two things needed to be considered. First, how the therapist felt towards the family – for example, very protective of one member, or angry towards another. Secondly, how that might resonate with the therapist's family script and their need to know the likely scenarios which would arouse such reactions, as these are the dangerous repetitive situations which could impel the therapist to act inappropriately.

As an example, Byng-Hall outlined how the concept informs what he does in the clinical situation:

When difficult argumentative family scenarios arise, which seem to get nowhere but are repeated nevertheless, I begin to feel like trying to stop one. This alerts me to reflect on what is going on. I may realize that I may have already tried in some ineffectual way to stop them, probably along peacekeeping lines (I know that from the inside), and had felt a bit defeated and now wanted forcefully to call a halt. I become curious and ask them if this happens at home. If so, I ask if they feel any sense of 'here we go again' – at which I often get rueful smiles of recognition. They all hate these scenes. I tell them that this is such a common phenomenon, and isn't it awful? – because what ever you do it only gets worse, but you feel you just have to try. I call these episodes vicious circles. Now we get into an exploration of how to deal with these at an interactive level. I say that having the feeling of 'here we go again' is so valuable. It alerts everyone to try to do something different even if it is only slowing it down. How about signalling to each other when you begin to feel it coming on? – and so on. This can lead to a discussion about the usual pattern, and they work out strategies that might help. I then explore the family history by asking what happened in the parents' families of origin around these issues. Often it suddenly makes sense of why each parent responds as they do. We discuss how it is useful to know each other's 'trigger' points. This can be a route into some empathy and understanding. The outer interactive family and inner family issues are brought together, for both family and therapist. You will have noticed the almost parallel paths taken between them and me. Of course it is never as neat as this but I have found it a very valuable sequence of events; even if it takes several sessions, and is repeated, hopefully there will be some differences each time.

In the preceding example the notion of countertransference has been employed to highlight the correspondence between what is taking place between the therapist and family in the here-and-now and the spontaneous and habitual family scenarios that occur at home. The therapist in this case accepts the peacekeeping role as it is familiar to him and also systemically resonates with the family's dynamics.

In response to the question of whether the observer group's role behind the screen was used to aid the therapist with their counter-transference issues, Byng-Hall said that it could be used as a form of supervision after the session, although in his supervision groups he tended to explore each supervisee's family trees before the therapy session. Elsewhere he has noted: 'In particular the caring scripts are sought – what made you want to be a family therapist? I have recently become interested in the caring roles taken up in childhood of therapists' (Byng-Hall, 2002a). In our interview he continued:

Many of us have been 'parental' children, perhaps doing some looking after of a parent or a sibling – a first family therapy training, as it were. It is important to know the styles of caring that they used then and see when it shows in their therapy and help to ensure that it was appropriate. We also look for triggers, which are likely to draw them in. As the whole group becomes aware of these issues, it can become part of the way they can help their colleagues.

Byng-Hall has also written of the difficulty of addressing counter-transference disturbances in family therapy given the fact that many trainees have one-to-one therapy although they are going to be practising primarily with families.

So we have to find ways of keeping in touch with our inner family. I was lucky to have an analysis, which was enormously helpful. As I never had family therapy training, because I started the first training in the UK with Rosemary Whiffen in 1975, I had to find ways of doing this for myself. Teachers have a particular responsibility to know themselves. Whenever I theorized about human behaviour I made a resolution always to explore what relevance it had for me. I think I managed to keep to that, and many of these are published so that readers can see where I come from. Recently I found a way of telling my own story about how I had become a family therapist – a technique that can be used by others. (Byng-Hall, 2002b)

From a systemic perspective it would be expected that counter-transference would also be considered as a relevant factor between the supervisor and the therapist. If so, I asked, would the supervisory relationship then be assumed to impinge on the therapist's relationship with the family system?

Yes, this is crucial. I use attachment theory to understand relation-ships. A secure relationship is one in which you experience the attachment figure as having you in mind and available when you are in need. That provides a secure base from which it feels safe to explore and hence grow and learn, safe in the knowledge that if things go wrong he or she will be there for you. Families can also provide a secure base. This is true also for therapy in general. I have also conceptualized supervision groups as providing secure bases for trainees. This provides a setting in which the supervisees can feel able to relate to the supervisors in a way that can accommodate the difficult aspects of their relationships, including transference to the supervisor. After all, the really secure relationship is that in which negative feeling can be expressed and understood. The supervisor has to relate to and understand the group conflicts as well as be able to nurture the group. The supervisees can then bring their difficult feelings into the group to be understood, and are hence less likely to act them out in the family. It is a group phenomenon similar to the secure family base, where there are others who can share the care. It could be called a 'group criss-cross of transference/counter-transference'. That is so complicated that it may explain why the concepts are not used in the same way as in individual therapy.

In turning to the question of narrative in family therapy, I asked Byng-Hall what was meant by narrative.

Narrative and communications are the key to all relationships. I have been interested in and theorizing about this since 1973. What has interested me is how families could be helped to communicate with each other in order to empathize with each other's situations and collaborate to everyone's advantage. This communication includes family conversation in which there is always mutual influence: listening, influencing what is said, and vice versa. Accurate stories about what has been going on to inform those who were not there are essential. Family legends told about the past convey the family ethos about how the family should be now, and so on. Attachment research has shown that, broadly speaking, narratives that are linked to empathy are associated with better outcomes. I have found that research can reveal far more interesting phenomena than any armchair theorizing. Family therapy is currently a mixture of ideas, which are being explored, and various approaches advocated, with great enthusiasm. This has been our way. Eventually it will become clear which narrative approaches are useful in enabling the family to collaborate in finding solutions to their own problems.

Concerning the issue of competitiveness, I asked Byng-Hall whether the therapist would address this complex dynamic so often present in families, and which might emerge covertly between the therapist and some members of the family.

Families are amazingly complicated and fascinating. That's why I love working with them. It is true that competition between family members can be a major feature, which could easily lead to subtle attempts to make alliances with the therapists. Experience and knowledge of covert cues, including one's feelings evoked, help to spot these. Much has been written about how to establish a therapeutic relationship with all family members. This has been described as neutrality but I do not like that term as I try to make positive warm contact with each member from the beginning of the first session. That is consistent with attachment theory. In the first session I try to make sure that members feel that I have understood them sufficiently to be there for them. Just as important, they all see me relating to all members of the family and then observe how I keep glancing round the room to see how each is being affected by what is going on.

Discussion of case-study vignette

The following is a selection of John Byng-Hall's comments on how a family therapist might work with the clinical vignette selected for discussion.

Obviously there is no chance of working with the family; but there is a way of working systemically around family relationship issues. I was thinking that there is something about this girl that allows her to be ignored and seem to feel nothing. I also thought about the system, which includes the setting, the receptionist and so on. I suppose as a family therapist I would be struggling with how to think about the family system. I would probably be quite active in the session and gently ask questions about family interactions while leaving time for her to reply. I would want to take up the issue of her leaving home. I wouldn't sit in silence as from my experience silence doesn't help to make people feel secure. I might, as a family therapist, make some telephone contact with the family. I have used international conferencing calls for family discussions for those who use continents to leave home; but I doubt if this would be suitable even when she became talkative.

By way of explanation, I mentioned that the client's mother telephones from abroad on a daily basis and tends to do all the talking while the client remains silent.

Well then, I would need to be careful about not talking too much, like her mother. Then I would attempt to make some links to what had transpired in the waiting room prior to the session, to the fact that somehow she had been forgotten, and then look at what it is that *she* does to get herself forgotten. I would also be interested to know if she had any brothers or sisters and whether any of them had left home. I would ask if she knew how her mother and father had left their parental homes. This would be a way to get into the family script and then to ask about how her mother got on with her own mother.

It seems that the less she says, the more the mother calls. I might then make the suggestion that the client could write her mother a letter or email as a way of breaking the cycle. This is a 'too close/too far' relationship. I would point out her needing to go to the other side of the world in order to get away but that she still takes with her the longing to be mothered. To some extent the client may be receiving some mothering from her flatmate, as it was she who first brought her to the therapy. I would reflect on the systemic issues and the similarity between the clinical situation and her family issues. I would be concerned about my countertransference difficulties and of the possibility that I might work overtime with the client just like her mother and become too close. I might also consider working with her three flatmates, as they represent the client's family in this country at the moment.

Conclusion

My rudimentary familiarity with and understanding of family systems therapy leads me to believe that the relevance of second-order cybernetics, or the impossibility of separating the observer from the observed, has either not tended to be a major feature of family work or been too difficult to integrate fully into current models. Having said that, second-order cybernetics is nevertheless a hallmark of Systems thinking and is certainly implied in the literature and case-study material by some family practitioners. It seems to me that if the therapist's influence on the family system was given due consideration, then all of their interpretations, by definition, could only be thought of in interdependent terms. Furthermore, if this were the case, then as the practitioner interviewed here stated quite clearly, from his perspective all of family systems therapy would be centered on the therapist's countertransference. John Byng-Hall's general description of countertransference seemed to encompass both the feelings that the family puts into the therapist and the therapist's own unresolved familial transference difficulties. Byng-Hall highlighted this contradiction when he said that as far as he was concerned, countertransference is fundamental to the practice of family therapy, although this principle is not overtly stated; to which I would add: and the term is not generally featured in the family therapy training and texts written for this tradition.

Chapter 9

Psychotherapy Training and Countertransference

This chapter is based on interviews with three highly experienced psychotherapists who manage and teach on recognized established professional psychotherapy training programmes. One of the main aims of the interviews was to investigate the meaning and significance of countertransference for each organization. Of particular interest also was to know which definition of countertransference was emphasized and to understand how the concept was incorporated and addressed with students at the interview stage and during their training.

The original definition of countertransference as an unconscious distortion on the part of the therapist that interferes with the therapeutic interaction would suggest that it is a particularly salient aspect of psychotherapy training. It implies also that these discrepancies would be encountered between interviewers and applicants in the selection process encounter.

One of the questions put to trainers in this small survey asked for their opinions on the kinds of predisposing factors they thought attracted applicants to choose psychotherapy as a career. Their responses ranged between a more intellectual interest in human behaviour to a more spurious need for self-aggrandizement. Some practitioners have asserted that the choice of psychotherapy as a career is essentially related to trainees' 'unmet psychic needs' (Goldberg, 1993, p. 52). Emotional tensions and conflicts in practitioners' early familial relationships have been cited as a major influence in their opting to become psychotherapists. It has further been suggested that discordant nurturing experiences in childhood are a noticeable feature of their backgrounds. Some children assume a nurturing role in their families for a variety of reasons, sometimes because of their position in the family or as a consequence of a parent's being either physically or emotionally unavailable. Presumably this premature interpersonal responsibility leads to a strong nurturing identification, which subsequently exerts a vigorous pressure throughout the individual's life. It is not unlikely that this familiarity will draw them to opt for a career in one of the 'helping professions'. This career choice may also offer a possible way for the person to work through their own nurturing needs by ministering to the needs of others.

In 'Analysis Terminable and Interminable' Freud (1937) discusses the significance of the analyst's personality on the quality and outcome of their analytic treatment. He then makes the claim that there is no counterindication should a physician suffer from any physiological condition similar to that of their patient, and he further suggests that this may even enhance their treatment ability. Freud then compares the difference between the physician's role and the role requirements that are cardinal to the practice of psychoanalytic work:

> ... Whereas the special conditions of analytic work do actually cause the analyst's own defects to interfere with his making a correct assessment of the state of things in his patient and reacting to them in a useful way. It is therefore reasonable to expect of an analyst, as a part of his qualifications, a considerable degree of mental normality and correctness. (p. 248)

There is in fact a paucity of research and literature on the childhood factors that may induce a person to choose psychotherapy as an occupation. However, the results from a research project carried out by Merodoulaki (1994) suggest that psychotherapists were as children significantly more likely to play a conciliatory role in the context of parental discord compared to the relevant control group. A significant difference was also found between the control group and therapists, who mostly recalled their childhood as troublesome, and which they connected to one kind of separation or another. Other findings from Merodoulaki's study suggest that this cohort of therapists as children commanded an unusual degree of power in the family.

Interview (1) Psychoanalytic training

Jonathan Bradley is a child psychotherapist and trainer on the psychoanalytic child psychotherapy training at the Tavistock Centre in London. He began the interview by outlining the ethos and function of this Tavistock programme, which was set up predominantly to provide training for therapists to work with children, including very young children, and adolescents, as well as their parents, mainly in the National Health Service. One of the major aims of the programme is to produce psychotherapists who are adaptable to the changing needs of the NHS but who also are able to provide psychoanalytic psychotherapy, principally long term, to a range of clients. A further aim is to help trainees specialize in particular areas of work such as hospitals, special-care baby units and adolescent units.

In response to my question about the characteristic spirit of the training course, Jonathan Bradley said that this revolves around the recognition that in the clinical setting children are able to get access to the unconscious determinants of their behaviour and bring these out into the open, through words, play and drawing. This helped to explain the extensive length of the training programme, as there is a requirement to understand children of different ages and to understand also something of the way in which children express their fantasies, so that these can become available for them to think about.

A particular question that is often raised by psychotherapy trainees is whether there is a significant difference between the technique required to access unconscious material with children and that required in the case of adults. Bradley remarked that he thought the techniques differed in many respects, despite the fact that some people would say that the play of children under the conditions of the specific therapy room setting corresponds in important ways to the dreams of adults. Unlike children's social play, the play with which psychotherapy engages is concerned with internal figures, which are externalized in drawing and on the play table and in the manipulation of dolls, animals and similar small-scale objects. For example, Bradley noted, a child may develop a scene where initially there is muddle of animals on the table, not a fence in sight, without any possibility of protecting one kind of animal from another. This scene might allude to the child's internal confusion in quite a dramatic way by highlighting the child's sense of vulnerability and lack of defence against aggressive attacks. There may also be a vested interest in retaining that confused scene – rather than beginning to divide it up, introduce fences or make some distinctions between wild and tame animals, a parallel of what might occur in the analysis of an adult's dream. The big difference, on the whole, Bradley said, is that a child doesn't lie on a couch, can be volatile, and tends to move around a great deal, even to the point of trying to wreck the room. It is therefore important to know how to work with children, and this is what makes for the complex nature of the course work.

To sum up, it seems that the difference between working with an adult and a child is that the former is generally agreeable to lie on a couch and free associate, while the latter will have a marked tendency to act out. Bradley gave some examples of the types of behaviour with which the child psychotherapist might have to contend and the particular difficulties that can arise when working with children:

> From the outset with certain children you find that their actions are violent and their need to get rid of bad feelings prompts them to run away or physically or verbally attack; at the same time they may be extraordinarily isolated and hard to reach. So the way in which a child agrees to therapy is different from the adult, and unless you engage the child by showing that you can have access to thoughts that are very worrying to them, you are not going to get very far, because they don't give consent in the same way as an adult. An adult, unlike a child, will arrange an interview, sign up, attend weekly and pay their bill. It is very different for children: they have to like the therapist and to feel that he or she has interesting things to say.

The difference between adult and child psychotherapy suggests that one of the salient attributes required for working with children is the ability to engage with the child at the child's level. This was why Bradley insisted that the structure of the Tavistock training was very important:

> We make a distinction between the pre-clinical programme, which is at least two years, and normally three, and the clinical training. In many ways the essential characteristics needed for our training are brought out in the pre-clinical course, so that we are finally inter-viewing people who have been with us for three years. An essential feature of our pre-clinical course is an infant observation component, which requires the student to go into a home on a weekly basis to observe a baby over a period of two years. They are then expected to bring that observation in written form to a small-group discus-sion. This is particularly important because they are asked to be an observer and they have to negotiate that boundary between par-ticipation and non-participation and must also struggle to do that when a baby becomes a little toddler. Some of the observations involve very difficult scenes, which naturally bring to mind the observer's own infancy, and the trainee must then learn to make the distinction between what is their own experience and the experience

they are observing. Of course one's own experience can be both a hindrance and help in understanding someone else, so from the outset this training does therefore immediately involve the notion of countertransference.

As far as the relationship between the theoretical and clinical components of the course is concerned, Bradley explained that the teaching begins with Freud and then follows the psychoanalytic developments formulated by the Kleinian tradition. In the clinical setting the internal counterparts of the child's ordinary relationships make it possible for the conflicts they experience to be played out with the therapist. It is the therapist's responsibility to point out the difference between the internal picture and the external scene that is taking place in the therapeutic interaction. Furthermore, given the need to operate in the public health sector, technique needs to be adapted to different situations, such as short-term and applied work.

I asked whether Harold Searles's proposition that infants and children have a natural curative ability to help their mothers, and by extrapolation to assist the therapist, was of any relevance to the Tavistock training programme.

The idea, as such, was not considered I was told. However, it raised for Bradley the matter of the importance of close observation in the clinical setting. Taking up the question of how to think about a piece of apparently helpful behaviour on the part of a child, Bradley commented:

> Perhaps you can imagine a situation where a child would want to be 'helpful' in the session by telling the therapist where to sit and making sure that the room is nice for them and by being generally kind to the therapist. That might be a very different activity in quality from a child who, after emerging from a period of depression, perhaps brought about largely owing to the rejection of help, would suddenly feel in a generous mood and would say something genuine to look after the therapist. In this scenario the child may offer the therapist a sweet after realizing that he or she has, in reality, been having a difficult time. What is important is to be aware of all these things; but you can't pretend to try to impose a belief, such as that curative care is innate and should therefore be the focus of the session. It is exceedingly important to be able to distinguish what is a more veiled attack, what is much more to do with persecutory anxiety, and what the child would do if I don't help them, from the

genuine concern that they may express. This is the bread and butter of the interaction, which cannot afford to be too dominated by the theoretical model – although you need an available theoretical model in order really to get into the nuances of the actual communication.

Next I asked Bradley for his views on what might be the predisposing factors influencing a person to opt for the profession of psychotherapy.

It is not at all uncommon for trainees to come who have been very much affected by their childhood. This can be in an apparently ordinary way, though it can be important to them. So an issue that can seem quite ordinary – say, a move from one district to another, a difficulty in getting on at school, conflicts with siblings – can have taken root and sometimes leave the impression 'I shouldn't have been as miserable as that'. All of these difficulties can destroy us or allow us to find some spark in ourselves which enables us to work through it. It seems very important to consider not only what gets you into something but what you do with it afterwards. So what might be of help in getting one into training can be quite an impediment to our being open within training. Therefore a very important part of the clinical training is the personal analysis of the trainee. Our training requirements are quite strict: a student is expected to attend personal analysis four to five times a week throughout the training, which takes about four or five years after the pre-clinical training. So the ability really to look at one's own agenda and be able to make those connections, which include those predisposing factors, is important, and they need to be made available, rather than remain inaccessible to conscious processes.

Bradley considered that one of the most significant elements of the Tavistock training was related to the requirement of the pre-clinical training, which deals with infantile issues. As the therapist is duty bound to find an acceptable formula to tell the child or adult client that they have an infant self without enraging the person, so they will be agreeable to bring this heartfelt and troublesome part of themselves into the therapy. The infant observation element enables the trainee to become at ease with the infantile aspects of an encounter; a lack of this experience could lead to a breakdown in the therapy situation:

It isn't observation in a vacuum, it's observation in action. Even in the midst of a bad attack from an adolescent the therapist may still be able to find the words to reach the part of the client that they don't want you to see. Adolescents are often quite amenable if you can find the appropriate words to name their experience.

I asked Bradley if the activity of observing he was referring to was comparable to Bion's notion of containment.

By 'observation' I realize I mean quite a complex thing, I don't mean just something you see with your eyes. I also mean being able to meet your own experience so that it affects you, stirs you. For example, the communication of pain to a therapist may be expressed rather violently so that you really get the message, and you have to allow that to lodge and to distinguish those feelings not only as an attack but also as a desperate need to communicate. This means you have to be in touch emotionally with what it means to be in that kind of a state. So observation means allowing some kind of empathy to take place.

The notion of the capacity to experience another's experience and be able to empathize and respond appropriately rather than needing to project the experience back into the object in order to be rid of it is very much associated with the work of Bion. It is an arduous requirement and may be deemed fundamental to the practice of psychotherapy, at times stretching the therapist to their limits, especially when working with children. The child psychotherapist can expect to be consistently confronted with issues of a florid and infantile nature which are likely to elicit emotions that relate to both projection and countertransference.

Bradley referred to Bion's description of alpha functioning, which fosters 'reverie' and then allows experience to be handed back in a way that can promote growth. He stated his view that the most difficult aspect of the therapy for the therapist is that at times they may feel the patient is capable of receiving only relatively little back; so the real task for the therapist becomes the ability to contain, and hold onto, those thoughts and feelings that the patient is unable to accept at any given time.

In the light of the preceding comments my next question focused on the kinds of attributes the selection committee would be looking for in a child psychotherapy trainee.

As Bradley explained, the programme is composed of two parts, and many more people are drawn to the observation course, which is the largest MA course of its kind in the country. Relatively fewer then go on to do the child psychotherapy training, so the criteria for each are different:

> In the second you would be looking for them to have come to some rather profound view of themselves and therefore to be more able not to project their issues onto their clients and more able to learn and deal with some quite difficult concepts – above all able to work with children and not be afraid to work within a particular psychoanalytic framework.

As an example of the sort of question he might ask in order to glean the personal information needed as to whether the student was ready to train as a child therapist, Bradley said he would ask them about how they experienced the infant observation component: 'This immediately leads them into something very personal, so usually that sense of where they have come from and their own development arises very naturally and you very quickly get a view of them.'

In addressing my central topic of questioning, the topic of countertransference, he stated that he would attempt to avoid the theoretical debate and that he viewed the concept as something that required one to be in a receptive state and also be aware of oneself. He regarded this as linked with its main aim, which is to gain access to those aspects of the patient that have to be kept separate from the patient's main presentation:

> There could be one kind of communication going on and you become aware of something else taking place which is not presented in the same package. This could register in different ways, it could register somatically; and then you have to know how to locate that somatic disturbance in you. Was it something that was going on before or did you suddenly get a headache? You can't assume that because you are feeling sleepy that it means the patient is boring; but what is it in you that has needed to close down, what has the patient touched in you that may give you a clue about something in them that is unavailable? This first requires you to come to terms with what it is in yourself that you find unbearable. In other words, you don't have the right of instant access to everything the patient brings just because you have been in analysis.
>
> I think of countertransference as the ability to be able to work in a fog. My own view is that it isn't a kind of grand high road, it is a terribly obscure place to be in where necessarily things are

confused, that you might just be able to throw some light on, which can then be brought into the mainstream of communication.

The expression of countertransference as being in a 'fog' sounded like a graphic representation of an experience that is primarily or initially unconscious. As Bradley went on to say, 'Fog is the area where you are not sure what is you and what is the patient, and it is usually an unconscious communication and often a quite split-off part of the patient.' The crucial matter at hand for the therapist under these obscure conditions is the ability to reflect thoroughly on their feelings prior to any verbal communication to the patient. At the same time, he commented that sometimes the term is used by therapists to mean speaking about what they are feeling: 'I feel that is rather a dangerous pursuit if it is not linked to some understanding of what comes from yourself and what is really lodged in you from the patient.'

Addressing the concept of projective identification, Bradley expressed the view that people sometimes seemed to cannibalize the term, meaning that if you feel angry, you should express it rather than try to understand where that anger comes from. He commented:

I believe very strongly that what distinguishes therapeutic work from non-therapeutic work is the capacity to contain something and to feed back in an acceptable way. Obviously the ordinary life of the therapist is in the reply; but there is a thin but very clear distinction between re-projecting back into the patient what you have received and allowing yourself to speak as an ordinary person, sometimes with passion. There is this caricature of the neutral, characterless therapist, who speaks and interprets as if they are absent from the room, which is really unacceptable.

Comment

The particular training of the Tavistock programme tends towards the more mainstream end of psychoanalysis and is particularly committed to a Kleinian developmental model and its accompanying technique. This is not surprising given that the training is geared to working with children and adolescents. What is very clear is that people who expect to train as child psychotherapists must be prepared to confront areas of their own childhood that have hitherto remained concealed. The initial and lengthy so-called 'observation' component of the course suggests that the student is a neutral bystander. However, these observations of the mother–baby scenario cannot fail to arouse a range of competing and disturbing emotions in the trainee and comparisons linked to their own childhood experiences. Trainees are thus immediately confronted with their own transference issues, which will heavily influence their observational reactions. If these entanglements are then subjected to scrutiny, as Jonathan Bradley implied, it would appear that the connection between the transference/countertransference struggle and this mode of relating will be central, although under these conditions at least the transference difficulties would in effect be induced in the trainee. It would also explain one of the rationales for opening with this practical part of the training and its subsequent influence on the matter of the trainee's professional suitability.

The idea that such a career choice could provide a protective cover by engendering a sense of personal detachment is clearly fallacious. Likewise, the important predisposing childhood factors are not contraindications, as without this interest and sensitivity to one's internal and childhood experiences the necessary motivation for such work will be lacking. As Bradley intimated, the trainee's professional competence to a large extent depends on the painstaking deliberation of their personal motivations for this work. It seems clear that the course encourages trainees to consider and acknowledge the inevitable infantile residues that are part and parcel of their psychological makeup. It is also implied that the clinical benefit of this self-development focus is to reduce the trainees' more florid transference/countertransference responses.

The importance of paying particular attention to the personal and clinical implications of countertransference was considered to be a core issue in the Tavistock training. Bradley referred to 'holding onto', or the salient capacity of being able to sit with, countertransference experiences over a period of time. It may be said that this ability on the therapist's part will be reciprocally experienced by the patient and eventually enable them to think the unthinkable and counteract the need to 'act out'. In order to fulfil this task the trainee is first required to confront and acknowledge their unmanageable impulses, affects and memories, mainly through the personal therapy component of their training.

The injunction for trainee analysts to undergo their own personal analysis was first put forward by Freud. He argued that in order for the practitioner to fulfil their professional obligations it was imperative that they release their own resistances from the sway of the unconscious. This requirement is clearly explained: 'It may be insisted, rather, that he should have undergone a psycho-analytic purification and have become aware of those complexes of his own which would be apt to interfere with his grasp of what the patient tells him' (1912b, p. 116). Nevertheless, Anne Macashilll, Principal Lecturer at the School of Health and Community Studies at Sheffield University, in a paper in which she examines studies carried out in Europe and America to test this claim, concluded: 'The research studies fail to demonstrate that having the experience of personal therapy produces more effective therapists' (1999, p. 151).

Interview (2) Psychodynamic training

Lesley Murdin is a psychoanalytic psychotherapist, lecturer and clinical supervisor. She is currently Director and Head of Training at Westminster Pastoral Foundation (WPF). Lesley has been a chair of the psychoanalytic section of the United Kingdom Council for Psychotherapy and its Ethics Committee. She has published papers and books in the field of psychotherapy and counselling and is at present writing a text on transference for the Palgrave Macmillan psychotherapy series.

Murdin opened the interview by talking about the general attitude and spirit that guides the WPF training programmes. She said that the fundamental ethos of the training was determined by the fact that WPF was originally, and still is, a therapy service providing counselling and psychotherapy to clients. The training had evolved in order to supply therapists for that service. So the ethos has always been very much a matter of focusing on the well being of the clients. This has made it a very practical training, rooted in the clinical work, and is the central determining factor as to whether somebody qualifies or not. This is ascertained largely through supervision, but also through their discussions in seminars and through their own writing about the clinical work. Murdin said that the ethos can be seen to some extent from the mission statement of the charity, which is that it provides affordable, high-quality therapy and that the training has been developed in order to offer this kind of a service.

Murdin also pointed out that the idea of flexibility was also contained in the ethos of the WPF training model, as it had originated from a group of analytical psychologists, with a few Institute of Psychoanalysis analysts involved as well. This meant that from the very beginning it was a pluralistic, eclectic training with a strong Jungian input; but since then the staff were selected from all branches of analytical practice. Murdin continued by explaining the kinds of problems that that have arisen from this eclecticism.

In some ways this has made it very difficult, as some students complain that they don't know what they are supposed to think. In fact there isn't a 'supposed to think model' that they can take away with them. They have to evolve their own model. It's flexible, which I think makes it very demanding from the point of view of the trainee. It means they have to think for themselves, and since the university is involved now there is also an emphasis on academic performance. The trainee is not able to accept any one model as 'the truth,' because they are expected to be able to critique whatever they are being asked to look at, at the time, in the light of other models. So it is very broadly based, fluid and constantly changing, and I hope will continue to be like that and not settle into any rigid view of what's right and how to do it – which means it's always difficult and depends on the individual.

In reply to my question concerning the factors that attract a person to the profession Murdin noted that all of the people WPF trains have had some experience of psychotherapy themselves and have found it helpful. This often predisposes them to an idealized view – that they are going to help other people in the same way that they were helped. Murdin also suggested that the fact that many people who have come to train at WPF have been teachers, social workers and health professionals implied that they have always been interested in the way human mind works:

This would be a perfectly respectable motivation, in that you want to learn and to earn money – and why not? So I think the predisposing factors, as far as we are concerned, would be an initial career which would involve some discovery that people can change.

One of the things WPF would look for in their selection process would be an attitude towards other people, and the ability to accept other people, without wanting to change them into an image of oneself. Murdin remarked that 'a certain degree of tolerance, acceptance and enjoyment of what other people are telling you all seem important factors'.

Not only is the motivation for doing the work brought up in the selection process, it is also considered to be a factor that would continue to arise throughout the training. The WPF training is divided into two stages: the psychodynamic counselling followed by the psychoanalytic psychotherapy training. Murdin teaches the final seminar on the initial training. As she said,

> This is an issue which often comes up: why are we doing this work and what do we hope to get out of it? And what does it do for the therapist? Are you relying on the work, on the people you see for some personal satisfaction? Which might or might not be all right, because I think it needs to be acknowledged that there must be some satisfaction; but the counsellor needs to ask themselves what that satisfaction is – if it's productive or counterproductive for working with people. So I would say, yes, it is overtly addressed in the context of the work they are doing.

Murdin went on to state that she felt there were two particularly salient areas of the training. One was the personal therapy, which is required throughout the training and for some time before the student starts, as well as supervision. These two components where students work on themselves as the instrument of the work, mainly in therapy but also in supervision in a different way, are the two absolute essentials, and which may continue after the formal training is completed. This development must go on throughout one's working life, Murdin asserted.

In terms of the actual content of the course, the area of clinical concepts, where students are applying theory to their own experience, is probably the most important; but all the elements of the training are interdependent. There is also a seminar which Lesley felt was very important, entitled 'Ontology'. She explained that it was constantly being refined and re-defined. The seminar addresses how the subject constructs himself or herself, which can include religion, philosophy, politics and personal history, and students are expected to examine their own value system – what they think is important: 'I think that is an extremely crucial part of our training, which is very much emphasized.'

As for the personal attributes of a WPF student, Murdin continued,

> We look for some experience in working with people on a one-to-one basis and for someone we feel we are able to sit with. This is because we expect our trainees to be seeing clients from the first weeks of their professional training, after they have completed the

introductory course, which is spread over one year. So it has to be somebody that has that indefinable something, which makes them reasonably comfortable to sit with. So we are looking for personal suitability. I suppose we try to find out about that in the selection process by asking them what they've made of their life experiences, what they've made of any previous therapy they have had.

Murdin went on to talk about a particular research project that examined the WPF selection process in terms of attachment theory and the adult attachment interview:

We found that the people we have accepted have been in the more secure end of the spectrum rather than the insecure end of the spectrum. This is not something that we have been measuring but it seems to be what our selection process leads us to. I suppose that is part of what I am trying to describe when I say we want the trainee to be someone we feel we could talk to. It's rather vague but we have to allow ourselves sometimes to make selection decisions that aren't entirely based on a measurable factor. So somebody who might have a lot of experience, or a lot of previous training courses all in place, might still not meet that final implicit criterion that we are looking for.

Murdin said that people have to show they are capable of learning, that they can change, that they can be sufficiently vulnerable to say, 'I don't know', and be able to learn from somebody else.

In addressing the notion of countertransference, she remarked that clearly an important element of the training was that people were expected to know something about the historical vagaries of the term and the fact that it had all sorts of meanings and still does have. She went on to say that she thought that if you make it too broad and general it loses its point and is not worth using – if it is used to mean everything that the therapist feels:

I would want to go back to what I think of as a more specific use of it, as a response to the patient's transference, or the use that the patient is making of you. What I try to do, and help trainees in supervision to think about, is: how can it ever be distinguished from your own attitudes, your own emotional state that is going on outside of the sessions? That is, from my point of view, what is useful is specific to the person you are with, rather than what you bring in the first place. I suppose I think of countertransference as the therapist's free association to the patient: that they are bringing you material – emotional states that perhaps require an emotional response to, and maybe for part of the session, or so, I would become immersed in the emotional response. Then I try to stop myself about halfway through a session and think: what is going on here? Is what I am feeling just me, or is it related to the material that is being brought? And I try to have some sort of view about it which may, or may not be right. If I can, I will say something about it and see where that goes. Of course, as Freud said, you don't judge it by the immediate verbal response but more by the subsequent associations that the patient then brings, which will again alter my feeling state and my responses and give me more information, or confuse me further.

I try to be in the state that Freud described as 'evenly hovering attention', and allow myself to be moved in whatever way is called for so that I can have some idea of what kind of care this needs to be, what kind of transference is being shown to me. Sometimes what the patient shows and what I feel are inconsistent: that's when I think countertransference as a term becomes important, because some people will say 'I feel very angry and that is the client's anger'. I think that can be a cop out. This is very much bound up with the whole concept of projective identification, which I think can be a way of evading one's own responsibility for what is happening. So I think it is a term that needs to be used with a great deal of care. Nevertheless, it can be extremely valuable because the therapist's emotional state may be a guide, an indicator of what is not being said, or acknowledged, or it may just be a function of my free association to the material.

Murdin explained that under these conditions she tries to be very tentative and always willing to think that she might be wrong, that it was just her and not something that was going on for the patient. However, she also said that 'sometimes issues that turn out to be countertransference can be useful later; in that case, it may be more a matter of bad timing'.

Much emphasis was placed by Murdin on the clinical significance of countertransference in the training at WPF. The trainees are expected to be aware of what they are experiencing in a session and are required regularly to address these issues in their supervision presentations. There is a consistent expectation for trainees to think about their emotional responses to the client, to analyse them, to separate them into what is useful and constructive and what they think they need to deal with and take to their own therapy. Murdin indeed remarked that 'this requirement should become second nature to them'. In the seminars countertransference and the matching concept of transference are seen as important elements about which trainees need to think in relation to their clinical work; thus a lot of the focus in the seminars is about linking theory to practice:

> We expect them to be trying different ways of making use of their countertransference experience, either for themselves or in terms of what they can say to a client, and to put that in a way that opens things up, so they are not saying things like 'You make me angry', which an initial, raw trainee might want to say. They need to understand also how easy it is to become persecuting, or simply dangerous, if they are too easy with their countertransference. So at first they may lose some of their spontaneity; but for me one of the main purposes of the training is to prevent people from doing harm.

I asked Murdin if she thought that the concept of projective identification was a difficult notion for trainees to integrate in their clinical work. She said that from her experience it was a concept that trainees really liked; but that given the fact that it was a concept that could be difficult to grasp, and that if the student got hold of the idea that what they are experiencing actually comes directly from the client, they could sometimes use it in an inappropriate way:

> I think that what we need to do is to help them exercise a bit of restraint about it and to think that although it is a form of communication and a defence on the part of the client, it must not be used to say 'So I'm not a part of this, it is all the client'. Trainees need to know that they have to take responsibility for their own feelings and responses and they have to take responsibility for what they say and the effect that this has on the client. We therefore encourage students to think about countertransference, which is a concept with an honourable history; but I think it can easily be misused, especially by people who are fairly new to psychoanalytic work.

This led on to the question of the kinds of criteria that would disqualify a student from reaching the professional training standards required by WPF. Murdin commented:

> We always have to balance the well being of the clients, both now and in the future, against the hope that the trainee will learn. If there

were any question of a trainee harming clients then we would certainly stop them immediately, even if that were in the middle of the year. I can only remember one occasion when we did this, when a trainee was getting so over-involved in the material that the clients were suffering in a measurable way. What we always try to do is to give the trainee feedback. We take it as our responsibility to help them as much as possible to learn and to develop what they are not doing well enough – but the patients are the bottom line. We have never had to fail anybody on the psychotherapy training because by that time we have had them for four years; but we may certainly make people take longer, and we frequently do that.

This in turn led on to the usefulness and application of counter-transference in the wider context of the training environment, and to my assumption that countertransference experiences would play an important and relevant role in the selection interview for training applicants. Murdin explained the way in which the structure of the WPF selection process took the issue of countertransference into consideration in interviews for potential trainees. The process, she said, was quite rigorous,

Because we have applicants here for a case-discussion group, so we see them interacting in the group. This is followed by an individual interview when we see how they cope on a one-to-one basis, under conditions which create a lot of stress and anxiety. Mostly I think it works well; but we make mistakes occasionally, and they and we suffer as a result. I suppose I would like to know how to reduce that but in relation to countertransference in that context we want to know that they have sufficient self-awareness, and we are looking for the potential to use that. We are of course using our own counter-transference in interviewing them, to see what they do to us, to see what they seem to be evoking emotionally, and that, too, would be a part of the selection process. We ask the selection interviewers to say something about how they felt with the person at the beginning of the interview and how they felt at the end. So often people come in a terrible state of anxiety and it can be agony being with them. By the end, it is to be hoped they have settled down, and one has more of an impression of what they can be like.

I asked Murdin what happens if the interviewer finds they have experienced strong countertransference reactions with a particular applicant and feels unsure about the validity of their own responses: would a further interview be suggested? She said that this situation rarely happened because the interviewer would be expected to put to the interviewee their experience of them and then to see what they make of it:

> This can of course be a difficult thing to do, and I would never do it at the end of the interview because they might feel left in a rather disturbed state; but we need to know that they can deal with some fairly plain speaking about how they come across. So if somebody makes me feel very anxious or uncomfortable, I would want to say something about it, to see, for one thing, if they could help me to understand what was going on and, for another, to see how they would deal with confrontation of this kind. I usually say to people: 'I would like to know what kind of trouble you are going to give us if you come on our course. What do you think are the sorts of problems you might encounter? Or that we might encounter with you?'

Comment

This second training programme discussed has developed from various branches of psychoanalytic thought, which would explain its somewhat eclectic feel in relation to its more inclusive content, that includes a seminar on ontology, and to its style of teaching, which is not committed to any one specific psychoanalytic doctrine. The focus on countertransference issues seems to be integral to all aspects of the training and its relevance is also clearly considered from the very first meeting between interviewer and training applicant.

Although my interviewee defines countertransference according to its original Freudian meaning (the therapist's personal motional response to the patient's transference), her subsequent comments suggest an interpersonal way of working and a reciprocal way of thinking about the ideas that inform the practice. Murdin also highlights the perplexing participation of countertransference in her own description of it as the therapist's free associations to the patient.

The likelihood of countertransference responses emerging from inappropriate verbal interventions was also seen as a significant element of the training. This practical component gives trainees the opportunity to understand how their countertransference reactions could be restrained through the application of more neutral technical formulations. The importance of technique was also flagged up in her warnings to students about their interventions, which have the potential to be experienced by their clients as persecutory.

The tension that exists between harm and cure is an important area that seems to be given careful consideration in this training. Murdin refers to this issue on a number of occasions and also underlines its significance by citing the principal medical adage, 'First do no harm'.

Interview (3) New ideas on training

Professor David Livingstone Smith is currently Visiting Professor of Philosophy at the University of New England in Maine. He was formerly a psychotherapist and is the author of a number of texts and journal papers, many of which are devoted to problems related to the scientific status of psychoanalysis. Smith is also the Co-founder and Director of the New England Institute for Cognitive Science and Evolutionary Psychology.

In the final of the interviews for this chapter, and in contrast to the previous two, Smith questions the scientific status of the psychoanalytic model of human nature and offers a damning critique of some of its basic assumption and concepts. By extrapolation, he is sceptical of the quality of the training programmes currently on offer. In his interview Smith puts forward an innovative and radical training model in order to address the methodological inconsistencies that he considers are inherent in the majority of therapeutic models currently available.

I began the interview by asking Smith how he would envisage the ethos of his ideal training in psychotherapy:

> First of all I believe in science. Science is how we acquire knowledge, and psychotherapy can only be the application of a body of knowledge about the nature of human beings. So in my ideal training people need to know science, to understand scientific reasoning and they need to understand relevant areas of science – traditional psychology for instance. They need to know something about cognitive affective neuro-science, and they certainly need to know about evolution and evolutionary psychology.
>
> Science is organized criticism. So it is very important in my ideal training that people are not expected to believe anything in particular but are instructed in the methodology of reasoning. I don't mean in the fashion that one finds in so much psychotherapy and psychological research, where there is a kind of intellectual terrorism that often

requires the research be undertaken in ways that are rather naïve and often are simply not appropriate to the object of study. Attempts to test propositions that are held dear to psychotherapists and psychologists are often done in ways that miss the point. For example, critiques of Freud's explanation of slips of the tongue by psycholinguists do not factor in the causal significance of an emotionally charged context. Bernard Baars is one of the few people who have attempted to test scientifically the theory of slips, by creating an emotionally charged situation in an ingenious way. Baars had male college students perform a verbal task administered by a sexually attractive woman. He found that they tended to commit sexually suggestive speech errors more frequently than a control group.

Smith went on to say that in psychotherapy there is a fundamental problem, which is that psychotherapy is supposed to work, even though we don't really know how to investigate what works, and when things work, and we don't understand why they work – which poses a problem for any psychotherapy training. He therefore believes that psychotherapy training should not be geared primarily toward practice but more towards how we might acquire an understanding of the relevant aspects of human nature which can inform practice. His view is that training should not be eclectic but should be broad, because there is no good evidence to show that anyone knows how to do psychotherapy in a consistently effective way. 'My personal view is that psychotherapy is mainly superstition anyway, so I want breadth, and I want the emphasis to be mainly on knowledge and its acquisition.' Therefore, according to Smith, a fundamental component of the training should be dedicated to the philosophy of science:

What does it mean to say that something is scientific or not? What are the criteria that might justify stating that a particular claim is true or false? This is pure methodology, and science is nothing but methodology. Often people who don't know science identify science with the results of science; but real science continually transcends itself and proves formerly accepted 'truths' to be wrong. It's the methodology that is crucial. This is precisely what the world of psychotherapy lacks, which is why psychotherapy does not progress. Psychotherapy is morbidly obese: it doesn't develop or progress, but it just keeps getting broader. Training programmes are still teaching things that were initially formulated a hundred years ago without any objective way of establishing whether they are wrong. This is an intellectual scandal.

As far as I am aware, there is no training that addresses and investigates these propositions from a scientific perspective. So I asked Smith, from what he had said it seemed there was no training that would fulfil his criteria adequately. 'Yes,' he responded, 'I think the world of psychotherapy is largely a world of cults and the trainings in psychotherapy are inductions into cults.'

Smith continued by saying that there were several reasons why he felt this state of affairs would be unlikely to change:

I think that to a very great extent the field of psychotherapy is a refuge for the grandiose – that it is one of the few such areas left which has retained at least a modicum of credibility. It is not too intellectually demanding, can be quite lucrative and gives a false sense of knowledge. So the would-be psychotherapist can assume the mantle of wisdom and expertise without actually possessing any. This is tremendously attractive to a certain type of person: it's easy; it offers an illusion of superiority, which is very attractive; but it's false. Psychotherapy also has a sort of religious function. People are seeking salvation from the terrors and tragedies of life and initiation into a deep and secret knowledge of the human soul, or something like that. When you talk scientifically it spoils the fun and ruins this orgy of pretention to knowledge that these people like to indulge in. I think the field will fall into disrepute and cease to be taken seriously by thinking people before it will manage to get its act together.

Smith went on to clarify his pessimistic predictions for the entire profession of psychotherapy:

I think Freud was right when he said there is something about being human that is antagonistic to understanding human nature. So when we try to understand ourselves, we are actually operating against the grain. I think that this is always going to be a problem. I might be wrong but I think the key to understanding psychotherapy and doing it properly involves precisely those aspects of our nature that we don't want to know about. Without scientific rigour, we have nothing to force us to stay on track.

In response to my question about possible predisposing factors that attract people to the profession, Smith said he thought they were probably quite varied:

Just off the top of my head I would guess that some of them are more kosher than others. In one sense doing psychotherapy for a living is like being paid to listen to gossip all day. All human beings have an inclination towards gossip. I'm using the term 'gossip' very broadly, not necessarily based on repeating stories but certainly being privy to the social dramas of others. That's a powerful factor attracting people to the profession of psychotherapy. Doing psychotherapy is like watching soap operas, and you also have the added factor of the gossip of supervision. Some people go into it because they want to have secret knowledge; they want to know how human beings work. That was certainly a motive of mine. Others want to be healers, to do good. The whole idea that one can somehow magically heal the psyche without the benefit of anything that can reasonably count as knowledge about how the mind really works is so stunningly narcissistic that it leaves one speechless.

In a nutshell what Smith seems to be saying is that there is a close association between grandiosity and the need to heal. Smith remarked that he believed it was 'cheaply acquired pseudo-knowledge'. He continued:

Let's face it, it's not exactly rocket science. It is easily acquired, completely unverified, and gives the illusion of genuine knowledge. That's grandiose; it's like being an astrologer. It's reassuring because you can feel good about yourself, deeply flattering because you are idealized by your patients. So there are various motives; and in terms of addressing them, I think the point in psychotherapy, as in everything else, is not what brings you there but what you are able to do once you get there. In my ideal training these considerations are addressed only indirectly. If, for example, someone has embarked on a course of training because they are looking for cheap knowledge, and they find themselves on an intellectually demanding, methodologically rigorous programme, they simply won't get what they were looking for. At that point they can choose to stay in, or opt out. I'm less interested in people's motives than in their competence. Anyway, it is impossible really to know people's motives; it's entirely speculative.

Smith said he believed that an important element of psychotherapy training should be dedicated to the testing of theories against data – which, he said, was not exactly supervision, as he has grown suspicious of what he calls the 'supervision industry' because it is nothing but 'the blind leading the blind', and he thinks that too much credibility is given to supervision:

It is a nice little gimmick for dealing with the disreputable face of psychotherapy. Supervision is supposed to be some sort of a safeguard against malpractice. But that is transparently ridiculous to anyone ouside the belief-system. Supervision has no more scientific basis than psychotherapy. It's no safeguard. I think that the best form of supervision is group supervision, also known as the clinical seminar format, because it lends itself to critically testing theory against data, to generating predictions.

Smith also expressed the view that the use of case-study material was a very poor way of teaching. He went on to say: 'First of all, case studies are full of lies; second, they are used tendentiously to support one therapy or another, and I think their prominence in psychotherapy training doesn't make sense.'

Given his strong, controversial beliefs about the training and profession of psychotherapy, I asked Smith if he felt that in his ideal training set-up he would expect the trainee to come with any particular personal attributes.

One of the reasons that these questions are really difficult to answer is because I have certain personal beliefs about what makes a good psychotherapist; but I am also simultaneously critical of those beliefs, as they are not evidentially validated. So take the following with a grain of salt. The trainee psychotherapist should be critical and self-critical. They might not start out that way but must be capable of becoming so. They also need to be persistent, and certainly need to have high frustration tolerance, which might be the most important characteristic of all. In practice, I don't actually believe in applying these criteria too rigidly as I think people change. So what you need to have in a psychotherapy training is a basic intellectual capacity to understand the material, and then you need mechanisms to filter out those that can't hack it. I think this is better than pre-judging. I'm in favour of minimal pre-judging. This is analogous to natural selection. Nature generates enormous diversity and selects ruthlessly.

In practice I have always shelved my prejudices about what makes a good psychotherapist, and if students conform to a group of conventional academic prerequisites, as far as I'm concerned they are suitable for a psychotherapy programme.

Smith had a great deal to say on the significant topic of counter-transference. It is an area on which he has written and lectured and is therefore a subject with which he has become closely associated. He began by saying that he was not happy with the concept for a number of reasons:

One of them is best illustrated by a wonderful quotation from some-one named Holmes that I often repeat, which is that 'transference is a theory that only applies to one person'. Countertransference is also a role-fixed concept, and as such it cannot really meaning-fully come under the umbrella of science. I mean, there simply can't be deep psychological phenomena that are specific to a particular role; these have got to be embedded in something broader, and that is precisely what the notion of countertransference does not address. To talk about 'countertransference phenomena' is to dignify countertransference inappropriately, because, as we both know, there are numerous notions of countertransference. It is extremely ambiguous and vague, if not actually incoherent. When people go on about countertransference one needs to inquire exactly what they have in mind.

The question we need to ask is what psychoanalysts were trying to get at with the notion of countertransference. To my mind, they were probably trying to get at two things. One is the way analysts mess things up in therapy, which is taken to reflect the analyst's mind operating in ways that are inconsistent with doing psychoanalysis. Traditionally there are two areas to consider under this heading: one is their defensiveness, and the other is their inappropriate expres-sion of unconscious wishes. This is often attributed to the analyst's 'residual neurosis', which is one of the greatest euphemisms of all time.

The second broad version of 'countertransference' is understood as the analyst's unconscious awareness of their patient's uncon-scious concerns, which is the Paula Heimann version. Alternatively, countertransference is understood as those mental states experi-enced by the analyst as a result of a sort of primitive communication, which is the Bion version. According to the Kleinian spin, then, the patient intentionally but unconsciously elicits phantasies or affective states in the analyst. This view is more positive, as it has to do with resonance. This conception of countertransference was probably started by Jung originally and then picked up and made popular in the fifties by the neo-Kleinians.

What we need to look for is how we can conceive of these things in a more scientifically sophisticated fashion. Now, with regard to the first version of countertransference, there is in my view a great deal of self-deception in the service of psychoanalytic grandiosity around this, because the idea is basically that you can be cured of counter-transference – in that original disruptive sense – in principle, if not in practice. The old chestnut that these disruptions occur because an analyst hasn't been analysed thoroughly enough is nonsense.

Smith continued by asserting that countertransference, in the first sense, is perfectly natural because human beings are built by evolution to deceive themselves in the interest of exploiting others:

Psychoanalysts and psychotherapists are human beings; this is part of human nature. It is there because it *works* and it works in every area of life, so you can't be cured of it, just as you can't be cured of breathing. It is just part of being a human being.

He said that he thought there was something dreadfully wrong with a field that does not acknowledge this and sees it instead as pathological:

It's self-serving, because it creates this mythology that there are some people who are relatively free of these tendencies. It en-courages people to conceal them. The real pathological case, if you want to use that kind of language, would be the analyst who didn't countertransfer; as self-deception, it is crucial for social human functioning. The best that we can do is to hold these tendencies in abeyance for brief periods of time. It's ludicrous to think that anyone can sustain this consistently for fifty minutes. Maybe twenty minutes here and there, but this requires vigilance and discipline, which doesn't come from being 'well analysed'.

As Smith explained, this way of viewing countertransference taps into basic human tendencies that Freud and his contemporaries didn't and couldn't understand because the scientific knowledge was not available at that time. He went on to say that now we have no excuses, as this knowledge has now been in existence for over thirty years.

As for countertransference as resonance, Smith said that we have to do the same thing: we have to understand what is going on. He referred to the evidence from work in evolutionary psychology, sociobiology and cognitive science that has been carried out on resonance. 'We know that human beings are built to resonate with each other. There are neurons in the brain *that respond to perceptions of others just as though one was doing it oneself*; it is the neurological basis of empathy.' Smith asserted that this attitude was not emphasized in the psychoanalytic literature at all. Psychological resonance is not a technique, nor is it a special property of therapists, it is the property of human minds, human brains:

> That is where the countertransference literature goes terribly wrong. In essence, this is seen as a special ability acquired from one's training, or at least a capacity that is in some mysterious way galvanized by one's training. This is sheer nonsense. We would be better off looking at resonance as *an innate, evolved psychological capacity for unconscious communication.*

Smith went on to refer to the extensive research carried out by Paul Ekman (1985) on the expressions of emotions. Ekman's studies show that there are universal forms of emotional expression which are involuntary; and in evolutionary terms it seems we recognize them unconsciously in very sophisticated ways. An example would be the automatical wrinkling of one's nose. Smith said he thought it was obvious that human brains were designed by natural selection to detect these subtle nonverbal expressions, and that so-called countertransference could be identified as a special case of a process in which all human beings engage. He further asserted that one then, of course, needs to be open to the probability that this process is happening both ways in therapy.

In the light of these hypotheses the term 'countertransference', which Smith described as originally denoting the 'therapist's reaction to the patient's transference', loses plausibility. The 'counter' of 'countertransference' implies that the therapist comes in as an innocent and is subjected to the seething sexual and aggressive impulses of the patient, which then evoke a counter-response. If, however, one accepts the evolutionary hypothesis, or just accepts the idea that both patient and therapist are members of the same species, then, as Smith asserts, they would both be subject to similar reactions and responses.

In relation to the initial definition of countertransference as a distortion of perception and thinking, Smith declared:

If it weren't for these distortions, we would just see things as they are. How then do we explain why there are about thirty different forms of psychoanalysis and all are contradictory? With regard to the newer version of countertransference, it is asserted that the analyst's inner processes allow them to make inferences about the client's unconscious issues. This idea has a basic plausibility; however, there is no research and no evidence to establish this, other than anecdotal evidence.

Smith was also in disagreement with the communicative principle, which considers that these failures on the therapist's part are due to 'therapist madness', again on the basis that it is entirely natural and normal for all human beings to be prone to deceive others as well as themselves. 'The problem is that if we are self-deceptive by nature, we cannot to any extent be introspective about when we are deceiving ourselves. This is where the patient's unconscious communications give you something that transcends your own treacherous subjectivity.' However, if deception is an ineluctable attribute of human nature then we must all be caught up in a continuous cycle of interpersonal and intrapersonal deception with little hope of discerning the wood from the trees. This view of human behaviour and interaction is not dissimilar to Sartre's view of individuals as mired in bad faith, needing to remain divided from themselves and from others.

Smith agreed that his comments on the spuriousness of introspection is evocative of the early psychoanalytic work of Margaret Little, who wrote (Little, 1951) of the mirror that the patient also holds up to the analyst:

Yes, the mirror metaphor is immensely useful: you need a point outside of yourself that is methodologically trackable. The whole rationale of insight-oriented psychotherapy is that through training your subjectivity becomes purified, that it becomes a reliable guide. The new ideas on countertransference suggest the same – that you can just look into yourself. These ideas that the truth can be revealed to you date back at least four hundred years to Descartes. But this is a false and misleading doctrine. The truth about some aspects of yourself will never be revealed to you, no matter how diligently you introspect. You need a point of reference outside of yourself, and even then it is hard to hear.

With respect to the training associated with any therapeutic approach and the practice of the latter, what needs to be possible is that it be acceptable for people to criticize each other's views. Smith remarked: 'You can't have it all internalistic. That's like relying on introspection. You need to be able to say, as Michael Fordham said, "Thank God for all my enemies, who keep me sane".' This, Smith emphasized, should be part of the psychotherapeutic culture 'like it's part of the intellectual culture in science and philosophy – a culture that honours and encourages criticism'.

Comment

The psychoanalytic model of human nature is founded on the premise that human beings are naturally resistant to acknowledging and being aware of the conflicting infantile sexual and aggressive desires that have fuelled their childhood relationships and that continue to exert a pressure on all their adult relationships. The psychoanalytic process is therefore devoted to exploring and addressing these unconscious dilemmas as they arise in the patient's associations in relation to the analyst. To some extent, the therapist is expected to be relatively free of resistance in order to be able to assist the patient in this process. It is generally agreed that this comparatively neutral analytic position can to a reasonable extent be achieved by the analyst's undergoing his or her own personal training analysis. It is at this point that David Smith's thesis diverges radically, as he asserts that we are all by nature self-deceptive and no amount of training analysis can stop us operating against the grain. In keeping with his scientific and evolutionist stance, Smith claims that the notion of countertransference defined as a form of unconscious interpersonal resonance must, therefore, also be an ability that applies to the patient.

Although self-deception and resistance are fundamental to the psychoanalytic theory of human nature, the fact that one person, namely the analyst, can aid another, the patient, to become more aware of their own unconscious dilemmas, presupposes that it is possible to override what Smith believes are innate deceptive and self-deceptive survival mechanisms. The preceding radical and controversial argument presented by Smith takes issue with the entire field of psychotherapy and specifically with psychoanalysis. The idea that transference (defined as a distortion) must also be a feature that applies to the therapist is also in keeping with his thesis.

Yet Freud's brief exploration into the realm of countertransference almost a hundred years ago seem to have anticipated, albeit in a very rudimentary way, some of the current thinking in evolutionary and cognitive psychology. His initial development of the concept acknowledged that the analyst as well as the patient would be prone to distort reality. We also see Smith concurring with the second definition of countertransference as a type of involved clear-sightedness of the patient's experience, which developed out of the Kleinian tradition. Where the 'new' countertransference elaborated by Smith, and developed by evolutionary theorists, differs is in the claim that it is an unconscious survival ability that has developed over time as a means of detecting the deception of others.

The fact that evolutionary and cognitive psychologists are involved in rigorous empirical research, some of which has yielded some interesting and useful data, is to be applauded. The fact that psychoanalysis and psychotherapy research is lacking in scientific rigour suggests that it will remain open to both internal and external criticism. To assert that human beings are unconsciously deceptive, self-deceptive and insightful is a psychoanalytic dictum. The likelihood of these human traits applying to only one member of the therapeutic dyad must be considered to be untenable. Nevertheless, evolutionary psychology has yet to prove the motivations behind these human characteristics or that they have developed out of the ruthless need to survive.

The recent research from evolutionary psychology combined with the methodological inconsistencies in psychoanalytic theory has led Smith to critique the entire field of psychoanalysis and psychotherapy. He firmly believes that training for the profession, if it is to survive, needs to be placed on a more systematic and scientific footing. In his view most, if not all, psychotherapy training currently on offer is lacking in methodological rigour. He also maintains that trainings should be less partisan and more broadly based in order that the scientific discrepancies in a range of psychotherapeutic models be compared and addressed. Smith refers to the scientific spirit of collaboration and berates the lack of co-operative criticism across the different schools of psychoanalysis and psychotherapy. He does, however, point out the implausibility of being able to achieve such a task, given that from both a Freudian and an evolutionary perspective, human nature is considered to be innately and inherently self-deceptive and suspicious of others.

Conclusion

The psychoanalytic psychotherapy programme offered at the Tavistock Centre which has been outlined by Jonathan Bradley is a specific training in that it is primarily focused on working with children. Although this Tavistock programme is dedicated to working with the unconscious, its trainees, as Bradley pointed out, are confronted with the further complication of having to struggle with the unstable and mercurial behaviour that is typical of children and that inhibits their ability to free associate in the way adults are generally able to do. Presumably the importance that is placed on the course's infant observation component is to a large extent related to trainees' needs to recognize the ways in which their very personal countertransference responses are likely to be exacerbated under these particular clinical conditions.

The informative and diagnostic purpose of attending to countertransference issues has been clearly highlighted by Lesley Murdin. She considered this to be a fundamental and consistent feature of the therapeutic interaction, needing to be addressed throughout the WPF training but also to be recognized as a significant part of the interpersonal dynamics between applicant and interviewer at the training's selection stage.

In contrast to the approaches of the first two interviewees, David Smith has presented a challenging and controversial view of the fundamental principles that he believes are missing from the psychotherapy trainings currently available. Smith's voice is very much of a minority voice in so far as he rejects the concept of countertransference as being a disordered, partisan and even illogical concept, and he does so on the basis of evidence that is now emerging, and gathering, in the field of evolutionary psychology.

Chapter 10

Relational Patterns
and Paradoxes

Being-with-others is intrinsic to human existence, and the attendant frustrations and suffering that overarch this reality are one of the more pressing factors that induce people to seek professional help. This given of existence also suggests that the function of psychotherapy would, ipso facto, be to prioritize these interpersonal features. The unconscious tendency to transfer infantile relational patterns onto the here-and-now analytic interaction is at the centre of psychoanalytic thought and practice, and though Klein's subsequent revisions emphasized the child's current conflicts, the presupposition of transference as an intrapsychic repetitive distortion was never in dispute. The insurmountable problem of the analyst as a neutral observer was cogently argued by Margaret Little (1951) and systematized in the interpersonal approach devised by Harry Stack Sullivan (1953; 1964), which was based on the idea that the therapist is also subject to comparable misrepresentations. Other writers, such as David Mann and Gerald Schoenewolf, have emphasized the conspiratorial connection between transference and countertransference in order, it would seem, to counter the prevailing view of an asymmetry and lack of common ground between patient and analyst. However, the antecedents of transference as a patient-centred concept are still firmly entrenched in the dominant psychoanalytic model, while the post-Freudian formulation of countertransference as a form of discernment appears to have held strong.

This dominance is consistent with the principles of psychoanalysis and corresponds to its distinctive relational focus, which is based on the *difference* between patient and analyst. It is a one-person psychology in the sense that the patient's relationship to the analyst is based on a misconception which the analyst must interpret primarily in relation to the past. Although it is accepted that the analyst's idiosyncrasies and transference residues will on occasion interfere with this process, the practitioner is obliged to fulfil his or her main professional duty by illuminating the difference between the patient's wishes and conflicts in relation to the parents and the here-and-now relationship. It is hoped that in this arduous stage of 'working-through' the patient will become aware of and accept that their relationship to the analyst is based on a mistaken identity that is rooted in the past. The dismantling of these illusions, which are predicated on incestuous and aggressive impulses, is expected to facilitate the mobilizing of the patient's inner resources and enable them to loosen these parental ties, culminating in the final separation from the analyst.

The consistent refrains that consolidate the psychoanalytic process are the need to accept that relationships are disappointing and that separation and loss are inevitable. The benefits of acknowledging this unsatisfactory state of human affairs, that is woven into the psycho-analytic paradigm of human nature, is also intimately linked to the themes of vulnerability and loss of omnipotence. As Ian Craib has stated: 'I think what is valuable in Freud, and the other psychoanalytic theorists who followed him, is the always implicit, sometimes explicit message that we can never quite be what we want to be' (1994, p. 34).

The psychoanalytic relationship is based on the belief that the analyst is in the position to unravel the patient's convoluted, self-deceptive verbal and non-verbal patterns of relating. In principle, the here-and-now analytic relationship is the vehicle which enables the patient to separate and to perceive both the analyst and their own family-related frustrations in a more realistic light. Paradoxically, however, it is not unusual to glean from comments expressed by ex-patients that they continue to perceive their analysts as idealized objects. Yet, this contradiction is not altogether surprising since the psychoanalytic process is founded on the idea that it is possible and meaningful for one person individually and sensitively to discern the illusions and self-deceptive machinations of another – a capacity and disposition that can be regarded as reinforcing omnipotence. Further, the existence of the two very different countertransference definitions serves to reinforce the analyst's powerful and influential position, since he or she may opt generally to discard one in favour of the other or, at his or her own discretion, to use both on different occasions.

The variance between psychoanalysis and the communicative paradigm could not be more stark as the latter is based on the proposition that the patient and therapist are part of a unified system. Furthermore, the patient's realistic need to focus on and grasp the trustworthiness of the situation (via unconscious perception) is deemed appreciably more intense than the analyst's, owing to their lack of power in the encounter. 'Therapist madness', by contrast, is a concept that is overtly exclusive to the practitioner. In his attempt to redistribute the balance of power between analyst and patient Robert Langs was not satisfied to grant equal status to both parties, but has seen fit almost to reverse the activities (transference and countertransference) that have traditionally identified the two members of the psychoanalytic couple. Although the 'madness' of the therapist is understood to be akin to self-deception, it is not transferential in so far as it is viewed as not based on distortions linked to the past but rather connected to ontological and ontic issues that define the human condition. Unconscious perception, in this schema, which is a capacity granted to the patient, corresponds to the definition of countertransference as a form of insight and acute understanding.

This revolutionary inversion of the psychoanalytic paradigm does not appear to have dealt with the dilemma of the patient–therapist imbalance, as it can be seen to have tipped the scales in the opposite direction. However, as I understand it, one of the rationales for this counteraction is related to the idea that the person (therapist) who is responsible for analysing and interpreting the material of another is also the one who is more prone to confuse and distort the other's (patient's) difficulties with their own dilemmas. The fact that the patient has none of these responsibilities and is only expected to free associate suggests, in this author's view, that their material will be more authentic.

Self-deception, science and paradox

Although the principles that define the communicative model are profoundly at odds with the tenets of psychoanalytic thought, it is Langs's strivings to prove mathematically the universality of his findings which have led to criticisms similar to those levelled against Freud and his need for psychoanalysis to be recognized scientifically. Langs has pledged his allegiance to scientific investigation; he claims that his framework suppositions are universally applicable and has stated that his model is 'readily testable' (Smith, 1989) but without providing the necessary data to support these claims. In the paper 'Reconsidering Communicative Psychoanalysis' Piers Myers (2000b) puts forward a methodological proposal according to which the relationship between the therapist's behaviour and the patient's narratives may be observably tested. In his concluding remarks Myers states:

The burden of this paper is that lack of clarity in the central claims of communicative psychoanalysis has served to obscure the challenges faced by its proponents. There has been a failure to set out what these claims mean in terms of observable data, and this runs counter to its advocates' espousal of a 'scientific approach'. (2000b, p. 216)

The communicative approach is committed to the belief that human beings disclose their true interpersonal concerns primarily through encoded communication. In evolutionary terms, the thrust to survive has necessitated the development of antennae that can detect the deceptions of others, given that deception offers an evolutionary advantage. As we have also seen, it is easier to deceive others if we are unaware of our own deceit (simply put, we are all good liars and even better at kidding ourselves). However, at the same time, though what we overtly say cannot be trusted, we give ourselves away in the stories we tell each other. This view of human nature suggests that our authentic experiences tend to slip out automatically, most often unbeknown to us. An acceptance of these premises would require us then to doubt the truth of many of our conscious machinations. John Gray (2002) has explored this lack of human neutrality in relation to scientific investigation:

Science will never be used chiefly to pursue truth, or to improve human life. The uses of knowledge will always be as shifting and crooked as humans are themselves. . . . These are not flaws that can be remedied. Science cannot be used to reshape humankind in a more rational mould. Any new-model humanity will only reproduce the familiar deformities of its designers. It is a strange fancy to suppose that science can bring reason to an irrational world, when all it can ever do is give another twist to normal madness. These are not just inferences from history. The upshot of scientific enquiry is that humans cannot be other than irrational. (p. 28)

Gray also concludes that human activities are mostly unconscious and that 'No degree of self awareness can make us self-transparent' (p. 69).

Paradoxically, even though Langs is resolutely committed to the idea of the authentic nature of scientific data, the Langsian theory of the human condition is clearly in agreement with Gray's central thesis. Furthermore, owing to the model's lack of developmental theory and Langs's psychoanalytic antecedents, the communicative paradigm tends to be perceived as inherently linked to psychoanalysis and therefore somewhat scant. In this author's opinion, Langs's attitude and these aforementioned factors have sadly tended to obscure and undermine his more significant creative relational contributions. My own research was prompted by these concerns and was intended to help facilitate, access and untangle some of the philosophical here-and-now properties of that approach.

Self-deception and being-with-others

The Existential movement has explored in great depth the individual's struggle to accept both the freedom and the limits of the human condition and our inherent reluctance to engage openly with others. In the main, existential psychotherapy tends to examine these dilemmas only in terms of the client's world-view outside therapy. The communicative emphasis on boundary disturbances, which routinely arise in the here-and-now interaction, reinforces the view of the individual as averse to assimilating and accepting the restrictions of life identified by philosophers of the Existential tradition. The proclivity to relate hypocritically, which is indicated in the term 'bad faith', can also be recognized in the spontaneous need to express interpersonal emotional concerns covertly and in the recipient's diminished ability to hear them.

The theme of self-deception is embodied in the notion of bad faith. Individuals take flight into bad faith from the conflicts that inevitably emerge in their interactions with others. The human tendency to objectify the other is concisely depicted in Sartre's vignette of the 'Man at the Keyhole' (Sartre, 1943), who, on becoming aware of being observed, is caught by the 'look' of the other as he realizes that he can be objectively described and labelled as a snoop or eavesdropper. Knowing that other people can objectify us in this way also motivates us to objectify ourselves and to 'pin down' the other before they do the same to us. Sartre pursues his argument by claiming that human interaction is impelled by a need to control other people because of this threat.

It is suggested that Sartre's central thesis of the incessant struggle for power and control, which is considered to be part and parcel of all human interaction, is exemplified in the communicative undertaking to address the relational struggle within the consulting room. The communicative therapist is expected consistently to expose himself or herself to the 'look' of the client, and cannot maintain a position of proud, detached observer under the client's perceptive gaze. An example: a therapist who arrives late for a session is required explicitly to acknowledge the client's negative perception of the disturbance that will be expected to emerge in the latter's ensuing narrative. What is identified by Sartre as the inexorable feature of bad faith is highlighted and supported by the communicative model as the natural tendency to oppose and hinder this procedure. From a communicative perspective, 'bad faith' here refers to the therapist's refusal, or inability, to consider his or her own contribution (arriving late) to the theme of lateness that may be expected to be concealed in the client's narrative material.

The communicative approach also emphasizes the unnerving openendedness and incompleteness of the human condition, focusing, as it does, on the client's aptitude for supervising the therapist and the treatment process. This is paralleled by the view of the therapist's fluctuating disposition and need to receive guidance from the client. Langs's model is explicit about our unconscious capacity to accept the ontic and ontological boundaries of existence, although his model contains a more pessimistic view of our *conscious* capacity to acknowledge these human limitations, which is in contrast to the philosophy of Existentialism and Sartre's thesis. A very strong focus on the relational quality of the encounter echoes Sartre's injunction that psychoanalysis needs to attend to the interpersonal subject/object vicissitudes, as Betty Cannon explains: 'Sartre believes that the mechanistic, authoritarian approach to psychoanalysis, in which the analyst is only subject and the analysand perpetual object, is mistaken' (1991, p. 8). Essentially, Sartre's thesis illuminates the way in which the desire and struggle for power and control limits the possibility for relating authentically. His work also underscores the paradoxical features of the human condition. Human beings are both limited and free and can only exert their freedom by the attitude they take to their essential limitations. Bad faith is the device that people employ to deny their uncertain and vulnerable position in the world, which is why they attempt to control other people in the same way as they control objects. This author postulates that an integration of the principles represented by the concept of bad faith offers the therapist a very valuable set of tools, as these principles demand that the therapist consider both the significance of their own contribution to what takes place within the client–therapist interaction and their potential to exploit their position.

A further major feature of Existentialist thinking that is high-lighted in Sartre's work relates to the notion of consciousness or self-reflection. In the text *Understanding Phenomenology* (Hammond,

Howarth and Keat, 1991), this notion is defined from a Sartrean perspective: 'consciousness is nothing more than self-awareness' (p. 108). Sartre argues that human beings are predisposed to focus on the specific activity in which they are involved at any given time, and so tend to remain unaware of, or omit to give attention to, the many other possibilities on which that they could reflect from a variety of other perspectives. Sartre's example 'the Girl in the Café' (Sartre, 1943), who ignores the fact that her companion has taken her hand, is cited as an everyday occurrence of how people limit their consciousness and their choices by negating an aspect of their experience. Communicative psychotherapy offers a model of human nature that attests to the significance of unconscious perception, which can be discerned through encoded communication. Both of these features are antagonistic to a philosophy of existence, given that the Existential tradition eschews the idea of hypothetical models of human nature, including such abstractions as 'the unconscious'. While the author acknowledges the difficulty of bridging this divide, it is also contended that the existential dilemmas that are underlined in bad faith give strong support to the communicative emphasis on the relational, contextual or being-with aspects of the therapeutic encounter.

Although Sartre's account of bad faith was put forward as an inextricable human trait, his theory of consciousness nevertheless views it as a trait for which we are *responsible*, which to some extent can be transcended, albeit with great effort. This tension is also recognizable in the communicative defence of 'therapist madness' and acknowledged in the communicative paradigm. However, as David Smith has pointed out (Chapters 2 and 9), if self-deception offers an evolutionary advantage then it cannot be thought of as mad – it must be seen as a normal component of human nature and human relating. Sartre's evocative descriptions of bad faith furnish us with easily recognizable examples that reinforce a view of the ubiquity of human self-deception and its relational obstacles. It is suggested that a more thorough focus on the therapist's, rather than the client's, relational concealments can encourage the development of a reciprocal strength and authenticity in the client. As Cannon observes:

> Despite the dangers to oneself which self-revelations might pose, secrecy provides another kind of danger. Consequently, Sartre points out that 'this dark region that we have within ourselves, which is at once dark for me and dark for others, can only be illuminated for ourselves in trying to illuminate it for others' (L/S: p12).

This becomes clear when one understands that for Sartre the beginning of self-reflection lies to a great extent in the reflection of others on the self, to which one can now add disclosure to others who see and (one hopes) comprehend oneself. One can probably do this only if one has previously undergone a 'radical conversion' to a philosophy of freedom – that is, if one can bear to have the other see oneself differently from the way one would have wished. (1991, pp. 99–100)

A concentration on the struggle to engage, which is implied in Langs's model and emphasized in an explanation of why we are pulled into bad faith, must focus on the relational defences that are inherent features of human interaction. We tend to experience anxiety under the gaze of other people and are likely to be drawn into a mode of interaction which will offer protection from our being seen in a light that conflicts with our preferred (and would-be fixed) self-image. The practice of psychotherapy provides us with ample opportunity to hide behind the role in order to escape this disappointment. However, this tendency is also, and importantly, grist to the mill, because it provides the therapist with the very tools with which the vicissitudes of bad faith can be explored between client and therapist in the here-and-now. Sartre's thesis also reinforces the laborious and deeply challenging nature of communicative psychotherapy, in as much as the therapist is required continuously to confront their own defensive use of power and to expose what protects us all from the terror of facing the relentless concerns that impede our ability to relate. The two major mechanisms of bad faith pointed to by Langs's relational model are the impulse to recount stories that are apparently disconnected from the current scenario and the impulse to disturb the boundaries of the relationship. These impulses together allow the individual to remain estranged from the reality of any immediate conflict and to deny their essential isolation and limitations.

The exposing features of this approach differ from counter-transference self-disclosures advocated by some analysts in so far as interventions are based on *the client's* discrete (but penetrating) narrative-encoded observations rather than on the therapist's sub-jective emotional experience. They also contrast with the classical countertransference view, which claims that the analyst's distorted affects should be examined outside the therapy so that they can be excluded from the encounter as quickly and as thoroughly as possible. The notion of self-deception developed from evolutionary psychology suggests that self-deception is a necessary, albeit pernicious, survival mechanism as its primary function is to obscure the conflicts between people. The ontological description of bad faith also implies that it is a deeply-rooted characteristic of existence. At the same time, the notion of countertransference is a metapsychological term that refers to both resonance and misrepresentation, between which the analyst is expected subjectively and single-handedly to differentiate, unlike the patient, who is generally predisposed to misjudge and misconstrue reality. Moreover, in contrast to the classical psychoanalytic position, which implies that other people's emotions can be accessed through our own affects, the communicative and existential models each claim that it is only through other people that we can become aware of ourselves.

Relational paradoxes

Although communicative theory accepts in principle the implausibility of providing a fixed frame, Langs's focus on ground rules and his rigid boundary imperatives nevertheless imply that the provision of a 'secure frame' is both desirable and possible. For Sartre, anxiety, or what he terms 'nausea', is evoked on those rare occasions when the individual becomes aware that neither the environment nor other people are amenable to his or her control. An appreciation of the abhorrent nature of this awareness reinforces the idea both of the impossibility and of the meaninglessness of 'secure frame' conditions, suggesting instead that the therapeutic agenda should be devoted to an investigation of this existential struggle and interpersonal predicament.

The Jewish philosopher Martin Buber (1922), who is also associated with the Existential movement, made the distinction between two alternative types of encounter: 'I–it' and 'I–thou'. To say 'I' of necessity means to refer to oneself in relation to another, for although 'I' denotes the difference between people, to be an 'I' means that there must also be a 'you' – which means that 'I can never be totally separate'. Therefore, in common with other Existentialist thinkers, Buber considered that the person is always *in relation*. To relate in an 'I–it' mode means to encounter the other person in a piecemeal, analytical, objective way. The 'I–it' meeting can therefore only ever be a partial and one-sided interaction between people. An 'I–thou' meeting, by contrast, is an encounter that acknowledges the whole person and requires the 'I' to be fully present. 'I–thou' is an interdependent interchange, which acknowledges 'thou' as separate and gives to the 'thou' the space to be their own, inimitable, unique self. As Rose Graf-Taylor (1996) has commented:

> Mutuality must be understood in the context of dialogical relation. It is not merely a reciprocal exchange or equity between two people. It is the quality of the relationship maintained through a commitment of the partners to be present, responsive, and responsible to each other and to the relationship. (p. 332)

Nevertheless, Buber admits that the 'I–thou' interaction is an ideal which can never be adhered to, and that even on those occasions when we can, it is likely rapidly to deteriorate and revert back to 'I–it'. Buber also took issue with Carl Rogers' humanistic conviction that people are inherently trustworthy and good, or that the therapeutic encounter could be a meeting between two equals. He argued instead (Rogers, 1960), in a true Existential fashion, that the human condition is constituted by opposites (see further Friedman, 1996).

The difficulty of granting equal status to others, which difficulty hijacks the chance of genuine interpersonal exchange, has been a consistent Existential focus. It is suggested that a dovetailing of the two approaches serves to illustrate more emphatically the disconcerting and challenging nature of communicative practice and the therapeutic importance of attending to the existential dynamics that are built into, but only implied, in the model. It is further posited that by emphasizing the cardinal pressures and relational dilemmas of existence, the likelihood of applying the method in a customized, prescriptive and essentially defensive way may be reduced.

The Existential tradition asserts that participation, being-with-others and the relational realm cannot be eliminated from our being-in-the-world. Ernest Spinelli (1994) has clarified the significance of this maxim; he does, however, describe 'relational' as the therapist's attempt to place himself or herself in the client's shoes. The existential psychotherapist Hans Cohn (1997) also endorses this relational imperative. However, both Cohn and Spinelli's clinical examples are uniformly focused on clarifying and understanding the client's experience of relationships outside the therapeutic setting, and do not appear to include or consider the here-and-now interaction – a puzzling exclusion, given that their approach is grounded in a philosophy which gives priority to the incessant difficulties of how we are with others and the significance of being in the here-and-now. Existential

psychotherapy encourages clients to reflect on the ontic and ontological aspects of their existence. The relational process of communicative psychotherapy attends to being-in-the-world as it reveals itself
between patient and client. This author postulates that the communicative paradigm is in fact essentially grounded in the philosophy
of Existentialism, as the general thrust of the work in the consulting
room mirrors the ontological dilemmas of human existence in the
wider context of how we are with others in the world at large.

Existential philosophy has also inspired and contributed to the
development of the person-centered approach to psychotherapy; but
unlike its predecessor, the person-centered approach tends to empha-
size the growth facet of existence rather than the relentless dual
tensions that Existentialism asserts to be the hallmark of the human
condition. In this sense the humanistic movement would not qualify
for inclusion in a paradigm that is grounded in an examination of the
dynamics and vicissitudes of existence.

Relational dynamics and systems theory

Systems theory has revealed that change cannot be precisely pre-
dicted – that it is born out of crisis, or chaos, and that it can be
recognized by the repeating patterns exhibited in the movement of the
system as the latter continuously moves between chaos and order.
The patterns which illustrate that a system is in chaos are known as
fractals. The term 'fractal' is derived from the Latin *fractus*, meaning
irregular or fragmented. Benoit Mandelbrot's (1977) discovery of the
paradoxical nature of chaos led to the understanding that the natural
world has developed in what is known as a 'self-similar' way. 'Fractal
self-similarity' can be found in trees, coastlines, cauliflowers, the
vascular system and throughout the human body. Through the notions
of fractals and self-similarity it has been possible to uncover how the
world has evolved through interaction, and how a system's pattern is
generated and contained within itself. These repetitive patterns can be
discerned by either magnifying or shrinking an aspect of the system,
showing that self-similarity continues to repeat itself to infinity. This
process may be likened to the fragmented holographic image, which
becomes progressively less clear but continues to retain its durability in
a holistic way:

> A coastline is produced by the chaotic action of waves and other
> geological forces. These act at every scale to generate shapes that

repeat on smaller scales, a pattern roughly similar to the one at the large scale. In other words, chaos generates forms and leaves behind tracks that possess what scientists refer to as self-similarity at many different scales. (Briggs and Peat, 1999, p. 102)

Taking a simple example like a tree, it is easy to see the way in which its general form is repeated throughout the system from its trunk to its branches, twigs, and so on. Its seed has the potential to develop into a tree but is dependent on the quality of the soil, the climate and other environmental factors before being able to 'reiterate' its self-similarity over time. That is, not only are the elements of the tree, a particular system, related but they are also interrelated and dependent on other systems.

To apply these remarks to the world of people, when we notice that someone is mean or generous with money and then look more carefully at their behaviour, these same traits tend to be repeated at various levels; so that someone who is in this context, say, generous is also likely to be giving in terms of their time, emotions and their general openness to the world. These repetitive patterns are also noticeable between couples, in families and in organizations. If the management policy in an organization is characterized by a lack of communication, this same dynamic will be repeated throughout the entire system, and will influence staff members' relationships with each other and interactions with their clients.

The mechanism that powers and controls this interactive process is feedback. It is feedback which maintains this steady state, sometimes to the detriment of the system. This is why people often disapprove of whistle blowers as they are prepared to reveal the underlying chaos within a system that to all intents and purposes appears to be stable. This example also shows how change can occur suddenly and unpredictably under chaotic conditions and can lead either to new possibilities and transformation or to disintegration. It is no wonder that we often prefer to stay in frustrating, stagnant but familiar situations, knowing that if we confront them we cannot be sure of the outcome. Systems thinking and chaos theory graphically illustrate the vital role that chaotic or crisis situations play in creatively moving the system from a simple to a more complex form of organization and growth.

Generally speaking, it is only family therapy that has employed some of the principles of this compelling, non-linear view of the world and its contents. However, the research, case studies and publications presented from the family systems tradition do not tend to take into consideration the major systemic imperative that the therapist is also an *integral* part of the therapeutic system.

The notion of repetition is a familiar term to both the intrapsychic and object relations orientations within psychoanalysis, and refers to the innate tendency automatically to repeat and regress to earlier patterns of behaviour and relating, understood as a means of staving off the anxiety that precedes and accompanies change. The compulsion to repeat acts as a form of resistance to change, as the familiar and haunting echoes of infantile experiences and past relationships (however problematical) are felt to be safer than the new and unknown. The compulsion to repeat was also used by Freud to help to explain the character of the death instinct, and may be linked to the 'oceanic feeling' of which he writes (1930), as in the need to retreat to a quiescent, stagnant or immobile place, where being can be replaced by a fantasized non-existence.

From a Systems perspective, the psychoanalytic concept of repetition can be taken up in various ways. For example, the need to regress – a need to return to a more dormant state – may be characterized as a form of ego-fragmentation but in fact can, paradoxically, impel the person to deal with the threat of separation and isolation that precedes change and possible integration. Repetition can also be activated unconsciously as a form of feedback or homeostasis in order to provide the individual with a temporary, albeit spurious, sense of balance. Repetition to an earlier stage of development can also reveal the individual's patterning, 'fractal nature' or narrative over time, and should also offer clues as to the environmental factors that are inhibiting their potential for growth.

The relational aspects of communicative psychotherapy have many characteristics that are consistent with Systems thinking. Notably, the therapist is expected to address the patient's experience of disorder in the immediate context of the therapeutic environment. Chaos in the therapeutic system can be inferred from the patient's self-similar narrative communications that coalesce around a theme that links the manifest stories to the therapeutic arena, to the patient's current interpersonal life outside the therapeutic setting and to the patient's past interactions. These stories can be described as underlying fractal patterns that alert the therapist to the particular disorder in the system. It is conjectured that the potential for new order, and the emergence of new patterns of relating, may occur as a result of the therapist's ability to acknowledge and examine the way in which the same pattern is being repeated in the immediate encounter via the narrative feedback from the patient.

Paradoxically, even though communicative psychotherapy has been described as essentially systemic, its prescriptive procedures may counteract the therapist's ability to maintain a relational systemic focus. It has also been suggested (Prince-Warren, 1994) that the explicit focus of this approach on technical procedures may also decrease the therapist's empathic capacities.

The tenets of humanistic psychotherapy do not match the systemic view that self-organization emerges in response to the tension between confusion and symmetry. However, the humanistic belief in the self-actualizing tendency of all living systems, which can be either potentiated or frustrated by the wider system or environment, does in some way take into account the essential idea of interconnectedness. Integrative psychotherapy, as its name suggests, is predisposed to consider and incorporate the contributions of ideas and methods from competing schools of psychotherapy, which implies a propensity to recognize some of the similarities between approaches. Nevertheless, it would seem that the motivation to integrate generally has behind it the desire to widen and extend the therapist's range of techniques.

The traditional psychoanalytic approach takes as one of its central tenets the patient's predisposition to transfer material from the past onto the current situation. It is, therefore, a linear model in the sense that it calls attention to the asymmetrical factors that separate analyst and patient. However, non-linear theory has shown that all systems are exceedingly sensitive to their initial conditions, which means that the attitude and position at the onset will have a powerful influence on the system's trajectory. If it is assumed from the beginning that the patient's communications are distorted while the therapist's are relatively insightful, these same patterns will tend to be repeated at every level, like a self-fulfilling prophecy.

All of us who work from within a dynamic therapeutic approach by definition understand that there are times when we need to call on great reserves of emotional strength to tolerate the chaos and confusion that inevitably accompany our work with clients. We also know that an integral part of the therapeutic task involves making distinctions and judgements about the truth of our own and our clients' internal, affective states, which will always be open to doubt. Nevertheless, it seems to me that if we are prepared to adopt, as a first principle, an acceptance of the shared and similar, rather than different, qualities that exist in ourselves and in our clients, this will help to give a more authentic quality to what takes place in the therapeutic encounter. Furthermore, the commitment to such an attitude will allow the therapist to be guided in important ways by the client's perceptive and insightful contributions.

I would like to express my gratitude and debt once again to all the participants who so readily agreed to have their informed opinions and reflections included as a major part of this book's ongoing debate, and who did so in such a scholarly and scientific fashion. It has been enormously satisfying to me personally to see how each contributor, in his or her own way, has acknowledged the paradoxical and contingent nature of their chosen position, and the indeterminate, often mystifying and interdependent features of the therapeutic process.

It is my hope, as author, that the views expressed in this book will stimulate a move within the profession to challenge the present climate, characterized as it is by insularity, avoidance and dogmatic schisms, and to loosen what is so often at present a tenacious clinging to and defence of our preferred models. I look forward to seeing this debate extended to the wider system that exists across the competing therapeutic schools of thought, as these are the essential elements that constitute the system of psychotherapy. If we consider all of the schools of psychotherapy as forming one system, this may allow us to explore the idea of encountering one another in a way that makes it possible to recognize and acknowledge the commonalities within the system as a whole, and this in turn may lead us to uncover some as yet untapped and rich resources among ourselves and to determine some important and fruitful areas of future research and collaboration.

References

Alexandris, A. and Vaslamatzis, G. (eds.) (1993) *Countertransference: Theory, Technique, Teaching*. London: Karnac Books.

Badcock, C. (1995) *PsychoDarwinism: The New Synthesis of Darwin and Freud*. London: Flamingo.

Bertalannfy, L. von (1968) *General Systems Theory*. New York: George Braziller Inc.

Bion, W. R. (1959) 'Attacks on linking', *International Journal of Psycho-Analysis*, 40: 308–315.

Bion, W. R. (1962) *Learning from Experience*. London: Heinemann.

Bion, W. R. (1970) *Attention and Interpretation*. London: Tavistock.

Bohm, D. (1980) *Wholeness and the Implicate Order*. Boston: Routledge & Kegan Paul.

Bollas, C. (1987) *The Shadow of the Object: Psychoanalysis of the Unthought Known*. London: Free Association Books.

Borossa, J. (ed.) (1999) *Selected Writings: Sándor Ferenczi*. Harmondsworth: Penguin Books.

Briggs, J. and Peat, F. D. (1999) *Seven Life Lessons of Chaos*. New York: HarperCollins.

Buber, M. (1922) *I and Thou [Ich Und Du]* (trans. R. G. Smith), 2nd edn. Edinburgh: T. & T. Clark, 1950.

Burgoyne, B. (1994) 'Response to Langs and Badalamenti from a Lacanian psychoanalyst', *British Journal of Psychotherapy*, 11: 105–109.

Butz, M. (1997) *Chaos and Complexity: Implications for Psychological Theory and Practice*. Washington, DC: Taylor & Francis.

Byng-Hall, J. (2002a) 'Relieving parentified children's burdens in families with insecure attachment patterns', *Family Process*, 41: 375–88.

Byng-Hall, J. (2002b) 'My story why I became a family therapist', in J. Hills (ed.), *Rescripting Family Experiences: The Therapeutic Influences of John Byng-Hall*. London: Whurr Publishers.

Camus, A. (1942) *The Myth of Sisyphus [Le Mythe de Sisyphe]* (trans. J. O'Brien). Harmondsworth: Penguin Books, 1975.

Cannon, B. (1991) *Sartre and Psychoanalysis*. Kansas: University Press of Kansas.

Capra, F. (1996) *The Web of Life: A New Synthesis of Mind and Matter*. London: HarperCollins.

Cheifetz, L. G. (1984) 'Framework violations in the psychotherapy of clinic patients', in J. Raney (ed.), *Listening and Interpreting: The Challenge of the Work of Robert Langs*. New York: Jason Aronson.

Clarkson, P. (1995) *The Therapeutic Relationship*. London: Whurr Publishers Ltd.

Cohen, M. B. (1952) 'Counter-transference and anxiety', *Psychiatry*, **15**: 231–43.

Cohn, H. (1994) 'What is Existential analysis?', *British Journal of Psychiatry*, **165**: 699–701.

Cohn, H. (1997) *Existential Thought and Therapeutic Practice*. London: Sage.

Collins English Dictionary (1986), P. Hanks (ed.), 2nd edn. London: Collins.

Coltart, N. (1992) *Slouching Towards Bethleham: And Further Psychoanalytic Explorations*. London: Free Association Books.

Craib, I. (1994) *The Importance of Disappointment*. London: Routledge.

Crowe, M. and Ridley, J. (1990) *Therapy with Couples*. Oxford: Blackwell.

Dallos, R. (1997) *Interacting Stories: Narratives, Family Beliefs, and Therapy*. London: Karnac Books.

Darwin, C. (1859) *On the Origin of Species By Means of Natural Selection*. London: John Murray.

Davis, M. and Wallbridge, D. (eds) (1981) *Boundary and Space: An Introduction to the Work of D. W. Winnicott*. Harmondsworth: Penguin Books.

Dawkins, R. (1976) *The Selfish Gene*. Oxford: Oxford University Press.

Dixon, N. (1971) *Subliminal Perception: The Nature of a Controversy*. London: McGraw-Hill.

Dupont, J. (ed.) (1988) *The Clinical Diary of Sándor Ferenczi* (trans. M. Balint and N. Zarday Jackson). Cambridge, MA and London: Harvard University Press.

Ekman, P. (1985) *Telling Lies: Clues to Deceit in the Marketplace, Politics and Marriage*. New York: W. W. Norton.

Ekman, P. and Friesen, W. (1974) 'Detecting deception from body or face', *Journal of Personality and Social Psychology*, **29**: 288–98.

Ferenczi, S. (1933) 'The confusion of tongues between adults and the child', in *Final Contributions to the Problems and Methods of Psycho-Analysis*. London: Hogarth Press; repr. London: Karnac Books, 1980.

Frank, K. A. (1999) *Psychoanalytic Participation: Action, Interaction, and Integration*. Hillsdale, N.J. and London: The Analytic Press.

Frankl, V. (1946) *Man's Search For Meaning*. London: Hodder & Stoughton, 1964.

Frankl, V. (1967) *Psychotherapy and Existentialism*. New York: Washington Square Press.

Freud, S. (1895) *Studies in Hysteria, The Standard Edition of the Complete Psychological Works of Sigmund Freud* (ed. J. Strachey), 24 vols. London: Hogarth Press, 1953–73, vol. 2.

Freud, S. (1897) Letter to Wilhelm Fliess, 21 September 1897. In Pre-Psychoanalytic publications and unpublished drafts, *The Standard Edition of the Complete Psychological Works of Sigmund Freud*, vol. 1.

Freud, S. (1900) *The Interpretation of Dreams, The Standard Edition of the Complete Psychological Works of Sigmund Freud*, vols 4–5.

Freud, S. (1910) *Five Lectures on Psycho-Analysis and other Works, The Standard Edition of the Complete Psychological Works of Sigmund Freud*, vol. 11.

Freud, S. (1912a) 'The dynamics of transference', *The Standard Edition of the Complete Psychological Works of Sigmund Freud*, vol. 12.

Freud, S. (1912b) 'Recommendations to physicians practising psychoanalysis', *The Standard Edition of the Complete Psychological Works of Sigmund Freud*, vol. 12.

Freud, S. (1914) 'On the History of the Psycho-Analytic Movement', *The Standard Edition of the Complete Psychological Works of Sigmund Freud*, vol. 14.

Freud, S. (1926) *Inhibitions, Symptoms and Anxiety, The Standard Edition of the Complete Psychological Works of Sigmund Freud*, vol. 20.

Freud, S. (1930) *Civilization and its Discontents, The Standard Edition of the Complete Psychological Works of Sigmund Freud*, vol. 21.

Freud, S. (1933) 'Anxiety and instinctual life', *The Standard Edition of the Complete Psychological Works of Sigmund Freud*, vol. 22.

Freud, S. (1937) 'Analysis terminable and interminable', *The Standard Edition of the Complete Psychological Works of Sigmund Freud*, vol. 23.

Friedman, M. (1996) 'Reflections on the Buber–Rogers dialogue: thirty-five years after', in M. Friedman (ed.), *Martin Buber and the Human Sciences*. New York: State University of New York Press.

Fung Yu-Lan (1958) *A Short History of Chinese Philosophy* (trans. D. Bodde), 2 vols. New York: Macmillan.

Giannetti, E. (1997) *Lies We Live By: The Art of Self-deception*. London: Bloomsbury.

Gibney, P. (1996) 'To embrace paradox (once more, with feeling): a commentary on narrative/conversational therapies and the therapeutic relationship', in C. Flaskas and A. Perlesz (eds), *The Therapeutic Relationship in Systemic Therapy*. London: Karnac Books.

Gill, M. (1984) 'Robert Langs on technique: a critique', in J. Raney (ed.), *Listening and Interpreting*. New York: Jason Aronson.

Gitelson, M. (1952) 'The emotional position of the analyst in the psycho-analytic situation', *International Journal of Psycho-Analysis*, 33: 1–10.

Goldberg, C. (1993) *On Being a Psychotherapist*. New Jersey: Jason Aronson.

Graf-Taylor, R. (1996) 'Philosophy of dialogue and feminist psychology', in M. Friedman (ed.), *Martin Buber and the Human Sciences*. New York: State University of New York Press.

Gray, J. (2002) *Straw Dogs*. London: Granta.

Greenson, R. R. (1967) *The Technique and Practice of Psychoanalysis*, vol. 1. New York: International Universities Press.

Grinberg, L. (1993) 'Countertransference and the concept of projective counteridentification', in A. Alexandris and G. Vaslamatzis (eds),

Counter-Transference Theory, Technique, Teaching. London: Karnac Books, pp. 47–65.

Grotstein, J. S. (1987) 'Making the best of a bad deal: a discussion of Boris's "Bion Revisited"', *Contemporary Psychoanalysis*, **23**: 60–76.

Hammond, M., Howarth, J. and Keat, R. (1991) *Understanding Phenomenology.* Oxford: Blackwell.

Harris, T. (1994) 'Response to Langs and Badalamenti from a social scientist/psychotherapist', *British Journal of Psychotherapy*, **11**: 109–114.

Haskell, R. E. (1987) 'Social cognition and the non-conscious expression of racial ideology', *Imagination, Cognition and Personality*, **6**: 75–97.

Haskell, R. E. (1990) 'Cognitive operations and non-conscious processing in dreams and waking reports', *Imagination, Cognition and Personality*, **10**: 65–84.

Haskell, R. E. (1999) Unconscious communication: communicative psychoanalysis and subliteral cognition', *Journal of the American Academy of Psychoanalysis*, **27**: 471–502.

Heidegger, M. (1927) *Being and Time* (trans. J. Macquarrie and E. Robinson). London: Harper Row, 1962.

Heimann, P. (1950) 'On countertransference', *International Journal of Psycho-Analysis*, **31**: 81–4; repr. in M. Tonnesmann (ed.), *About Children and Children-No-Longer: Collected Papers.* London and New York: Routledge, 1989, pp. 73–79.

Heimann, P. (1959–60) 'Countertransference', in M. Tonnesmann (ed.), *About Children and Children-No-Longer: Collected Papers.* London and New York: Routledge, 1989, pp. 151–60.

Heisenberg, W. C. (1958) *Physics and Philosophy: The Revolution in Modern Science.* New York: Harper; repr. Harmondsworth: Penguin Books, 1989.

Hinshelwood, R. D. (1989) *A Dictionary of Kleinian Thought.* London: Free Association Books.

Hodder & Stoughton Latin Dictionary (1965), A. Wilson (ed.). Sevenoaks, Kent: Hodder & Stoughton.

Holmes, C. (1991) 'The wounded healer', *Society for Psychoanalytic Psychotherapy Bulletin*, **6**: 33–36.

Holmes, C. (1998a) 'Bad faith in psychotherapy', *Journal of the Society for Existential Analysis*, **9**: 24–34.

Holmes, C. (1998b) *There is No Such Thing As a Therapist: An Introduction to the Therapeutic Process.* London: Karnac Books.

Holmes, C. (1999a) 'On snowflakes and psychotherapy', *Psychotherapy Review*, **1**: 166–170.

Holmes, C. (1999b) 'Confessions of a communicative psychotherapist', in E. M. Sullivan (ed.), *Unconscious Communication in Practice.* Buckingham: Open University Press.

Holmes, C. 'Relational patterns of being in communicative psychotherapy'. Ph.D. thesis by published works, University of Middlesex, 2001.

Honderich, T. (ed.) (1995) *The Oxford Companion to Philosophy*. Oxford: Oxford University Press.

Husserl, E. (1925) *Phenomenological Psychology* (trans. J. Scanlon). The Hague: Nijhoff, 1977.

Jacques, E. (1953) 'On the dynamics of social structure', *Human Relations*, 6: 3–24.

Jacques, E. (1955) 'Social systems as a defence against persecutory and depressive anxiety', in M. Klein, P. Heimann and R. Money-Kyrle (eds), *New Directions in Psychoanalysis*. London: Tavistock, 1955; repr. London: Karnac Books, 1977, pp. 478–98.

Jaspers, K. (1969) *Philosophy*, 3 vols (trans. E. Ashton). Chicago: University of Chicago Press.

Joseph, B. (1985) 'Transference: the total situation', *International Journal of Psycho-Analysis*, 66: 447–54.

Jung, C. G. (1908) 'Sex and battering in psychotherapy', in J. Masson, *Against Therapy*. London: Atheneum, 1998.

Kierkegaard, S. (1844) *The Concept of Anxiety* (trans. R. Thomte). Princeton, N.J.: Princeton University Press, 1980.

Klein, M. (1932) 'Early stages of the Oedipus conflict and of super-ego formation', *The Writings of Melanie Klein, Vol. 2: The Psychoanalysis of Children*. London: Hogarth Press, 1975, pp. 123–48.

Klein, M. (1946) 'Notes on some schizoid mechanisms', in *The Writings of Melanie Klein, Vol. 3: Envy and Gratitude and Other Works, 1946–1963*. London: Hogarth Press, 1975, pp. 1–24.

Klein, M. (1952) 'The origins of transference', in *The Writings of Melanie Klein, Vol. 3: Envy and Gratitude and Other Works, 1946–1963*. London: Hogarth Press, 1975, pp. 48–56.

Kohut, H. (1977) *The Restoration of the Self*. New York: International Universities Press.

Kohut, H. (1984) *How Does Psychoanalysis Cure?* (ed. A. Goldberg and P. Stepansky). Chicago: University of Chicago Press.

Kuhn, T. S. (1962) *The Structure of Scientific Revolutions*. Chicago: University of Chicago Press.

Kumin, I. (1985) 'Erotic horror: desire and resistance in the psychoanalytic setting', *International Journal of Psychoanalytic Psychotherapy*, 11: 3–20.

Lagache, D. (1953) 'Freudian doctrine and the theory of transference', in *The Work of Daniel Lagache: Selected Writings*. London: Karnac Books, 1993.

Langs, R. J. (1973a) *The Technique of Psychoanalytic Psychotherapy*, Vol. 1. New York: Jason Aronson, 1973.

Langs, R. J. (1973b) 'The patient's view of the therapist: reality or fantasy?', *International Journal of Psychoanalytic Psychotherapy*, 2: 411–31.

Langs, R. J. (1974) *The Technique of Psychoanalytic Psychotherapy*, Vol. 2, New York: Jason Aronson.

Langs, R. J. (1976) *The Bipersonal Field*. New York: Jason Aronson.

Langs, R. J. (1978a) 'Transference beyond Freud', in R. J. Langs, *Technique in Transition*. New York: Jason Aronson.

Langs, R. J. (1978b) 'The adaptational–interactional dimension of counter-transference', *Contemporary Psychoanalysis*, **14**: 502–533.

Langs, R. J. (1979) *The Therapeutic Environment*. New York: Jason Aronson.

Langs, R. J. (1980) *Interaction: The Realm of Transference and Counter-transference*. New York: Jason Aronson.

Langs, R. J. (1982) *The Psychotherapeutic Conspiracy*. New York: Jason Aronson.

Langs, R. J. (1983) *Unconscious Communicatioin Everyday Life*. New York: Jason Aronson.

Langs, R. J. (1987) *A Primer of Psychotherapy*. New York: Gardner Press.

Langs, R. J. (1992) 'Boundaries and frames: non-transference in teaching', *International Journal of Communicative Psychoanalysis and Psychotherapy*, **7**: 3–4.

Langs, R. J. (1994) *Doing supervision and being supervised*. London: Karnac Books.

Langs, R. J. (1997) *Death Anxiety and Clinical Practice*. London: Karnac Books.

Langs, R. J. (1998) *Ground Rules in Psychotherapy and Counselling*. London: Karnac Books.

Langs, R. J. (2004) *Fundamentals of Adaptive Psychotherapy and Counselling: Theory and Practice*. London: Palgrave Macmillan.

Langs, R. J. and Badalamenti, A. (1992a) 'The progression of entropy of a five-dimensional psychotherapeutic system', *Systems Research*, **9**: 3–28.

Langs, R. J. and Badalamenti, A. (1992b) 'The thermodynamics of psycho-therapeutic communication', *Behavioral Science*, **37**: 157–80.

Langs, R. J. and Searles, H. (1980) *Intrapsychic and Interactional Dimensions of Treatment: A Clinical Dialogue*. New York: Jason Aronson.

Laplanche, J. and Pontalis, J.-B. (1973) *The Language of Psychoanalysis*. London: Hogarth; repr. London: Karnac Books and the Institute of Psycho-Analysis, 1988.

Little, M. (1951) 'Countertransference and the patient's response to it', *International Journal of Psycho-Analysis*, **32**: 32–40.

Little, M. (1960) 'Countertransference', *British Journal of Medical Psychology*, **33**: 39–41.

Lovelock, J. (1979) *Gaia: A New Look at Life on Earth*. Oxford: Oxford University Press.

Macaskill, A. (1999) 'Personal therapy as a training requirement: the lack of supporting evidence', in C. Feltham (ed.), *Controversies in Psychotherapy and Counselling*. London: Sage Publications.

MacErlean, N. (2001) 'How to work with a maverick', *The Observer*, 9 September: 20.

Macquarrie, J. (1973) *Existentialism*. London: Penguin Books.

Mandelbrot, B. B. (1977) *The Fractal Geometry of Nature*. San Francisco: W. H. Freeman.

Mann, D. (1997) *Psychotherapy: An Erotic Relationship*. London: Routledge.

Mann, D. (1999) (ed.) *Erotic Transference and Countertransference: Clinical Practice in Psychotherapy*. London: Routledge.

Maroda, K. J. (1991) *The Power of Countertransference*. London: John Wiley; repr. Northvale, N.J. & London: Jason Aronson, 1994.

Masson, J. (1985) *The Assault on Truth: Freud's Suppression of the Seduction Theory*. Harmondsworth: Penguin Books.

May, R. and Yalom, I. (1984) 'Existential psychotherapy', in R. Corsini (ed.), *Current Psychotherapies*. Itasca, IL: Peacock.

Meissner, W. W. (1980) 'A note on projective identification', *Journal of the American Psychoanalytic Association*, 28: 43–65.

Menzies-Lyth, I. (1988) *Selected Essays, Vol. 1: Containing Anxiety in Institutions*. London: Free Association Books.

Merodoulaki, G.M. (1994) 'Early experience as factors influencing occupational choice in counselling and psychotherapy', *Counselling Psychology Review*, August: 18–39.

Milner, M. (1952) 'Aspects of symbolism and comprehension of the not-self', *International Journal of Psycho-Analysis*, 33: 181–85.

Minuchin, S. (1974) *Families and Family Therapy*. London: Tavistock.

Mitchell, S. A. and Black, M. J. (1995) *Freud and Beyond: A History of Modern Psychoanalytic Thought*. New York: Basic Books.

Money-Kyrle, R. E. (1956) 'Normal counter-transference and some of its deviations', *International Journal of Psycho-Analysis*, 37: 360–66.

Myers, P. (2000a) 'Unconscious perception in the story of psychoanalysis: a vignette', *Free Associations*, 7: 76–97.

Myers, P. (2000b) 'Reconsidering communicative psychoanalysis', *International Journal of Psychotherapy*, 5: 203–218.

Nietzsche, F. (1882) *The Gay Science* [*Die Fröhliche Wissenschaft*] (trans. W. Kaufmann). New York: Random House, 1974.

Nietzsche, F. (1883) *Thus Spake Zarathustra* (trans. W. Kaufmann). New York: Dover, 1964.

O'Brien, M. and Houston, G. (2000) *Integrative Therapy: A Practitioner's Guide*. London: Sage.

O'Conner, J. and McDermott, I. (1997) *The Art of Systems Thinking*. London: Thorsons.

O'Hanlon, W. (1994) 'The third wave'. *Family Therapy Networker*, November–December: 19–29.

Ogden, T. H. (1982) *Projective Identification and Psychotherapeutic Technique*. New York: Jason Aronson.

Penguin Dictionary of Quotations (1960), J. M. Cohen and M. J. Cohen (eds). Harmondsworth: Penguin Books.

Prigogene, I. (1980) *From Being to Becoming: Time and Complexity in the Physical Sciences*. San Francisco, CA: Freeman.

Prince-Warren, M. (1994) 'The missing link: the role of empathy in communicative psychoanalysis', *International Journal of Communicative Psychoanalytic Psychotherapy*, 9: 35–39.

Racker, H. (1968) *Transference and Countertransference*. London: Hogarth and the Institute of Psycho-Analysis; repr. London: Maresfield Library.

Rayner, E. (1991) *The Independent Mind in British Psychoanalysis*. London: Free Association Books.

Robertson, R. and Combs, A. (eds) (1995) *Chaos Theory in Psychology and the Life Sciences*. New Jersey: Lawrence Erlbaum Associates Inc.

Rogers, C. (1959) 'A theory of therapy, personality, and interpersonal relationships, as developed in the client-centered framework', in S. Koch (ed.), *Psychology: A Study of a Science, Vol. 3: Formulations of the Person and the Social Context*. New York: McGraw-Hill, pp. 184–256.

Rogers, C. (1960) 'Dialogue between Martin Buber and Carl Rogers', *Psychologia*, 3: 208–21.

Rogers, C. (1961) *On Becoming a Person*. Boston, MA: Houghton Mifflin.

Rogers, C. (1980) *A Way of Being*. Boston, MA: Houghton Mifflin.

Roget's Thesaurus of Synonyms & Antonyms (1972), S. R. Roget (ed.). London: University Books, 2000.

Rose, H. and Rose, S. (eds) (2001) *Alas Poor Darwin: Arguments Against Evolutionary Theory*. London: Vintage.

Rycroft, C. (1968) *A Critical Dictionary of Psychoanalysis*. London: Nelson; repr. Harmondsworth: Penguin Books, 1972.

Sabbadini, A. (1990) 'Existential analysis and psychoanalysis', *Journal of the Society for Existential Analysis*, 1: 29–32.

Sandler, J., Dare, C. and Holder, A. (1973) *The Patient and the Analyst*, 2nd edn. London: Karnac Books, 1992.

Sartre, J. P. (1939) *Sketch for a Theory of the Emotions*. London: Methuen, 1962.

Sartre, J. P. (1943) *Being and Nothingness* (trans. H. Barnes). New York: Philosophical Library, 1956.

Sartre, J. P. (1946) *Existentialism and Humanism* (trans. P. Mairet). London: Methuen, 1948.

Schoenewolf, G. (1993) *Counterresistance: The Therapist's Interference with the Therapeutic Process*. Northvale, N.J.: Jason Aronson.

Schur, R. (1994) *Counter-transference Enactment: How Institutions and Therapists Actualize Primitive Internal Worlds*. Northvale, N.J.: Jason Aronson.

Schwartz, J. (1994) 'Is physics a good model for psychoanalysis? Reflections on Langs and Badalamenti', *British Journal of Psychotherapy*, 11: 372–75.

Schwartz, J. (1999) *Cassandra's Daughter: A History of Psychoanalysis in Europe and America*. Harmondsworth: Penguin Books.

Searles, H. (1959) 'Oedipal love in the countertransference', in Searles (1965).

Searles, H. (1961) 'Schizophrenia and the inevitability of death', in Searles (1965).

Searles, H. (1965) *Collected Papers on Schizophrenia and Related Subjects.* London: Hogarth Press; repr. London: Maresfield Library, 1986.

Searles, H. (1967) ' "The dedicated physician" in psychotherapy and psychoanalysis', in R. W. Gibson (ed.), *Crosscurrents in Psychiatry and Psychoanalysis.* Philadelphia and Toronto: J. B. Lippincott.

Searles, H. (1975a) 'The patient as therapist to his analyst', in P. L. Giovacchini (ed.), *Tactics and Techniques in Psychoanalytic Therapy, Vol. 2: Countertransference.* New York: Jason Aronson.

Searles, H. (1975b) 'Countertransference and related subjects', in J. G. Gunderson and L. Mosher (eds), *Psychotherapy and Schizophrenia.* New York: Jason Aronson, 1975.

Searles, H. (1979) *Countertransference and Related Subjects: Selected Papers.* New York: International Universities Press.

Searles, H. (1987) 'Overloving' – a misnomer', in J. Langs (ed.), *The Year Book of Psychoanalysis and Psychotherapy*, Vol. 2. Emerson, N.J.: Newconcept Press, pp. 259–70.

Segal, J. (1992) *Melanie Klein.* London: Sage.

Senge, P. (1990) *The Fifth Discipline.* New York: Doubleday.

Silverstein, E. A. (1984) 'Langsian theory and countertransference', in J. Raney (ed.), *Listening and Interpreting.* New York: Jason Aronson.

Singer, E. (1998) 'The interpersonal approach to psychoanalysis', in R. Langs (ed.), *Current Theories of Psychoanalysis.* Madison, CT: International Universities Press, pp. 73–101.

Skynner, R. (1987) *Explorations with Families, Group Analysis and Family Therapy* (ed. J. R. Schlapobersky). London: Methuen.

Slife, B. D. and Lanyon, J. (1991) 'Accounting for the here-and-now: a theoretical revolution', *International Journal of Group Psychotherapy*, 41: 145–66.

Smith, D. L. (1989) 'An interview with Robert Langs', *Changes*, 7: 117–21.

Smith, D. L. (1991) *Hidden Conversations: An Introduction to Communicative Psychoanalysis.* London: Routledge.

Smith, D. L. (1999a) 'Understanding patients' countertransference', in M. Sullivan (ed.), *Unconscious Communication in Practice.* Buckingham: Open University Press, pp. 17–34.

Smith, D. L. (1999b) *Approaching Psychoanalysis: An Introductory Course.* London: Karnac Books.

Smith, D. L. 'The evolution of the unconscious'. Unpublished paper, 2002.

Spillius, E. B. (1983) 'Some developments from the work of Melanie Klein', *International Journal of Psycho-Analysis*, 64: 321–22.

Spinelli, E. (1989) *The Interpreted World: An Introduction to Phenomenological Psychology.* London: Sage.

Spinelli, E. (1994) *Demystifying Therapy.* London: Constable.

Stanton, M. (1990) *Sándor Ferenczi: Reconsidering Active Intervention*. London: Free Association Books.

Stanton, M. (1992) 'Harold Searles talks to Martin Stanton', *Free Associations*, 3: 323–39.

Sullivan, H. S. (1953) *The Interpersonal Theory of Psychiatry*. New York: W. W. Norton.

Sullivan, H. S. (1964) *The Fusion of Psychiatry and Social Science*. New York: W. W. Norton.

Szasz, T. (1965) *The Ethics of Psychoanalysis: The Theory and Method of Autonomous Psychotherapy*. Syracuse: Syracuse University Press.

Tillich, P. (1952) *The Courage to Be*. New Haven, CT: Yale University Press.

Trivers, R. L. (1971) 'The evolution of reciprocal altruism', *Quarterly Review of Biology*, 46: 35–56.

Trivers, R. L. (1988) Introduction to J. S. Lockhard and D. L. Paulhus (eds), *Self-Deception: An Adaptive Mechanism?* Englewood Cliffs, NJ: Prentice Hall.

Van Deurzen-Smith, E. (1997) *Everyday Mysteries*. London: Routledge.

Warnock, M. (1970) *Existentialism*. Oxford: Oxford University Press.

White, M. (1986) 'Negative explanation, restraint and double description: a template for family therapy', *Family Process*, 25: 169–84.

White, M. and Epston, D. (1990) *Narrative Means to Therapeutic Ends*. New York: W. W. Norton.

Wiener, N. (1948) *Cybernetics*. New York: MIT Press; repr. 1961.

Wilson, E. O. (1975) *Sociobiology*. Cambridge MA: Belknap Press.

Winnicott, D. W. (1949) 'Hate in the countertransference', *International Journal of Psycho-Analysis*, 30: 69–75.

Winnicott, D. W. (1958) 'The family affected by depressive illness on the part of one or both parents', in *The Family and Individual Development*. London: Tavistock, 1965.

Winnicott, D. W. (1960) 'Counter-transference', in *The Maturational Processes and the Facilitating Environment*. London: Hogarth Press, 1965.

Winnicott, D. W. (1963) 'The capacity for concern', in *The Maturational Processes and the Facilitating Environment*. London: Hogarth Press, 1965.

Wolstein, B. (ed) (1988) *Essential Papers on Countertransference*. New York: University Press.

Yalom, I. (1980) *Existential Psychotherapy*. New York: Basic Books.

Young, R. M. (1994) *Mental Space*. London: Process Press.

Zohar, D. & Marshall, I. (1994) *The Quantum Society: Mind Physics and a New Social Vision*. London: HarperCollins.

Zukav, G. (1979) *The Dancing Wu Li Masters: An Overview of the New Physics*. London: Rider & Co.

Index